About the Author

Susan Campbell lives in the west end and rescue dog Ronnie.

She is a qualified Counsellor, Life Coach and Community Worker who made the bold decision to walk away from a senior management career in the voluntary sector in 2008 to pursue a long term dream of working for herself.

Since then she has nurtured a successful consultancy business in community development and coaching and rekindled a love of writing.

She is passionate about challenging inequality in all areas of life with a particular interest in mental health.

She is an avid supporter of Dogs Trust and has pledged a percentage of her Royalties from *Ronnie* to the organisation.

Acknowledgements

So many people to thank, but first, let's start with all of the dogs that have supported Ronnie Ronster's Dog Walking Service over the years and the dogs that have touched our lives:

Lola (Balola-Blanca) and Sophie, Little Millie, Handsome Jack (Vizsla), Jackson, Rosie (Jack Russell), Max (Collie cross), Oscar, Old Jack (Retriever), Hoover, Zak (Westie), Molly, Kiko, Hamish (Airedale), Noelle and Rachel Anne and Freya Blue, Sparkles, Rosie (Beagle), Holly, Ruby (black doodle), Old Max, Jacob, Bodie (Retriever), Scamp and Milly Moo.

Raja, Brodie, Ruby Doodle Doo, Miko, Peggy, Loki, Henry, Bub, Annie, Gebo, Iggy, Cole, Jack (Collie/Staff), Annie, Teddy, Marley, Lachie, Dexter (Westie), Kenzie, Ollie (Jack Russell), Otis, Mylo, Jack (Collie), Callie, Zak (German Shepherd), Magnus, Freddy, Solly, Missy, Penny and Bonnie, Zak (Collie), Breagha, Archie and Bertie, Dexter (Labrador), Mungan, Cooper.

Quinn, Betty, Cora, Hamish (Doodle), Sasha, Dusty, Stevie, D'arcy, Nessie, Lou, Cosmo , Elsa, Murphy and Cara, Molly the Collie, Del, Oskar, Bailey, Tiny, Mac, Aoife, Snoopy, Eddie, Bodie (Rottweiler), Leo, Fern, Mollie, Frankie, Spud, Ollie (Yorkie) Domino, Pippa, Indy, Stanley, Ty, Harvey, Nina, Kobe, Angus, Charlie, Belle, Ben, Hamish, Badger, Sausage, Marag, Breagha, Sandie and of course Jasper.

Thank you also to all of the owners for trusting us to take care of their dogs and for the support and friendships that have resulted.

Thanks too for my family and friends ongoing encouragement which propelled me towards the finish line.

Special thanks go out to a few.
Ashley for all she taught me about writing techniques and editing and the great enthusiasm she showed me when I first approached her with the idea. Nat for all of the hours she spent being a second pair of eyes during editing and just believing in me. Chris for producing the most beautiful photos for the book and his ongoing encouragement.

Morvern, my BFF, just for everything!

Elspeth for all of her design expertise for the cover through 999 Design, for using her vast contacts to promote the book and all of her ongoing support with PR.

Sharon for her words of wisdom.

And, of course, Ringwood Publishing for taking a chance on my first attempt at writing a book. Their ongoing support and advice has been invaluable.

Projects don't happen in isolation and I'm so grateful to have all of these amazing people in my life to share this precious time.

Last, but by no means least, Colin and Ronnie. From the day I showed Colin the first chapter, and he gave a huge sigh of relief that he wasn't going to have to tell me to find another hobby, he supported and encouraged the development of the book. He cracked the whip when I couldn't be bothered writing and added memories I had forgotten; a team effort all round. And Ronnie … well, without Ronnie, we wouldn't be here now.

Thank you one and all!

Dedication

To Colin and Ronnie, the two great loves of my life, and in memory of Aileen, our beautiful niece.

Foreword

Animals have always played a huge part in my life, particularly dogs. I feel the strongest connection with them, and love the unconditional acceptance they bring to relationships. Over the years, many dogs have touched my life, always enhancing and enriching it. But one in particular has had the most profound and life-changing effect ... Ronnie.

I'm not sure if it's because Ronnie is the first dog Colin, my husband, and I have had full responsibility for; other dogs have been family pets, or on loan while friends and family holiday. Or maybe it's the fact that he's a rescue dog. I know dog trainers will tell you that it's wrong to feel sympathy, as dogs live in the moment and leave painful memories behind, unlike humans. Still, being human, it's difficult not to worry about the possible, invisible scars a dog had been left with when it is abandoned.

Whatever the reason, I experienced a strong urge to write about our times with Ronnie, sharing the happy, challenging and downright inspirational aspects of dog ownership. It's not always an easy road and not a decision to be taken lightly. I often feel that taking on a dog is one step down from having children in the responsibility stakes, but I could be way off the mark on that one. I do know, however, that in the absence of children of our own, Ronnie definitely receives a lot more love and attention than he might have done had this not been the case. Maybe that's why he chose us.

I also hope this book will challenge people to think outside the box in terms of their career choices. I took the bold decision of starting my own business as a life coach a year before Colin moved across to the world of self-employment. This manoeuvred me into an excellent position to support him when he too decided to go it alone. Both our journeys had different bumps along the road, but the message is clear. If you want something badly enough and take the necessary action, the Universe will support you all the way.

In the following chapters, I have attempted to capture the essence of owning a dog and show how life-transforming it can be. I hope this encourages more people to think about taking on a rescue dog, perhaps pursuing a few dreams of their own in the process.

Now I want to introduce you to the most precious canine in the world. Meet Ronnie.

Chapter One - Let's just go and see

We spotted the familiar yellow and black Dogs Trust sign, lit up in the night, long before we turned into the car park of their Glasgow re-homing centre, on a wet December evening in 2008. I felt every cell in my body push forward in an effort to speed up our arrival.

Colin and I had made the mammoth decision to adopt a dog, and now the reality of that decision was staring us in the face. I had left my long-term job only six months previously, to follow my dream of starting my own life-coaching business. At that point, I was working from home which meant we could pursue another long-term dream; giving an abandoned dog a loving home.

Our excitement, anticipation, not to mention sadness, were palpable. I knew my heart was going to break at some of the sights we were about to see. As we got out of the car, I spotted some of the dogs in their kennels, and there was a medley of barks, yelps and howls coming from all directions.

We walked through the front door and observed several couples and families, all with the same look of excitement and trepidation that we were experiencing. I can still remember the strong smell of 'dog'; a smell that would be off-putting to some people, but only added to our anticipation. As we made our way to the reception desk, we heard puppy barks and squeals coming from three Border Collie pups, tumbling and playing behind the wooden desks. They were such a welcoming sight.

'No,' we said to each other.

We didn't want a Collie. It would be too much work as they need hours of exercise and stimulation every day. A more placid dog would suit us better, and anyway, we had only come to the Dogs Trust to find out ABOUT the procedure for adopting a dog. We were not actually going to take one.

A dark-haired woman approached us, wearing the Dogs Trust uniform of dark green trousers, a jumper with the logo just below her left shoulder,

1

and green wellies. She smiled and introduced herself as Cat. 'How can I help you?' she asked.

'We just want to find out how to go about adopting a dog?' Colin replied.

'No problem. If you'd like to fill out our standard form, I can then talk you through the process.'

She handed us the form, attached to a clipboard, and we sat down dutifully and began filling it in. The form asked lots of questions about our preferences in a dog, and what was most important to us. It was an impressive list, which seemed to cover all bases.

We were asked if it was important that our dog got on with other dogs and children, and travelled well in the car. 'Yes.' to all.

Had we previously owned a dog? 'Yes' Both Colin and I had had family dogs when we were growing up.

What age and size of dog were we looking for? We ticked the 'puppy to three years' box and the 'medium size' box.

Did we have a garden, and if so, was it enclosed? We live in a ground-floor tenement flat, which has a small, fenced front garden and a large enclosed communal back court area, so 'Yes' again to both.

How much daily exercise would we be able to give a dog? We carefully counted this out and came to an agreement of two and a half hours a day: three half-hour walks, morning, lunchtime and last thing at night, and an hour-long walk in the evening. This seemed reasonable and well within our reach.

Did we have children, and were we were thinking of having a child in the next year? Colin and I were in our early forties, and owing to an illness of mine, had not been able to have children. I had been diagnosed with endometriosis at thirty-five. And so it was a sad reply of 'No' to both of these questions. We were under no illusion that if we adopted a dog it would become our surrogate child.

All in all, we were pretty flexible in our needs. Our only fixed requirement was that the dog had short hair, to prevent triggering Colin's asthma.

Cat took our form and asked if we would like to take a walk along the kennels: the 'Walk of Shame', as Colin later named it. The next twenty minutes were heart-breaking. I could honestly have found room in the car for every one of the dogs, but for one reason or another, there wasn't a suitable one amongst them: long-haired, very old, three-legged etc. I suddenly realised that our criteria were not quite as flexible as we had thought, and my heart sank.

I also felt terribly guilty about dismissing the older and disabled dogs, so in need of a good home. The reality was that both Colin and I wanted the opportunity to create many happy memories, and share many happy years with our new dog.

One dog stood out for me: Blue, the Greyhound. The kennels were all in a row and there was floor-to-ceiling glass in each of them to maximise the viewing power of potential new owners. At the bottom of the glass was a series of small holes, to allow the dogs to come up and sniff people's hands.

Blue was lying in her bed by the window. Unlike the other dogs that came running to the glass (including the three-legged terrier) Blue never moved. Her eyes were dead and her head lay heavily on her stomach, as though life had just been too difficult for this beautiful dog. I turned to Colin and said, 'I really like her.' He gave me a hard stare.

'Susan, she's lovely, but she's bigger and older than we wanted, and we're only looking.'

I could see that my hubby was working really hard to keep a detached and practical approach to our search. I, on the other hand, in what was and remains a common theme in my life, was letting my heart rule my head.

'You're right,' I sighed, and dragged myself away from the kennel, stealing one last distressing look at gentle Blue.

We walked back to the reception area remorseful and dejected. Cat sat us down.

'Don't worry if there were no suitable dogs in the front kennels,' she said. 'We have another hundred out the back. I'm sure we can find a suitable match for you.'

We nearly fell off the chairs. Mixed emotions were running through me. How wonderful that there was still the opportunity for us to find a dog, but how sad that there were so many abandoned and unloved dogs in the world.

'Just give me a few minutes to check our files and I'll see who we have,' Cat muttered, as she walked over to a table which had index cards stuck to the wall above it. She began taking out cards at random as we waited nervously for her return.

I glanced around the room. There was a Christmas tree in one corner, with boxes wrapped in Christmas paper underneath it. There was tinsel draped over pictures on the wall. I felt the familiar butterflies dancing around in my stomach. Various emotions were running through me as we approached my favourite time of year; excitement mixed with the fear that accompanies any new adventure.

There were photos on the wall of some of the dogs, and photos of all the staff at the centre, pictured with their dogs alongside a photo of the centre cat. 'Brave cat!' I pointed out.

I decided to visit the bathroom to pass some time. Nerves were getting the better of me. Inside the cubicle was a photo of an old, blind dog, desperately in need of a home. Above the photo was the title 'Sticky Dogs'; the ones the centre found it particularly difficult to re-home. As I washed my hands I noticed there were 'Sticky Dogs' stuck all over the bathroom, and in every cubicle. Colin worked in sales and I knew he would be impressed when I told him about this particular PR campaign. My guilt returned and I exited the bathroom quickly.

I sat back down next to Colin, who was chewing on a fingernail. Cat was on her way back. She produced a blue folder and said; 'Looking at your forms, I think this dog fits your criteria really well. Meet Ronnie.'

She opened up the folder and there was the most beautiful photograph of an eighteen-month-old Lurcher-cross. How strange. We both had a keen interest in Lurchers, having read a fantastic book about one on holiday in the Canaries, and then reading up on the breed on our return. For me, it was love at first sight. Colin was trying desperately to remain stony and impartial, but I could see him melting in front of me. She urged gently: 'Ronnie has been with us for the last three months, and we can't understand why no one has taken him. He's the most adorable dog. Would you like to meet him?'

Colin and I looked at each other in excitement and he held two hands up. 'Well, what harm can that do?'

Cat walked towards the reception area, picked up a walkie-talkie and said 'Can you bring Ronnie up to reception, please?'

We stood by the front door with the eagerness of children awaiting the Christmas gift they had always dreamed of. Suddenly, out of the darkness, came this gangly, over-enthusiastic, grinning, multi-coloured dog. The handler who brought him to us was struggling to stay on her feet. I crouched down to meet him and he licked my face and hands with great exuberance.

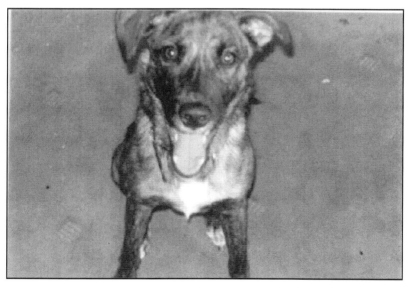

Love at first sight

His fur on first sight looked coarse, but when touched, felt luxuriously soft. It was different shades of brown mixed with black, and he had a white chest. We would later find out this was called 'brindle'. His ears were like velvet. What else can I say about his ears? They were colossal and moving about in all directions. One minute they were stuck back solidly to his head, the next they sprung cheekily forward over his eyes, and then they were sticking out to the side like the wings of an aeroplane. This dog had style.

For a pooch that had just spent three months in the pound, he was surprisingly full of the joys of life. We would discover later that this was, indeed, Ronnie's greatest blessing to us.

'Would you like to take Ronnie for a walk?' the handler asked. 'There's a field just over the back, where you can get a better feel for him.'

Again Colin spoke that memorable line: 'Well, what harm can that do?'

We set off around the corner with Ronnie. The enthusiasm with which he pulled us towards that field was unmatched by any other dog I have known. As we approached the grassy area, we suddenly realised that we had both just come from work and were dressed totally inappropriately for the task in hand. We were dressed for the boardroom, only visiting the Dogs Trust to find out the procedure for adopting a dog. How we had both deluded ourselves!

'What the hell,' we reckoned, 'it's only a bit of mud.'

There was a wooden boardwalk that took us into the middle of the field, which I manoeuvred treacherously in my high-heeled boots. Colin was braver than me and ventured out beyond the wooden planks into the muddy grassland with Ronnie. I stood back and watched the two of them. It was pretty dark in the field. There were a few lights dotted around, and some light was coming in from the street lamps. I could still make out the two silhouettes of man and dog, perfectly synchronised.

Colin, in his best business suit, could not take his eyes off Ronnie as he was pulled energetically through the mud. I could hear him repeating, 'Good boy, Ronnie, good boy. Come on, Ronnie, come on. Who's a good boy then? Yes, you are, you are. Come on, Ronnie, let's go.'

He attempted to run with him, but the mud made this impossible if not a little dangerous, so he slowed down and continued his wholehearted conversation with Ronnie. It wasn't one-sided either, as Ronnie's tail never stopped wagging, and I could see those ears flapping about frantically as he ran.

The rain started to get heavier and it was time to return to the centre. They both came bounding back towards me and as we walked back along the board walk, Colin turned to me and asked, 'So what do you think then?'

'I think he's perfect!' I nodded.

As we arrived back at the centre, windswept, wet through, but oblivious to both, we knew something extraordinary had just happened. We got to the reception desk and Cat asked us what we thought.

'We'll take him!' was our unanimous reply.

Chapter Two - What next?

Cat looked surprised. I sensed she was just about to ask for Ronnie to be taken back to what was turning into his not so 'temporary accommodation'; rejected again. I had the distinct impression that Ronnie had made several trips back and forth from his kennel, as a result of his *'joie de vivre'*.

It's funny how the characteristic that may have put other people off was the very thing that was drawing us to him. He had an energy about him that was transmitting 'Whaheeeey!' This was nectar to a life coach and, as it pretty much sums up Colin's life attitude, I knew we were all a brilliant match.

'Oh, that's fantastic! Ronnie, you have a new home!' Cat exclaimed, as she bent down to give him a hug.

Ronnie's tail continued to wag as he grinned at us all, going from one to the other to be petted. I knew he didn't have a clue what was going on, but he was getting caught up in the excitement of it all as other staff members joined in.

'If you just take a seat, I'll get the paperwork and talk you through what happens next.'

Walking over to the blue plastic seats, we sat down with Ronnie, who was filthy from his escapades in the field. We couldn't take our eyes off him. He climbed cheekily onto the seat next to us, which I'm sure he wasn't allowed to do, so Colin helped him off. His muddy paw prints were all over the chair. Just past the reception area, I found a plastic container full of old towels and took a couple from the top. As I returned, I could see Ronnie sitting quietly in-between Colin's legs. He looked so snug and safe, and they both appeared entirely at ease with each other. I wiped down the seat and attempted to get the worst of the mud off Ronnie.

Cat came back with forms and information sheets. Again, it was extremely thorough. We were given information on: training; grooming; what to do if he barked too much; what to feed him; and some of the issues we might experience when re-homing a rescue dog.

'Here's the form you'll need to get your vet to sign to register Ronnie,' Cat instructed. 'You need to bring that in with you when you pick him up. We also need to organise a home visit. Don't worry about this. We're not checking how clean your home is. We just want to make sure it's suitable for a dog.'

'God, you're thorough,' smiled Colin.

'We need to make sure it's safe and secure,' she responded. 'You should be aware that you're adopting Ronnie. If anything goes wrong, you can't re-home him yourself. He has to come back here and we would then find him a new home.'

'That's fine,' We both nodded. We had been on the Dogs Trust website so we knew this.

'You also need to attend a training event, and the next one is Thursday morning. Can you make that?' We both agreed to be there. 'It's just to run through some of the things that may happen with a rescue dog. Again, it's nothing to worry about. You can take Ronnie home with you next Thursday after the training.'

Next Thursday! That was less than a week away. We would have him for Christmas.

'That's wonderful,' I said, followed quickly by, 'Oh no, we can't! We're away overnight next Saturday, for a Christmas party. We can't leave him so soon.'

'Next Thursday is the final day we're letting dogs leave the centre before Christmas. It's the cut-off date. If you can't take him then, you won't be able to take him until after New Year,' Cat warned.

I felt a stab in my guts and a dead weight in my stomach. Ronnie was now curled up on the floor between us. It was the quietest I had seen him and he looked absolutely endearing. The thought of this little dog having to spend Christmas and New Year in a cold kennel, with more than a hundred other dogs, was unbearable. If we could, we would have taken him home right then. How far we had come in a few hours!

'I think we should give the party a miss, Colin. This is more important,' I declared, somewhat sanctimoniously.

'Looks like it,' Colin agreed. What perfect dog owners we were going to make.

Cat was called away and we were left deliberating our dilemma. Could we take him with us? The party was in the Inverkip Marina hotel in Ayrshire, and we were staying with friends who had two beautiful labradoodles, called Dougie and Daisy. No. We had been told that Ronnie got on well with other dogs, but could we risk this so soon?

I imagined returning to a war zone with the three dogs nursing broken bones, cuts and sporting bald patches as we waded through the tufts of fur.

And anyway, leaving him in a strange environment while we were out tripping the light fantastic would just not have been right. The reality was that neither of us would have felt like tripping anywhere for worrying about how he was holding up. We also had no idea if he was a destroyer, and I visualised returning to our friends' home to find Ronnie trapped under their overturned Christmas tree, entangled in tinsel and bobbles, close to electrocution from the fairy lights.

Missing the party seemed the only option, but that would mean letting our friends down, and passing up an evening of festive fun we had so been looking forward to. We had both made such an instant connection with Ronnie, and contemplating spending Christmas without him was taking all of the joy out of the season. He would be alone in a cold kennel when there was a warm, loving new family ready and willing to take him home now.

Cat returned. 'It's fine. I've just spoken to my manager and we'll make an exception. You can come and pick Ronnie up the following Sunday.'

In came the high again. I felt the brick in my stomach dissolve as the butterflies flew back in. We looked at each other with enormous relief, mixed with trepidation. Ronnie would be coming home for Christmas after all.

The centre was now closing and it was time for us to leave him for the first time. The handler who had brought him to us returned. Colin and I were both already feeling the sadness of separation, but Ronnie went out the door with her quite happily.

He was gone, and we stood for a few moments in disbelief. What had we just done? We had signed the papers and, subject to checks and training, Ronnie was now ours. Even though we had both known it was highly likely that, by coming to the Dogs Trust, we would see a dog we wanted (though we had never outwardly expressed this to each other), the speed with which this had all happened had left us spinning.

We walked to the car in shocked silence, and drove the twelve miles or so home. It was dark and raining, and the only sound on the journey was that of the windscreen wipers brushing backwards and forwards, keeping the rain at bay. It wasn't until we got to Glasgow Cross, a couple of miles from home, that the silence was broken.

'What have we done?' Colin exclaimed.

'I know. We're in shock, Colin, but it's okay. Everything is going to be okay.'

It was dark on the roads, but I remember the Christmas lights in some of the shops breaking up the dimness and shining like multi-coloured halos of hope in the night. I'm a great believer in Angels, and their power to support and guide us through life. Being brought up Catholic, Angels figured heavily in my indoctrination. Having left several of the teachings of Catholicism behind me as I entered adulthood, Angels had firmly remained. My parents did a great job of bringing me up in that faith in terms of giving me a strong moral compass and sense of justice, but I was always at odds with the contradictions of some of its teaching. There's none of that in the instructions I've read about Angels though, just love, acceptance and hope, and my set of Angel cards, which I use often in challenging times, are an ongoing source of support and reassurance. I had set an intention to the Angels on our journey to the Dogs Trust.

'Dear Angels, please let us find the perfect dog for us. ' I now congratulated them on their fantastic job of finding Ronnie.

We opened our front door and felt the welcoming warmth of the central heating. I put the kettle on and we began to imagine how we were going to incorporate our new family member into his new home.

Colin was on a roll. 'This is where we'll put his food and water dishes,' he pointed to a suitable spot in the kitchen. 'And I think his bed should go here in the hall, between the piano and our bedroom. This can be his little safe area that's close to us too.'

'Perfect.' I made the coffee and as we munched on mince pies, Colin composed a text to all our friends and family. It read:

> We just thought you would like to know that Ronnie, an eighteen-month-old Lurcher-cross will be leaving the Dogs Trust on Sunday, 21st December, to start his new life at Sauchiehall Street. He's looking forward to meeting you. Merry Christmas. Ho Ho Ho!

Chapter Three - Homecomings

What a night. On returning home from meeting Ronnie, we headed next door to our local pub to celebrate Colin finishing work for a three-week festive break and, more importantly, to toast our new family member. To be honest, I think we both just needed a drink to calm our nerves, and give us some time to reflect on what we had done.

Texts flowed with notes of congratulations all evening, as well as calls from family and friends. Somehow, we never tired of recounting the story of our adventure, and this helped to reassure me we had done the right thing.

Our friend John was up from London and joined our celebrations, alongside Steve who owned The Alamo; a beautifully refurbished guest house just around the corner from us, with amazing views over the Kelvingrove Art Galleries and Museum. The love and care he has put into refurbishing this property is immense and he happily showed us photos of each room. They were decorated exactly to my taste: rich autumn colours, beautiful wooden beds draped in the softest pillows and duvets (the kind you dive into and lose yourself). We warmly congratulated him on his creations.

The night wore on and the events of the day were beginning to catch up with us. 'Think we'll make a move shortly,' Colin said to our company.

'Just wait here for one minute,' Steve announced, as he sped out the door.

We looked at each other, both wondering what was going on when Steve came bursting back and placed a room key in my hand.

'There you go. Have a night in the Alamo on me.'

'What? Steve ... no, we can't. That's too generous, really it is,' I stuttered, overwhelmed by his kindness.

'Seriously, the room's empty. You've had a fantastic day. Now have a fantastic night.'

'Oh, Steve, thank you so much,' we both gushed over drunken hugs and kisses.

'That's bloody lovely that! I've come all the way from London and you guys end up with a hotel room right on your doorstep! I'll just head back to my folks' house then!' John joked.

We nipped next door and filled an overnight bag before making our way across the street to our palatial bedroom for the night. Steve had even thrown in breakfast.

'Susan, today I finished work for three weeks, we got Ronnie, I found out ACDC are playing Glasgow next June, and now we're staying here. This is, without a doubt, the second best day of my life!'

We often recount that story of the day we first met Ronnie, and how exciting it all was. I'll always remember it as one of those very special times from our box of memories.

As the days moved on, we began the countdown to Ronnie's arrival, sorting the house and buying in all the necessary doggy goods. We had passed our house check. Having nervously awaited the assessor's meeting, it had all been very straightforward. He checked our garden was safe and secure. Then he gave Ronnie's bed the once over and we had a chat about rescue dogs, and the support the Dogs Trust provided if needed.

Now it was time to get into dog mode as collection day had arrived.

'Right, here goes then,' Colin said, as we turned into the Dogs Trust car park.

'I'm really nervous, Colin. We are doing the right thing, aren't we?' I asked, knowing that we were.

'Only one way to find out. Let's go and get him.' We climbed out of the car and made our way to reception.

We had completed the hour and a half journey from Inverkip to Uddingston, quietly anticipating what was about to take place. The party had been a great success. It had commenced with a mass-produced menu of festive delights followed by bounteous 'dad' dancing to Slade, Shakin'

Stevens, The Pogues and many other merry annual offerings. My sparkly dress and shoes were now safely tucked up in the overnight bag in the boot as we sped down the motorway towards our new family member.

The last part of the journey to the centre had become very familiar to us, as Colin had made several trips back to see Ronnie while on holiday. I had joined them a couple of times too, and we had romped around the field, all becoming better acquainted. The strong bond that was to become impenetrable over the coming years was beginning to form between us all.

The centre was busy, and there were several dogs heading in and out with potential new owners looking to adopt a dog in the New Year. It brought back affectionate memories of our first visit. Cat was at reception and greeted us with a smile.

'This is the big day then. He's waiting for you. I'll just radio ahead and get him brought up.' She picked up the walkie-talkie and said, 'That's Ronnie's mum and dad here to pick him up.' We all laughed as she realised what she had said.

Two other staff members took us aside and handed us a large yellow Dogs Trust bag. On the front was a sticker with 'RONNIE' written in black marker pen next to their motto: 'Give a Dog a Home'. It's funny, but I remember feeling a genuine sense of pride when I read this. 'RONNIE' would soon be ours. The bag is now framed and proudly hanging on our bedroom wall, having been kidnapped by my best friend Morvern, as she worked her artistic magic on it. Inside the bag was enough food for five days, more leaflets, a computer printout of all the veterinary treatment Ronnie had received since entering the centre three months earlier, and a bright yellow Dogs Trust lead to go with his collar. We were told Ronnie had passed his final health check that morning, and was good to go. Paying the £75.00 adoption fee completed the deal.

He came bursting through the door all legs and ears, and raced towards us with his over-enthusiastic welcome we had grown so fond of. Jumping up, he licked our faces, then got himself tangled up in his lead, and the chairs as he went around everyone saying 'hello'. I liked to think that by now he recognised us, but to be honest, everyone was getting the same lovely greeting. This was just his way.

Getting to know you

'Just to let you know that Ronnie got a little grumpy this morning when we were drying his paws,' one of the staff members warned. 'He's fine. He just doesn't enjoy this, so be aware when you're drying him.'

This remains the case. Ronnie has a great dislike of having his paws dried.

Cat approached us. 'Okay, I think that's everything. If you have any problems at all, you can contact us any time. Remember, we have our own dog psychologists too, if you're ever in need of advice. We're going to miss you, wee fella, but it's so good to see you leaving here.' She leant down and gave him a final hug. We left the centre to a chorus of, 'Bye,

Ronnie. Good luck. Come back and visit,' from all the staff, as we carried the big yellow bag, while being dragged out the door as Ronnie made his great escape.

He jumped easily into the back seat with me as we started our journey home, lulling us into a false sense of security. As soon as the car picked up speed, Ronnie began pacing furiously back and forth, crying and panting. I opened the back window slightly and he immediately stuck his nose out, sucking in all the air he could while leaving sticky saliva marks all over the window. The car we had was fairly big, but it was feeling increasingly small, as Ronnie took up more and more room, howling as he passed backwards and forwards across me.

We had been told at the training day that dogs often have upset stomachs when leaving the centre, as a result of the stress. Shortly into our journey there could be no doubt that this was the case for Ronnie. The smells that were coming out of him and into the confined area we were all sharing were revolting. Each time he passed me, a fresh waft of flatulence would fill my nose. What had he been eating? Whenever he went up on his hind legs to look out the back window, another high-pitched sound would come blasting out of his backside, much to our amusement. I was like a five year old, giggling at fart noises. It brought some much needed humour to the proceedings.

Colin was trying to soothe him from the front. 'It's okay, Ronnie. We'll soon be home. Calm down now, there's a good boy.' Both his and my words were falling on deaf, floppy ears, as Ronnie hurled himself from side to side, whining and gasping. His sharp claws dragged across my jeans each time he passed. I knew there were going to be aching scratches and bruises underneath, but my priority remained calming him down.

On turning into our street, the tension eased, knowing this ordeal was nearly at an end. Colin got out of the car first, opened the back door and caught hold of Ronnie's lead. He lunged out of the car and I followed, nursing my sore legs.

At the training day they had told us that when you take your dog home for the first time, you must take him to where he will be going to the toilet before introducing him to the home. This serves three purposes: it calms the dog down; lets him relieve himself; and enables him to get the scent of where he will be going in the future.

Ronnie pulled us across the road to an area of grass at Kelvingrove Art Galleries and Museum. While enjoying sniffing every blade of grass he dutifully did his business. As we returned to the flat, we were all a little calmer.

I opened the door and Colin let Ronnie off his lead. Again, we had been told to open all the doors in the flat, and let him roam freely between rooms, to get a feel for the place. Off he went, pacing frantically from one room to the next, sniffing his way through our home. We shut the front door behind us and left him to it. Anything that could have cut or hurt him had been removed, so he had free reign. We had even lifted the three rugs in the hall in case of any little accidents.

We sat in our kitchen, shell-shocked. The journey home had not been how either of us had visualised it. Had we jumped into this massive undertaking too lightly? What if he was going to be too much for us? How would I ever be able to control such a high energy dog if Colin was not around? So much for our decision to adopt a more passive natured dog.

As we sipped our coffee, Ronnie emerged from one of the rooms and joined us. He placed his head on my lap, looking up at me with his striking amber eyes. 'There, Ronnie. Everything's okay. This is your new home now and you're going to be very happy here,' I said, as Colin stroked his head gently. Calm had temporarily been restored.

Ronnie needed several walks that day owing to his upset tummy, and it was a pleasure to walk through the spectacular parks that are right on our doorstep. On returning from his evening walk, it was time for his first dinner. I scooped out the correct amount of dried food from the big yellow bag, into his shiny new bowl. Ronnie waited patiently, then pounced on his dish like a cat on a rat. Despite his massive enthusiasm, he was actually a very delicate eater. I have seen many dogs devour their dinner in seconds, but Ronnie chewed every mouthful like a connoisseur. There were many layers to this dog.

After dinner, we all settled down on the couch. It wasn't long before the unfamiliar noises from outside had Ronnie repeating the behaviour we had experienced on the drive home. He paced the couch like a polar bear I had once seen in Glasgow Zoo, demented by his captivity. This time, however, Ronnie began barking and this was new. We had commented several times on our visits to him how strange it was that we hadn't heard him bark. Now he was making up for lost time. With every external noise there was an assortment of internal barks.

They were such puppy barks too, high-pitched and overexcited. It was like he was just finding his voice, and it somehow didn't match his fully grown, gangly frame. We used to tell people, much to their amusement, that his voice hadn't broken yet, as he would often be in mid-flow, and the pitch would rise several tones, just like an adolescent boy.

We tried desperately to calm him down with toys, treats and distracting dialogue. Sometimes it worked, other times the noises were just too new and distressing to him. He was still such a young dog, and although he looked fully grown, we had to remind ourselves that his life experience to date was limited, and probably not that positive. That's the thing with rescue dogs. You just don't know their history, but the fact that he had been given away at fifteen months old didn't point to the happiest of starts in life. 'Colin, what are we going to do? The neighbours!' I groaned.

'It's fine. If anyone complains, we'll explain that we've just got a rescue dog and are settling him in. They'll understand.'

After several hours of on-and-off barking, Ronnie exhausted himself and lay quietly on the sofa beside us. It had been a gruelling day for all of us mixed with moments of pure pleasure when he snuggled up beside us, licking our hands and faces. Now it was time for bed. Prior to Ronnie's arrival, we had visited our local pet shop and purchased a sturdy dog bed. It was nestled in the safe place Colin had identified, between the piano and our bedroom.

The words of the Dogs Trust trainer came back to me.

'Many people ask us if it's okay to let your dog sleep on your bed. We don't actively encourage this, but really it's a matter of personal choice. If you asked all of the people that work here where their dogs sleep, you'd find the majority of them would say on their beds!'

'However, don't allow your dog to sleep on your bed on the first night. You're taking a rescue dog home and you have no idea how they're going to react. Imagine if Ronnie was to go for you in the middle of the night, not that he ever would, the lovely little pudding, or soil your bed. You'll not have made a strong enough bond with your dog yet, so give it a few nights and let them settle in.'

We had agreed that Ronnie should sleep in his own bed, and encouraged him towards the new burgundy bed frame with the soft, sheepskin inner cushion. He settled down with no objections as we got ourselves ready to retire.

'That's brilliant,' I beamed. 'He likes his bed.'

'Good stuff,' Colin gargled through a mouth full of toothpaste.

We both said goodnight to Ronnie and climbed into bed, shutting the door behind us. All was quiet for a minute or so … and then it started. Initially, it was a soft whimper. This led onto a louder wail, which then became an ear-piercing howl. This little guy did not want to be left on his own in a strange house, and was making it known in no uncertain terms.

Like parents of a new baby, we lay there, tense and uncomfortable. 'Give it a few minutes and see if he calms down,' I said.

'Okay, but I don't think he's going to settle.'

'Remember what they told us at the training: we need to persevere.'

Ten minutes passed and things were getting no better. The howls were heart-breaking and Colin made a suggestion.

'Maybe if we open the door, he'll feel more comfortable and settled. He'll get our scent and be able to hear us and that'll calm him down.'

'Okay,' I capitulated. I couldn't bear to listen to the wailing any longer.

Colin got out of bed and opened the door slowly. First, I saw the shadow of a black nose peeping around the door. Then a gust of wind blew through the bedroom as Ronnie leapt from his bed to ours in one majestic movement. If it had been a cartoon we would have seen the sparks and smoke flying behind him. He had snuggled down and settled for the night before Colin had even returned to his diminishing space in the bed. We both lay there, laughing uncontrollably: first at the ridiculousness of Colin's suggestion, as if Ronnie was just going to remain calmly in his bed with our door open; and secondly, at the way Ronnie had played us.

'What'll we do?' I asked.

'Leave him.'

We all snuggled down together for some much needed rest and Ronnie spent his first night, and every night since, nestled safely between the two of us.

Night night

Chapter Four - A dog is for life

Our home resembled Santa's grotto. There was tinsel and fairy lights draped over every picture, and my garland sparkled over the fireplace. The enormous Christmas tree was taking over the bay window, as its branches made it tricky to close the curtains, or access the music cupboard. Every year, I managed to squeeze a few more festive delights into our home and I loved it. The difference this year was that we had a new family member too, and we had no idea how he would react to this winter wonderland.

As it happened, he took it all in his stride. My fears of finding the presents destroyed, or the fairy lights chewed through, had been unfounded, as he casually ignored all of the splendour. I think the fact that he was getting far more exercise than the two and a half hours we had originally calculated had helped greatly. We had both taken him for many winter walks and he was beginning to make friends with other dogs in the park.

The transition from Dogs Trust to home was not without its challenges however. Colin had come back from one early morning walk shaken and distressed. All had been going well, with Ronnie happily enjoying his constitutional, when a woman and child in a buggy had approached. Ronnie's hackles had gone up and he had lunged towards them both, barking furiously. Colin had managed to pull him back, get him on the lead and calm the situation down. Understandably, the woman had got a terrible fright, and had not held back in letting Colin know how irresponsible she thought he was for letting such a *vicious* dog off the lead around children.

When Colin arrived home, the look of disappointment in his eyes told me he had real concerns about Ronnie's irrational behaviour. Colin is a very gentle and sensitive person, who doesn't react well to confrontation.

'I got a real fright, Susan, and don't understand why he did that. There was no catalyst that I could see.'

'I know it's really distressing, Colin, but we need to keep remembering that he's a rescue dog, and we know so little about his history.'

'I know.'

'It could have been anything. Maybe the buggy? Who knows? But no one was hurt and you got it under control.'

'What if I hadn't been able to though?'

'Let's not think about that. It's just really upsetting that it happened and you got a mouthful, but you know we would've reacted the same way if it had happened to us.'

'I know, and that's what's so disappointing. I think we need to keep him on the lead until we know him better, and can train him properly.'

Ronnie appeared blissfully unaware of the distress he had caused. He was standing in the kitchen, tail wagging, ready for a game of fetch. We both agreed it was best to ignore him so as not to reward his poor behaviour. On taking some advice, we were told this was possibly the first time he had seen a buggy. Thankfully it was an isolated incident.

Christmas morning arrived. I got up, lit the fire and all my candles in the living room, put the fairy lights on and stood back and marvelled at how beautiful the room looked with all the presents under the tree. Time to open them. After bringing in two piping-hot festive mugs of latte from our treasured coffee machine, we began unwrapping as the Christmas music played in the background.

Ronnie was right in the middle of it all. He had several gifts of his own and revelled in all the attention. Squeaky toys, chocolate treats, Christmas stockings full of delights and a shiny red festive collar with 'WOOF' written in silver letters, covered the floor. Family and friends had been so generous welcoming him into his new home. We have some beautiful photos of him lying covered in Christmas paper as the excitement got too much and he collapsed in a heap.

I wore the beautiful dress and jewellery Colin had presented me with, and we welcomed my parents, who had arrived to share dinner with us and meet Ronnie for the first time.

First Christmas

'Oh my! Hello, Ronnie,' my mum giggled, as he gave his usual enthusiastic and loving welcome, though he was now beginning to display guarding tendencies when people came to visit. These materialised in barking when the bell rang and continued until visitors were in the door. He looked a little confused about his behaviour as he was desperate to say hello, but felt the urge to protect his new home too. This resulted in frantic tail wagging and jumping up, mixed with pulling back and barking.

Following my mum through the door, my dad arrived to be leapt upon too.

'Hello, Ronnie. Get down! For goodness sake, Ronnie! He's a real scamp, isn't he? You've got yourself a real live wire there!' he gasped to Colin, as there was a chaotic clamouring to get into the hall.

Once we were all seated and settled, Ronnie jumped up and took great delight in making their acquaintance. They were captivated by him, just as we had been the first time we saw him. Embarrassingly, he was still suffering from an upset tummy, which meant our guests received the full force of his flatulence too. This just became a great source of amusement to us all, and thankfully improved with time.

As we sat down to the Christmas feast, Ronnie was incredibly well-behaved, lying under the table. I was determined not to have a begging dog, as there is nothing more off-putting when eating than having a drooling pooch staring pleadingly at you. Ronnie was taking good instruction on this and already showing signs of being very trainable. As a treat he did get a bowlful of Christmas dinner once we were all finished, and he savoured every mouthful.

We moved through to the living room next to the tree and enjoyed liqueurs and cheese and biscuits; the excesses of Christmas Day were endless.

'Colin, you excelled yourself again. Thank you for all your efforts,' my dad gushed. Colin is a fantastic cook, far better than me, and thoroughly enjoys creating the perfect festive meal. As we settled down to let the mammoth dinner digest, Ronnie jumped up beside my mum.

'Hello, little man,' she smiled as they snuggled into each other.

'What a plaster!' my dad said, 'Susan, your mother's a magnet to animals and children. They sense she has a good heart.'

'I know,' I replied. 'He's certainly taken to you, Mum.' She smiled contentedly and kissed the top of Ronnie's head.

'He's not a bad dog,' my dad said. Real praise indeed. 'Seriously though, it's a great thing you've both done, giving him a loving home. You've really landed on your paws here, Ronnie!'

'You certainly have. It must be so nice to be out of that cold kennel and be with your new family,' my mum cooed. Ronnie's tail tapped against the sofa, revelling in all the attention. Colin and I shared a satisfied glance as I experienced one of those Christmas moments when all just felt right with the world.

He lay his head on her lap and remained there for the rest of the evening. Despite what had happened earlier with the woman in the park,

Ronnie definitely enjoyed the company of women, and the position he took up with my mum was to become a favourite.

A post-dinner walk was called for and Colin spoke the magic word, 'Right!'

We had discovered that Ronnie did not respond to 'Walk', 'Walkies' 'Let's go out', or any other form of call to action. Quite by chance one night, Colin had said 'Right!', and Ronnie was off the sofa faster than a couple of teenagers caught snogging with the lights out.

We think he just learned this from Colin's reaction to taking him out. Whenever it was time for a walk he would stretch, take a deep breath and say 'Right!' How clever of Ronnie to have learned this so quickly. He can be completely crashed out, but just the mention of the word resurrects him, as he leaps onto the floor, tail wagging and ready to do the deed. Now, he even reacts to a stretch or change in Colin's breathing pattern. He's a clever cookie too, as even words that sound similar —'night' or 'bright' etc. — will get the same response, though not Ronnie's desired result.

When friends come round we have to explain in covert ways not to say the magic word. Ronnie has leapt off the sofa several times mid-conversation as our guests innocently share stories such as:

'How did your night go last week?'

'It was okay, though I'm not sure they had the right mix of people at the event.'

'Is that right? It's a shame when a night doesn't go as planned.'

Poor Ronnie would be on and off the couch like a bouncing ball as we explained: 'Listen, Ronnie reacts to a certain word that means the opposite of left, and even to words that sound like it. I know it's impossible to keep them all out of conversation, but just be aware that that's why he's bouncing around the room like this!'

After a lovely walk and some coffee and mince pies, my parents headed home and Colin pottered about in the kitchen. The day was nearly over and I was feeling the familiar sadness of another Christmas coming to pass. I sat on our sofa gazing at the twinkling tree and listening one final time to my festive music.

It had been a very quiet Christmas Day as Elizabeth and Jim, my sister and brother-in-law, had celebrated with Jim's family, and Morvern, my best friend, who usually spent the holidays with us, was travelling in New Zealand. We always had an open invitation to Colin's family, but my mum had been ill for several years and had now recovered, and I had felt it important to spend the day with my parents this year. I was really missing everyone at that moment, and could feel the tears brimming in my eyes.

As they fell, I felt a furry friend jump up beside me. He was looking at me with such intensity, head moving from side to side, and then he began to lick the tears away. Each time one fell he would be straight in there, wiping it away with gentle kindness. What a dog. I realised that while this was not going to be plain sailing, Ronnie had such a good heart that there was nothing that we couldn't work on and resolve.

A dog is for life, and that's exactly what Ronnie was going to be.

Chapter Five - Moments

Colin and I had enjoyed many long summer walks with our new family member. Some of them were more memorable than others. On one of Ronnie's last walks of the day, I had stayed at home and was getting ready for bed. The doorbell rang and Colin stood outside, looking frantic.

'What's wrong?'

'Ronnie hasn't come back here, has he?'

My heart stopped.

'No. Oh, Colin, what's happened?'

'He's run away. I think he saw a fox and he bolted. It's dark now and I can't see him. '

I froze, unable to take in fully what Colin was saying. I managed to blurt out:

'Oh my God! What are we going to do?'

'You wait here in case he makes his way home. I'll go and keep searching for him.'

I paced the floor going between the living-room window and the front door. I was beside myself. I had visions of Ronnie lying dead on the road, having been hit by a passing car, or worse, a bus. We lived next to two very busy roads and I couldn't see him standing a chance if he attempted to cross one on his own, especially at night. Then I jumped to picturing him being mauled by the fox; a savage death.

I heard a dog bark in the distance, but knew instantly it wasn't Ronnie. Then I heard someone coming out of the close, and mistook it for our gate opening. As I ran in and out of the flat between the window and the gate, I was exhausting myself, and behaving like a mother who had lost her child in a department store. Come to think of it, the feelings I was experiencing were reminiscent of times this had happened to me as a child.

I have a vivid memory of being separated from my mum in Marks and Spencer's. My stomach was aching with fear and panic as I weaved my way through unfamiliar adults, tears streaming down my face. We were only apart for a matter of minutes, but I experienced a feeling of total abandonment and vulnerability, thinking I would never find my way home and be lost forever. When I saw my mum pushing her way through the crowds and rushing towards me, the relief consumed me and I didn't care that I was getting a right good rollicking for wandering off. Safety and security had been restored to my little world as I grabbed my mum's hand tight and didn't let go.

Now I was regressing into similar emotions as Ronnie's absence went on for what seemed like an eternity. Suddenly, I spotted Colin stomping down the road with a very sheepish looking Ronnie at his side. The relief was enormous and I ran out to meet them.

'Don't speak to him, Susan.'

'But I'm just so relieved he's okay.'

'Just ignore him. We can't reward behaviour like that. He needs to learn he can't run away.'

Ronnie's ears were clamped back firmly to his head, tail between his legs, as he pleaded with those beautiful amber eyes for a pat. It killed me, but I followed Colin's stern instructions. He was right; he had to learn. We got back to the house and I heard Colin say:

'Ronnie, you can't do things like that. I'm really disappointed in you. We've given you a warm house, food and lots of love and you've let us down tonight. Go to your bed.'

Ronnie followed Colin's instructions and curled up in a tiny ball in his bed. As I passed him on my way back from the bathroom, his sad eyes followed my every move. I was desperate to kneel down and give him a cuddle, but I knew I would then experience the wrath of Colin. We had to be consistent.

'He's not coming into bed with us tonight, Susan.'

'Okay, but he looks really upset.'

'He's a dog. He'll get over it.'

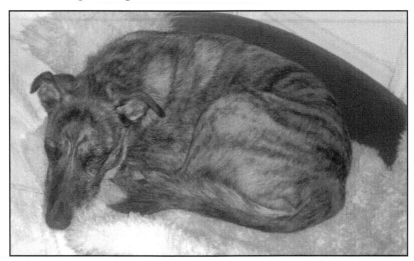

Scolded Ronnie

We lay there for fifteen minutes or so, neither of us able to sleep and me feeling increasingly guilty at the thought of Ronnie lying out there alone. I know on reflection it was ridiculous, and he was probably sleeping quite peacefully … but we weren't.

'I feel bad, Susan. Was I too hard on him?'

'You did what you thought was best, and he does need to learn.'

'I can't sleep.'

And with that, Colin got out of bed, opened the door and Ronnie was in like a flash, before Colin had time to change his mind.

'It's okay, Ronnie. We love you and just want to keep you safe. Snuggle in and get some sleep. We forgive you,' Colin said, as he gently kissed Ronnie's head and we all settled down for the night.

Another walk stands out too, in the list of memories we were now creating. It was a glorious summer's day and we had been in the putting green, playing fetch with Ronnie and his pals. There were a couple of gaps in the fence that, being a wee skinny malinky, Ronnie was able to get through. He had taken to running down to the river, just a stone's throw from the putting green, to cool off and replenish himself. He always ran back, as the thrill of a game of fetch was as powerful as a pocketful of treats.

On this occasion, we had finished the game and were walking along the riverside. Ronnie had made his way down to a nice little section of beach where he could paddle at the river's edge. We stood watching him with great pride as he slurped at the water and waded through the ripples. The water was so clear and glistening in the sun.

Then Ronnie began to wade in further than he usually did. Despite calls from us both, he continued to move forward, and by this time was half-way across the river, which was getting deeper and deeper. My heart was beating so hard I could hear it pulsating in my ears as Colin shouted, and it was as if he had got so far out he wasn't now sure what to do. By the time he got two-thirds across, he realised he was in trouble and stopped dead.

The river was moving fast and he was half-in, half-out, perched on top of a submerged stone, looking frightened and confused. His ears were pinned back to his head and fear was screaming out of his eyes. He was trembling and crying, and my heart was breaking for him. Now too far out for us to get him from this side of the river, I didn't know what to do.

'Wait here, Susan. I'll run around to the other side of the river and carry him out.'

Colin left me at such speed that I knew he was as worried as I was, as he turned on his heels and was out of sight in seconds. To get to Ronnie he had to run up the hill, past the putting green, out onto the street, cross a bridge and then run back down the opposite side. I couldn't see his progress and was willing him desperately to get to Ronnie.

'It's okay, Ronnie. Everything is going to be okay,' I tried to reassure him.

It seemed to take forever for Colin to get there, and at one point, when it looked like Ronnie was falling from the stone; I took my sandals off and began paddling towards him. It was useless though. The stones made it impossible for me to walk more than a couple of inches. I just kept talking to him and trying to keep him calm.

There was quite a crowd of passers-by forming now, curious, as we were, as to why this little dog was not swimming his way to safety. I know they were shouting advice and support, but I couldn't hear a word of it. I made my way back to the riverbank and decided to try again, wearing my sandals. But by this time, Colin had arrived at the other side. He took off his socks and shoes and walked into the icy cold water. I saw him grimace as his feet went in, with the shock of the temperature and the sharpness of the stones.

On a number of occasions, I thought Colin was going to hit the water as he stumbled and slid his way slowly towards Ronnie, who was looking more and more pathetic by the minute. At last, he was with Ronnie and as he scooped him up into his arms, a cheer went out from the audience. I felt the extreme tension I had been holding float down the river. Colin carried him back to the riverbank and I ran round to meet them both, thanking the crowd for their support as I passed. I felt like playing police officer and saying:

'Move along now, folks. Show's over. Nothing to see here. Move along, please.'

As I reached the other side, Ronnie's tail was wagging and he jumped up to give me his usual energetic greeting. He seemed a lot less affected by the trauma than we were. I picked him up and cuddled and kissed him, not caring that I was being soaked by his sopping fur.

'Oh, Colin, I'm so glad you got him safely back. Thank you, thank you, thank you,' I said as I kissed and cuddled Colin now, Ronnie jumping in-between us. 'But why didn't he just swim? I thought all dogs could swim?'

'I really don't know.'

To this day, Ronnie has never swum a stroke. While still enjoying a cool down and drink in the river, he has never gone far enough in to get stuck again, thank God. What a dog!

A final, more light-hearted moment I recall involves Ronnie's love of food. It has become a tradition in our home to host a New Year's Eve party. These soirées have taken many forms: from a full house to a handful of friends, depending on our energy levels post-Christmas. This was Ronnie's second New Year's experience with us, and it was a busy affair. The house was packed with people, and more arrived each minute as we got nearer to midnight.

Part of the tradition involves everyone going outside into our front garden to welcome in the New Year. Glasses filled with anything sparkly, we eagerly anticipate the first chime of the University bells, and watch the fireworks going off all over the city. I love it, and always feel it's such a fantastic way to start each new chapter of our lives. As we hug and kiss our way around the company, there's a real feeling of optimism about what lies ahead.

The buffet was set up in the kitchen and consisted of festive leftovers: Christmas cake; mince pies; festive shaped savouries and, of course, Colin's infamous sausage rolls. A party just wouldn't be a party without Colin's infamous sausage rolls. A tasty cheese board completes any buffet, and there were even Santa-shaped cheeses on there.

As we all piled back into the flat to enjoy the nibbles, Ronnie was conspicuous by his absence. Suddenly, I heard a roar of laughter coming from the living room. There was Ronnie proudly displaying an entire '100% extra-free' block of mature cheddar cheese in his mouth. He looked so pleased with himself, and somehow had not had the savvy to go somewhere private and demolish it. He had carefully planned his moment when we had all been outside toasting the bells, swiped in and was now the proud owner of a block of cheese twice the size of his head.

I removed it swiftly from his slobbering mouth and placed it with a heavy heart in the bin. Why couldn't he have taken the stinky Danish blue I detested so much? My dog obviously had the same taste in cheese as me.

Ronnie is a Lurcher-cross, and Lurchers are renowned for their scavenging tendencies. It's in their nature, and this is something we have had to contend with on an ongoing basis. We've learned from experience that we need to 'Ronnie-proof' the kitchen after we've cooked and eaten. If we forget, it's not long before we hear the sound of knives and forks hitting off crockery, as Ronnie pre-washes our dishes. Thank goodness for dishwashers.

The cheese incident is often recounted with great fondness by our friends who witnessed it, and it does bring a smile to my face. We got an e-mail from our friends Sharon and Robin after one of our parties which said:

'Just wanted to say a massive thanks from Robinofski and I for the most brilliant party. We are totally, TOTALLY profoundly in love with Ronnie, by the way. We spent ages talking about him on Sunday night, and we decided he has a really strong aura for a dog. He just makes such an impact; a really deep personality.'

Enough said.

Chapter Six - The blip of a PIP

'What's wrong, Colin?' I asked, exasperated by his erratic behaviour.

'Nothing, I'm fine.'

But I knew things were far from fine. He had not been himself for days and was uncharacteristically uneasy. On his head hitting the pillow, Colin always drifted off to sleep in a matter of minutes; something I envied. I often found it difficult to sleep so easily, and was awake long after I heard the deep hypnotic breathing that told me he had slipped into slumber, but this had not been the pattern for the last week or so. We would go to bed and he would still be tossing and turning, pulling the covers from me and sighing deeply into the small hours. I knew it was work-related, but recently, he wouldn't go into the detail of his distress.

For many months, Colin had been unclear about his sales targets, and seemed to have no management agreement of which areas he was expected to sell to. We had had many long conversations about how he could tackle this lack of clarity with his boss, but any action Colin took resulted in stalemate, as the issues were placed firmly with the indecisiveness of "Head Office".

It felt like he was leaving the house every day with no compass, no clear direction of where he was going, or what was expected of him week by week and this had been causing him great frustration. For the last week or so, things had changed and he had shut down communication. On returning home, he would watch hours of television, barely conversing and then head to bed for another restless night. It was miserable.

Ronnie was picking up the signals of an unhappy home. The second sense animals possess was in overdrive. His gaze would go between Colin and me as if trying to make sense of the change in our home's atmosphere and he would shove toys into Colin's hands in an effort to take his mind off his woes. While Colin still showed all the previous love he had for him, his enthusiasm for wrestling with Ronnie and playing fetch was waning. I was a poor substitute, and Ronnie knew this. I didn't have the strength or stamina of Colin, and our games just lacked the gusto they both so loved. Ronnie could often be found lying curled up in his bed, his soulful eyes perfectly replicating the mood. And so the ripples of the situation rolled over all of us as we bumbled through each day.

Then one afternoon, I checked our e-mails. Colin had sent one to our home account from work. I opened it with horror when I read the heading. It was a Performance Improvement Plan (PIP) to Colin from his boss. Having worked in management for many years before starting my own business, I knew how serious a PIP was, and that it was effectively a way of managing people out the door.

Each area of Colin's job description had been broken down in the PIP; targets, sales, teamwork, administration and overall performance. Beside each were statements which appeared to question Colin's ability in most areas, and an action plan had been drawn up with ridiculously tight deadlines to rectify the faults.

First, I felt sick, and then I felt a huge rush of loyalty for Colin. How dare his boss do this to him! Colin was one of the most hardworking people I knew, and always gave 100%; he had won awards for his selling skills and excelled in every job. His boss had head-hunted him from his previous role just under a year ago, boasting that Colin was the best salesperson he had ever known. What the hell was going on? Finally, my anger turned towards Colin. Why had he not told me about this? How did it get to this stage without me knowing?

I grabbed my phone and searched with shaking hands for his number. *No,* I realised, *this was not a conversation to be having on the phone.* It was only half past two, and Colin would not be home until six. The hours stretched cruelly in front of me. I felt like I was back at school, waiting to be summoned to the head teacher for some misdemeanour or other, not knowing what the outcome would be, and with no reference points to pull on. Our world could be about to come crashing down around us, and I didn't know what to do.

Ronnie came to me and rested his head on my lap. I reached for his lead which resulted in the usual excited leaps and yelps we had grown so fond of. It was as if every walk we took him on was his first. A long stroll in the park would help clear my head.

As we marched together, my mind was racing. I decided the best course of action was to distract myself for the meantime, and focus on what was around me. I was a *Life Coach*, for God's sake; I helped people all the time to overcome hardships and start afresh. Whatever happened, we would handle it. One of the fantastic benefits of studying life coaching was that I had a wealth of tools to pull upon in situations like this, though it was easier to support others, and not so effortless when applying them to myself.

I knew that the worst thing I could do right now was to go into catastrophic thinking mode. My coaching training had taught me that everything in the Universe is made up of energy, including us. Like attracts like so when we put out fear and worry we attract that straight back to us. When we put out love and positivity, our lives then reflect this. *You get what you focus on* was a common saying on my course. It's fascinating and follows the principles of *The Law of Attraction*. This type of thinking comes naturally to some lucky people, Colin being one of them, but most of us have to re-train our brains and mindsets to accommodate this welcomed guest. I so wanted to stay in a place of positivity with this current challenge, but was realistic enough to know that was going to be a struggle.

Over the past few months it had been wonderful to build up a relationship of my own with Ronnie. His morning walk was with Colin before he left for work, then I would take him out at twelve and four, spending the time in between either coaching clients or catching up with paperwork. I'm not sure how this had started, but we always had a pre-walk snuggle. I would go into the bedroom to put on my shoes and Ronnie would jump onto the bed. Before my shoes were on, he would be on top of me, cuddling in and licking my face, tail beating the duvet. We would cuddle up together for a few minutes, both enjoying the closeness. This was followed by excited leaps and yelps as I tried to get his lead on, then off we would head.

We had a couple of routes, both of them beautiful walks around the art galleries and down by the River Kelvin. One of the things I loved so much about having Ronnie was that I had discovered so many stunning areas to explore with him, and felt ashamed that they had been on my doorstep without me even knowing they were there. As we walked, sentences from the PIP kept coming into my mind:

Underperformance in sales targets

Must see significant improvement in this area

Systems need to be better.

I felt a stabbing pain in my solar plexus; a sharp reminder of the fear I was experiencing around the situation, and the pain I was feeling for Colin. I quickened my pace and pushed the emotions down into my gut, to be dealt with later. Knowing my reactions well, this would probably result in nausea and loss of appetite around dinner time.

Distracted again, we walked on. Watching the seasons change was another source of immense pleasure. I'd seen snowdrops, then crocuses, followed by daffodils and tulips, all blossom before my eyes. Watching the trees bud as they came back to life, breathed energy and enthusiasm into me every day. Now the summer roses were everywhere, and their colours and scent introduced the new summer season. How blind I had been to miss all of this pre-Ronnie.

We walked for miles that afternoon, and it certainly did help to calm my mood and quieten my mind. On returning, I attempted to work, but couldn't concentrate on anything. Colin would be home soon, so I started making dinner to distract myself further, though I was barely able to stomach cooking. As he came through the door, I lunged at him.

'What the hell is going on, Colin? Why are you on a PIP?'

Oh dear, my coaching tools had flown out the window alongside my calm mood and quietened mind. Ronnie skulked out of the kitchen, tail down and ears stuck firmly to the back of his head.

'What? Oh, you saw the e-mail.'

Colin shifted from one foot to the next. His head appeared too heavy

38

for his body as it hung down into his chest.

'Yes, I saw the e-mail, and thanks very much for letting me find out that way. What were you thinking?'

'I'm so sorry, Susan. I didn't want to worry you.'

'So you thought keeping it from me until it got to this stage was a better plan then? Good job, Colin!'

He was fiddling with a water bottle, ripping the wrapper off piece by piece and making one hell of a mess.

'No. I just thought I could sort it out before it got to this stage, and then you wouldn't have to worry at all. I know how you worry.'

'Don't you dare turn this on me! I've spent hours supporting you with your work stuff. Why didn't you tell me about this? I could have helped you. I just can't believe you would let me find out like this. I've been in a terrible state all afternoon. How did this happen? And will you put that bloody water bottle down for God's sake!'

Placing the water bottle on the work surface, he finally looked up at me with desperate eyes.

'They're trying to cut the sales team from six account managers to two, and looking at ways to get rid of people. We're all on PIPs. The problem for me is that my first-year contract is coming up, and they can get rid of me with no repercussions to them if I've been there less than a year.'

'But they're the ones at fault! You've had no proper targets or areas since you started, so how can they throw a PIP at you, when there's nothing in writing to base your performance on?'

'I know, I know, I know. I need to take some advice, but it's not looking good, and I'm really sorry you found out this way. I really am.'

'But what are we going to do? We need your salary just now. I'm not earning enough yet for us to be able to take this hit! I'm going to have to try and find a job now. My dream is over!'

'Oh come on, Susan. That's a bit dramatic. You're the one who's always telling me everything happens for a reason, and it's not come to that point yet. We'll be okay. If the worst comes to the worst, you know I'll get another job.'

'Well, excuse my drama! What the hell else do you expect? I can't always be in *life coach* mode, and I know I'm jumping ahead, but someone's got to think about what we do here. We can't pretend this isn't happening. Oh, just leave me alone. I need to be on my own just now.'

Ronnie was in the hall in his bed, curled up in a tiny ball. I felt awful for the shouting match that had just taken place, as I know how sensitive animals are to tension. My guilt increased as I looked into the sad eyes of our rescue dog. I knelt down and gave him a reassuring hug. Lifting his soft, floppy ear, I whispered my first lie to him.

'It's okay, Ronnie. Everything's going to be okay.'

Chapter Seven - Could we really?

Once again, we both slept badly that night, having only exchanged the barest of words before bed, the atmosphere in the room steeped with apprehension. As the hours stretched before me, I continued the wrestling match in my mind. Why did this have to happen just now, when we most needed the security of Colin's job? I realised, as I ran the events of the day over and over, that this was exactly what I had been trained in. Sometimes life sends tests to see how serious we really are about following our dreams. I batted that revelation away stubbornly, not yet ready to release my fury.

The birds were chirping their morning song as the light slipped through the gaps at the top of our curtains. This irritated me too. Ever since those curtains had gone up I had been meaning to get some nice material to drape over the top of the rail. What was the point of having blackout curtains if there were vast gaps preventing them from doing their job? Off I went again into my internal moaning diatribe.

Ronnie was awake too. He began his usual morning ritual of rolling around the bed to wake us up, licking our faces and barking 'Good Morning'. Not being a morning person myself, I was constantly amazed by Ronnie's enthusiasm for each new day. Lying between us both, he smiled and wagged his tail. It was impossible not to be affected by his love of life. My bitterness melted as Colin and I looked at each other.

'I'm sorry,' I whispered.

'No, Susan, I'm sorry. This should never have happened the way it did.'

We attempted to hug, but Ronnie made this impossible as he lolled between us.

'I do know that things will be okay. I just got such a fright,' I said.

'I totally understand. Who wouldn't have got a shock in the circumstances? I feel a huge sense of relief now it's all out though. It felt

41

dreadful not telling you.'

'These last few weeks must have been awful for you, Colin. I'm sorry you felt you couldn't speak to me. I know I must have sounded so selfish last night, but *please* can we make a promise to each other that, no matter what, we'll be honest in future?'

'I promise. I really do. It won't happen again. The last thing we need is for us to fall out when things are tough enough.'

'Right then. Let's put it behind us now. We'd better get up and get a plan together about what we're going to do.'

Colin had agreed with his boss that he could take a few days off to consider his options, and over that period his phone seemed to be ringing constantly. He spent hours discussing the situation with team mates, spoke with ACAS, and we also phoned my friend and fellow Life Coach, Nat. She had been an HR manager for many years before starting her own business, and was in a great position to advise us on employment rights. While it appeared that procedure had not been followed by Colin's company, the bottom line was that employers could terminate a contract before the end of the first year, without having to give any reason for doing so. Employment law and protection only kicked in after one year of service. We were stuffed.

Colin's boss seemed genuinely unhappy and uncomfortable with the situation he found himself in too, and together they had many conversations on the best course of action. During one of these exchanges, Colin negotiated a decent pay-off and a glowing reference. He went in the next day and resigned.

It was over in less than a week. On reflection, I couldn't quite take in the speed at which it had all panned out. Five days before, I had been aware that Colin was unhappy, but completely oblivious to the severity of the situation. Now, he was unemployed.

This brought immense changes to our day-to-day lives. I continued to work on my business, while Colin began the arduous task of finding another job. He re-established links with employment agencies. The world of sales is a precarious one and this wasn't the first time we had found ourselves in this unenviable position. He set up meetings to sit in front of people half his age, as he battled to project a positive spin on his current situation.

At least Ronnie was happy about the changes. Blissfully unaware of what was going on around him, he just loved the fact that Colin was home more. It meant far more walks off the lead, and endless games of fetch. He was in heaven.

Colin would get himself suited and booted, armed with his newly updated CV and references, and head off into town, ready to talk himself up and find out his options. After each meeting he would return, and in his usual upbeat fashion, tell me that everything had gone well, and that there were interview opportunities available for him. He was right, but there was just something about him, never spoken, that told me that the hideous way his last job had concluded had affected him more than he would ever admit. I could see it in his eyes and his buoyant behaviour was overplayed. Behind the smiles and positive anecdotes, the hurt and disappointment ran deep.

What followed were a couple of months of filling out application forms and attending interviews. It broke my heart watching Colin fighting to remain optimistic, when his trust had been so badly broken. He was becoming jaded, having to repeat his story over and over, and tired of remaining enthusiastic about working for another company, regardless of their promises of outstanding career progression opportunities and superb benefits. He was going into interviews unprepared and, as time went on, indifferent to the outcome. I'd never seen him like this before.

This was, of course, resulting in no job offers, which perpetuated the hopeless cycle Colin was now falling into. His heart just wasn't in it. I couldn't watch any longer and it was time for a chat. As he and Ronnie came bursting through the front door after one of their many escapades, I hustled Colin back out and into our local pub. It was a glorious summer evening so we took an outside seat as I began.

'Well, Mr Campbell, how are you feeling?' I asked as I sipped my cold and welcome glass of wine.

'I'm doing okay. Just getting a bit sick of repeating myself and finding positive ways of saying I was sacked! I'm still pissed off about what happened and I think it's coming through at times.'

'I think you're right. It's really difficult to cover up stuff like that, even when you think you are. It seeps out in body language, or in your tone of voice. Totally understandable though, Colin, after everything that happened.'

'I know, but I need to snap out of it. It's not doing me any favours and I need to find another job.'

'Is that what you really want, Colin? How do you feel about going back into sales?'

'It's all I know, and we need the security just now. I don't mind carrying on. What choice do we have?'

'Well, I'm just planting the seed, that maybe you could look at a change of direction. I know my initial reaction to all of this didn't exactly inspire what I'm about to say, but as you know, I'm a great believer in things happening for a reason. Maybe this is the Universe telling you it's time to try something new. You're certainly not enthusiastic about getting a sales job at the moment.'

Coincidently, before this had all happened, we had met with our financial advisor. This economic MOT had revealed that I was paying into an endowment policy from my previous mortgage that was running at a loss. Our advisor had suggested I contact the company to see what it would pay out if I cashed it in early. Her view was that as it was never going to produce the projected amount, the monthly fee would be better saved elsewhere, and the lump sum would be a welcome boost to our finances. At that time, there were no penalties for cashing it in early, and a nice little nest egg had been incubating away safely over the course of the policy. It had felt a little scary to cash it in, but the words I had read so many times during my own business start-up journey kept coming into my head.

'Great things involve great risks and you will be constantly tested. So many people give up at the first hurdle. Will you be different? You have to

44

ask yourself if you are prepared to do whatever it takes to make it work.'

Looking back now, I believe that it really was the Universe lining up to support us to take a new leap of faith. Colin wasn't meant to get another job at that time. Whether people believe or not in what many call 'mumbo jumbo, tree-hugging nonsense', I have found consistently that when inevitable challenges have come in one door, a solution has found its way through another.

'Do you really think I could do something else?' Colin asked as I saw a twinkle form in his eyes.

'Yes, I do. Why not? We have some savings now, plus what I'm bringing in. Maybe you could try something new, if you want to. You're always saying how jealous you are of my self-employed lifestyle, so put your money where your mouth is!'

'Wow, Susan. Maybe you're right. You're certainly right about me envying your lifestyle. I hated leaving you and Ronnie in the mornings to go and work the nine to five drudge. But what could I do?'

'What do you want to do? What about something with your music?'

'Mmmm. That would be the obvious thing, but I'm not sure that's the road I want to go down. The band's great, but it's something we do together. How would you feel about me being out most evenings gigging? It wouldn't do much for our life together.'

'That's true. The band's a hobby, but I know how much you love to show off! If you had to make a living from it though, the magic may go out of it. Well, what else interests you?'

'Okay, go with me on this one, as it's something that keeps popping into my head. You know how Ronnie needs walked so much and I've met lots of people and dogs over the last few months just with taking him out?'

'Yes.'

'Well, I'd like to try my hand at dog walking. I'm out so often with Ronnie and I really enjoy it, so why not see if people would pay me to walk their dogs too?'

I felt my stomach flip with excitement; a good sign. Intuitive reactions are generally right, and I liked what I was hearing. Something inside me just knew this was a first-class idea that I had to support my hubby with.

'That's a great idea, Colin. You're right. You already know loads of people and Ronnie has made friends with so many dogs. There must be people out there who would use your services. What we need to do is get a plan together and I'll coach and support you to get started.'

The excitement was building. I could feel the energy levels rising in both of us.

'Could we really do this, Susan?'

'Of course, we could. All it takes is an idea and lots of oomph, which you have, and things will come in to support you to make a success of it. That's how it all works, Colin. It's what I do for a living! The fact that it keeps coming into your head is a sign that you should pursue it.'

Ronnie really was turning our lives around. We were both becoming fitter and loving the positive energy he brought to our home. This was taking it to another level altogether though. Colin and Ronnie were going to set up business together, and make a living from spending every day together walking other dogs.

And so that evening, as we enjoyed that last of the sun's rays, 'Ronnie Ronster's Dog-Walking Service' was born.

Chapter Eight - Ronnie Ronster's Dog-Walking Service

And so they came; all of the signs and signals that were needed to convince Colin he was doing the right thing. He'd actually been receiving these for months whenever he headed out with Ronnie, but now they were becoming more frequent and less easy to ignore. Before he had even left his job, Stephanie, a neighbour, had sought out Colin and Ronnie's help. She had a beautiful Australian Blue Heeler called Sparkles, who was a canine with issues. Sparkles didn't get on well with other dogs, and the advice she had been given from a dog psychologist was to walk Sparkles for a couple of weeks with another dog, to help socialise her. She came to our door to ask if Ronnie could be her supporter. Of course, Colin agreed to help out, and every day, they would all head off at 6.00 p.m. to do a round of the park.

We had both felt chuffed that Stephanie had identified Ronnie as having the kind of energy Sparkles needed, and Colin saw this as a way of contributing something to the dog world. It worked well, and while Sparkles was still, at times, a nervous dog, she and Ronnie trotted along nicely together on their daily walks, and in time, Sparkles would became one of Colin's future clients. It was another indication of the specialness of our wee rescue dog.

Colin had also, from the early days of having Ronnie, linked up with a group of dog owners who met every evening in what used to be a putting green, across the road from our flat. Their dogs ran around together and burned off energy while the owners chewed the fat.

Colin and Ronnie had now established themselves as part of the pack, and the putting green was becoming Ronnie's favourite place in the world. To this day, whenever he gets a whiff that he is going anywhere near the place, he pulls so hard on the lead he nearly chokes himself, coughing most of the way there like an old man who has smoked too many Capstan Full Strength.

So who were Ronnie's pals? Well, there was Lola, a beautiful white Staffie rescued by Gaile, who was a graphic designer at that time. Then there was Harvey, an exuberant huge black Labrador owned by Chris, a photographer. Fleece the Collie and Skye the Parsons Russell were the best behaved dogs of all, being owned by Pat, the dog trainer. Noelle, the graceful Whippet, and cute-as-a-button Rachael-Anne, the miniature Shitsu, were owned by Veronica and Blair, both students, and Brodie the chocolate Labrador was owned by Herroch, the joiner from the Western Isles. These dogs were the first pals Ronnie made over the initial few months of his new life with us, and they were all to become invaluable in supporting Colin's new venture.

While Colin had been going through the soul-destroying process of looking for another job he had got chatting to Dave, the then-owner of our local pub. Dave and his business partner Steven had given up good jobs to invest in what had become a very run-down, bordering on seedy establishment. In its heyday, the Brewery Tap had been a thriving and popular bar, which prided itself on its welcoming atmosphere, wholesome food and real ales. Over the years, it had been neglected and then sold on to someone who didn't show it the love and care of the previous owners.

The results had been sad to watch. The clientele changed from faithful local regulars to people only interested in the ridiculously cheap alcohol, resulting in mayhem at closing time. Being situated next door to us, we would often come out on a Saturday morning to find half our fence broken off and strewn across our garden, and empty bottles of beer and wine perched precariously on my beloved plants.

And so it was with great pleasure that we had welcomed Dave and Steven as our new neighbours. They worked tirelessly on a complete conversion, and the result was a total facelift, new menu and competitive bar prices, to entice previous loyal customers back into its beautiful surroundings. Now called the Drawing Room, as it overlooked the Art Galleries, calm was restored and our garden fence and plants breathed a huge sigh of relief.

If we had no plans, Colin would pop in for a pint on a Friday evening, and on this particular night, he got chatting to Dave about the pros and cons of self-employment.

'Colin, all you have to remember is if you can find a way to make £100 a day, you're sorted. That's what it takes, and if you can't live off the proceeds of that, you're doing something wrong. Just £100 a day, mate.'

This had really got Colin thinking, and had obviously been one of the catalysts behind his urge to try dog-walking. He began working out the connotations of this with regard to number of clients and walks he would need to make this cherished £100 a day.

As we sat down together to make a plan this is where he started.

'Susan, if I have ten dogs and charge £10.00 per walk, that's £100 per day. That's all I have to do.'

'Wonderful Colin, but is £10.00 per walk the going rate? You need to do some market research, to find out what other dog walkers are charging, as that seems a bit much to me.'

So he began researching every dog walker in Glasgow, and came to the conclusion that the current going rate was £8.00 for an hour-long walk. We sat down again to restructure the plan. 'I've decided what I'm going to do,' Colin said purposefully.

'Okay. Let's hear it then.'

'I'm going to promote a special offer of £5.00 per walk for the first two months, to any clients who come on board in the first two months of my business starting.'

'Right. And what happens after that?'

'After that I'm going to charge £7.00 per walk so that I'm offering a competitive rate. The £7.00 rate will only be open to the clients who come on board in the first two months. Everyone else after that will be charged £8.00 per walk.'

'So you're going to have two rates on the go. Do you think that's wise?'

'Yes. I want to show my gratitude to clients who trust in me in the early days; reward their loyalty. I need to see if I can do this, Susan. If people trust me to walk their dogs at the start, they should be offered a cheaper rate. Once I get into my stride with it, and see that I can do it, I'll raise the fee, but reward their loyalty by not charging them as much as everyone else. Like I say, that's only open to clients who come on board early. My rate will be £8.00 as of month three for new clients.'

I wasn't nearly as enthusiastic of this plan as Colin was. During the business side of my life coaching training I remembered being told of the importance of consistent charging. We were advised that all clients should be charged the same rate, as people talk and would be more than a little pissed off it they found out that someone was getting a better deal than they were. I had to work hard to pull back and remind myself that this wasn't my decision to make.

'Well, it's up to you. It's your business, but I wouldn't do it that way. Just keep an eye on it, okay? So what are you going to do?'

'Okay, I want five clients by the end of the month. If I get that I'll continue for another month.'

Oh my God … he was only giving himself one month to test this out. I was into the second year of my business and still nowhere near where I wanted to be. What was he thinking? Once again, I took a deep breath and continued listening.

'I'll carry on for another month looking for one new client per week, which will give me ten by the end of month two. If I've got that, I'll know I've got a business, so I'll focus on it. If not, I'll start looking for a job again.'

'I don't think you're giving yourself long enough.'

'Susan, we can't mess about here. I know we have some savings, but they're not going to last forever, and it'll take me a few months to get a job. I'm not going to put us in any financial danger. We'll know soon enough if it's a goer.'

I supportively nodded my head, offering a reassuring smile, but inside I was alarmed by the pressure Colin was putting on himself and the convoluted charging plan he had come up with. I was going to have to trust him and let him find his own path in this, however, as much as I wanted to jump in and change it all.

'So when are you starting?'

'Well, we've got Dalmallyfest coming up, so I'll start the Monday after that. The last thing I want is people booking me and having to say: "Great, brilliant I'm super-reliable, but I can't do next weekend".'

'Okay then. That's Monday, 17th August.'

Two weeks away.

The race was on to get PR materials together to begin promoting the business. Together we set a goal. I went through the process I had used so many times with clients, and Colin took to it really well. He imagined a date six months ahead and using as many positive and inspiring words to convey what was happening with his business by that date, he wrote down a plan that was motivating yet realistic. It had to be clear, not woolly, and capture all of the timeframes he wanted to reach each part by, finishing up with a rousing final statement of his intent to achieve it. We then chunked this down into milestones with the action he needed to take each month to reach the goal. It included all of the practical things he would need to do as well as contingency plans in case things didn't go exactly to plan.

I've continually found that writing things down like this and making this positive statement to the Universe brings about progressive change. It may be that the goal changes or the way you get to where you want to be comes in from a different direction, but something changes when the intention is made. Doors start to open and people come into your life to propel you towards your dream. It's magical and something to do with the new positive energy a goal brings into your life.

He began taking the actions as he worked on his new website and searched for suitable business cards. Chris had offered to take photos of Ronnie and did a wonderful job, capturing the real essence of him in every shot, so it was torture picking the eight we wanted. Gaile suggested that she could create a business logo for us, and again we were taken aback by the quality of her work. The Ronnie Ronster's logo is a cartoon head-shot of Ronnie, grinning widely and wearing his signature bandana. It was perfect.

The website was coming along nicely. One of Colin's previous jobs had been Sales Manager for an Internet company, who sold search engine optimisation packages. This had come in handy to both our businesses, as Matt, one of Colin's friends, who still worked there, had done a fantastic job of designing my first website for free. It also meant that Colin knew his way around designing and launching his own for Ronnie Ronster's, and had support on hand whenever he needed it.

It amazed me how easy it actually was to set up. Colin chose the template from a selection of animal type ones that were available, and then did some research into other dog-walking services, looking at what they offered and charged. Putting his own unique slant on the text, he added the additional graphics that Gaile had designed to go with each section and service he wanted to offer. He was able to buy the domain name for Ronnie Ronster's Dog-Walking Service relatively cheaply, and within hours, his website was up and running.

'Do you think this is a bit cheeky, Susan?' Colin called me in from the kitchen to view his work

HANGOVER SERVICE

Book our 'Hangover' service in advance, and we will collect your dog at the agreed time for their first walk of the day, while you catch up on some well-earned shut-eye!

EMERGENCY HANGOVER SERVICE

Of course some hangovers just happen spontaneously. If you haven't pre-booked, but desperately need that extra hour (or two) in bed, call our emergency hotline, and if we can help you we will!

'No, I think it's really good. I'm not sure anyone will ever use the service, but I think people will like the sentiment.'

'What about this though?'

THE 'DIRTY STOP-OUT' SPECIAL

Let's not judge. We've all been there. But should you find you need our overnight service at short notice, just call and if we can help, we will!

'Well it's different. I've not seen that offered by anyone else. Keep it in just now and let's see what the reaction is.'

The graphics from Gaile worked so well for the website that we decided we needed to find a way of thanking her for all of her hard work. I came up with the idea of Colin walking Lola for free as an exchange. This would also mean that he would be seen out with another dog, helping to build his credibility.

And so, Lola became Colin's first client before his official start date, and Gaile continued to design the most amazing graphics which, mixed with Colin's flare for coming up with 'different' offerings, was bringing the website alive. I particularly liked 'P in the Park'.

IN THE
PARK

Ever been held up at work unexpectedly for a meeting? Or had to cut short an impromptu social occasion? Or simply been stuck in traffic worrying about poor Fido at home alone, cross-eyed and cross-legged, desperate for a 'comfort' break?

Well, worry no more. We understand that sometimes life puts obstacles in the way of the love and care you want to give your best pal. So, we have introduced our 'P in the Park' teatime special.

Doing exactly as it says in the name, we will take your dog for a pee (and a poo if needed) in your local park. This short walk service will give you peace of mind, and allow your pooch to wait for your return in comfort.

The website was complete and Colin could not believe his eyes. When he typed in the words 'Dog-walking Glasgow' Ronnie Ronster's Dog-Walking Service came up on page one of Google. We hadn't paid for any search engine optimisations packages, or anything to boost the site, it just happened. Colin was beside himself with excitement. He knew from his previous role how much money people paid to make this happen, and how important it was to be on that first page, and it had happened by chance, or had it? Was this yet another sign that all was well with the new venture?

It seemed so.

The following Monday morning, the phone rang, and I heard one half of a conversation Colin was having:

'Yes, it is. Oh hello. Yes, I'm Colin, and you are? Hello, Sabrina. How can I help you? Oh, how lovely; a puppy. Where is it you stay? Yes, I would be delighted to walk little Millie. How did you find out about the service? Thank you very much. Yes, I like the website too. You'll have to excuse my over-excitement, but you're my first customer to come through the website, so it's great to know it works.'

I was equally excited as I stood ear wigging at the kitchen door. Colin bounced back to me with the look of a thrilled little boy. I knew exactly what he was going through; having had the same reaction the first time I got a life-coaching client. It felt like the world was opening up to you. There were possibilities galore and you were taking charge of your life; a wonderful feeling.

Little Millie

'Well done, you. Tell me all about it.'

'Well, Millie is a four-month-old Cairn Terrier that lives in Dennistoun with Sabrina and John.'

'Dennistoun? Is that not a bit out of your way?'

'Yes a bit, but it's a start, and I'm happy to make the detour while I build up my clients. They live just beside a park, so I can walk Millie and Ronnie there. I can't believe someone's phoned already. This is amazing, Susan. She wants me to start next week. Monday, 17th August!'

Chapter Nine - Early days

We had both been lucky enough in our previous work lives to have had company cars. Lucky, that is, until we left. Fifteen months previously, I had handed back the keys of my/their Golf TDi on my final working day. By that time, I had already started the process of looking for a replacement. While a car was a necessity, it had to be on a shoestring. I couldn't justify spending a lot of money with my business at such an early stage.

And so 'Cheeky' came into our lives, a red Fiat Seicento. She was the smallest car in the world. Well, less of a car and more of a hairdryer on wheels. I had, however, prided myself on getting a top-of-the-range hairdryer, with power steering, electric windows and air-conditioning. I loved her. Petrol costs were halved and I could park in spaces the size of a postage stamp. We would whizz around the town together, nipping in and out of the tightest spots, and producing a mixture of pleasure and pity from onlookers.

Ronnie fitted nicely in the back — just — but it was an uncomfortable journey for any back-seat passengers, and these became few and far between. I can remember driving my parents the four miles from their house to ours, and feeling like I would never get up one of the hills, foot pressed firmly to the floor, but the weight in the car was just too much for her. It also amused me greatly to see Colin driving her. He's a big guy and his head would sweep the roof as he sped along. The driver's seat had to be pushed so far back to get him into a comfortable position that it hit the backseat.

We called her Cheeky because there was such a mischievous look about her, and it was an act of bravery taking her onto the motorway. I lost count of the amount of times I was 'road-raged', and driving at speeds of over sixty-five miles per hour resulted in mass shaking resembling an internal earthquake. But l loved her.

So, by the time Colin's first week of his new business came around, we had been using Cheeky as our main source of transport for two months. Colin's company car had been sent back a month after he resigned. They had been kind enough to let him keep it for an extended period, to help with his job search, but he was now experiencing the inconvenience of not having a car of his own. He really did look ridiculous behind the wheel of Cheeky, but he never complained, and in those first few weeks of his business, it was Cheeky who ferried the dogs back and forth between walks. How on earth did they all manage?

D-Day arrived. Colin and Ronnie headed out the door: Colin filled with anticipation and a full breakfast and Ronnie … well, he was just being Ronnie, thrilled to be heading out with his dad. Colin had no idea where this new chapter was going to take him. All he knew was he couldn't believe that he was going to spend his days walking dogs from now on, and getting paid for it. It was such a contrast to the stressful, target-driven environment he had come from.

I watched the comical sight of them both speeding down the road in my little red box on wheels, wondering how on earth they were going to fit any more dogs into its tiny interior. Their first stop was Dennistoun to pick up Millie, and with a park on her doorstep, there was no need to transport her anywhere. A leisurely stroll ensued, with lots of stops to talk to fellow dog walkers and park dwellers. Puppies are such people magnets and Millie was loving all the attention.

I sometimes feel for Ronnie as so many of the dogs Colin walks are much prettier than him, and he is often overlooked. We think he's just gorgeous, but he does have the look of a mutt about him, and I can understand why people are drawn to the other dogs. His main source of interest seems to be his curious looking shape and coat. He's been called a hyena, an African wild hunting dog, and one little boy exclaimed, with huge excitement on one of our walks: 'Look, Daddy. It's a tiger dog!'

I'm always delighted when someone takes the time to pet him or comment on how unusual he looks, and I know that Ronnie is too caught up in the fun of the walk to even notice he's being ignored. I guess it's that old parallel with children again. We so want the people and animals we love to be popular.

Colin dropped a tired Millie home and headed back to our flat. He left Ronnie with me as he made his way to Ibrox. Another call had come in the previous week from Neil, owner of Jack, a Hungarian Vizsla. His previous dog walker had entered the close he lived in to pick up Jack, to be greeted with the unwelcome sight of a flasher. It was with regret that she told Neil she couldn't walk Jack any more. Neil had been recounting this story to Gaile as they were friends, and Gaile told him all about Ronnie Ronster's. And so, another dog came on board on 17th August.

Again, it was the other side of the city, but Colin felt it was worth the travel to get things off the ground, and to be seen out and about with dogs. We lived in the West of the city, while Millie was in the East and Jack the South. Colin was already racking up the miles.

He made a flasher-free pick up of Jack and brought him home to meet me. Jack fitted into the back of Cheeky, with a little push from Colin. He really only had half of the back seat as Colin's driver's seat was pushed so far to the rear. When Colin arrived home with him, he was a little frazzled. In transit, Jack was a barker with a really low-pitched, booming bark. As they had set off, Colin, in fright, had hit his head off the roof of the car as Jack's first deafening bark pierced his left ear.

There was so little room in the car that Jack's head had been right alongside Colin's when he let out his initial woof. In this enclosed area, the start this had caused Colin and the subsequent jump it caused his body had propelled him upwards. As his head already swept the roof in ordinary circumstances, there wasn't very far for him to jump to, causing a nasty bang to the head.

He wasn't badly hurt and as he recounted the story to me, he began seeing the funny side as I commented that I would love to have been a passer-by. Jack was a young dog with the most beautiful rust-coloured coat and daft temperament. Full of fun and a little heavy on the old paws, he bounded into our home, tail wagging, knocking down anything in his way. He made little squeals of delight as I petted him and told him what a beautiful boy he was. Little did I know then, but this was the start of it. Our home was soon to become a haven for so many wonderful dogs.

Colin, Ronnie and Jack headed over to the park for another walk and a game of fetch, as I continued with my working day. An hour later, they returned and Colin made the journey back to Ibrox to take yappy Jack home, this time prepared for the onslaught to his ears.

The final walk of the day was Lola, Gaile's gentle white Staffie, and this was to prove the most challenging walk of the day. Colin had been walking Lola for a couple of weeks now, and she just wasn't responding to him. On arriving at Gaile's flat, Lola had given Colin a lovely welcome as usual, delighted to see him, but as usual, not so delighted at being taken from her comfy bed, down two flights of stairs for a walk. A battle of wills ensued, with Lola winning. She was a solid mass of muscle who knew her own mind. Colin managed to get her down the stairs after much pulling and cajoling with treats, but once on the pavement, Lola wasn't for budging.

Early days walk

Not quite knowing what to do next, Colin waited a few moments and then nudged her along a little bit by bit. She really didn't want to go anywhere, but Colin knew she must have desperately needed the toilet, so he held his ground. His patience was rewarded as two feet from her close door; Lola relieved herself and then promptly turned tail, pulling Colin vigorously back towards the comfort of her bed. There wasn't going to be any walk again today.

Colin decided it was time to speak to Pat, the dog trainer, about Lola's lack of compliance. Pat told him:

'She's not coming willingly because you're *asking* her to go for a walk, you're not *telling* her. Your whole body language and energy needs to show that you're in control, or she'll just keep resisting you.' This was to prove one of the best pieces of advice Colin received, and it worked a treat. Just by going in purposefully and with an assertive energy, the next day, Lola obliged, and they managed a stroll around the block. He's used this advice continually in his work with the dogs over the years.

And so, Colin's first day was over. This was going to be an adventure. Ronnie was happy as he had been on two walks with two new pals, and spent the day with his beloved dad. Colin was happy as he had learned that he could walk other peoples' dogs, even if only on a small scale so far. There was scope to grow and organise himself better, so as not to have to be driving back and forwards all day, but he was confident that would come with experience.

We also got our first taste of dog-sitting at the end of the opening week. Oscar, the graceful Whippet owned by Ian and Catherine, who were off to a music festival, came to stay for the weekend. He really was no bother at all, and being a friend of Ronnie's already, the two of them just played all weekend. They ran up and down our hall, tugging toys from each other's mouths, and tumbling about the place like spring lambs. Oscar also became a regular of the pack whenever Ian and Catherine needed us.

In the second week, two new dogs came on board. Jackson, the most majestic Lurcher I have ever seen, was owned by Jennifer, a school teacher. Ronnie and Jackson were already the best of pals. He wasn't a putting-green regular, but Colin and Jennifer had met often in the grounds of the Art Galleries, from early on in our ownership of Ronnie. Jackson would race around the grounds, and it was a truly spectacular sight watching him glide through the grass at the kind of speed which left all other dogs in his shadow.

There was a special connection between Ronnie and Jackson, and we always knew when he was around. Ronnie could pick up his scent from a good half a mile away and nearly pulled your arm off to get to his best pal for a run and a play. Now the summer holidays were over, Jen was heading back to school and wanted Jackson to get a good run every weekday. It would be a pleasure to have him as part of the pack, and an absolute thrill for Ronnie to have his best pal with him every day.

Ronnie and Oscar

Rosie the Jack Russell also came on board. Ursula, her owner, was a friend of Jen's, who had recommended us to her. Coming from the Dogs Trust too, we felt an instant connection to her. Never in my life had I seen a welcome that matches Rosie's. Her entire back end wagged and she leaped so high off the floor she could lick your nose, and sometimes, when she was in a particularly frisky mood, she'd nip it. Colin was about to start receiving this greeting every day, and experience the immense pleasure of welcoming these dogs into our lives.

Both Jackson and Rosie were local dogs, so Colin could walk to and from their homes, which was just as well: there was no way in the world that Jackson would have fitted into Cheeky with his elegant long legs and greyhound frame.

Ronnie and Jackson

In the second week, I also performed nursing duties to Millie. She had a stomach infection and needed to have medicine every few hours, and just be cuddled and loved the way we all do when we're not well. She was dropped off every day after her morning walk, and in-between the dispensing of medicine from a syringe into her little pink mouth, she lay on my lap sleeping as I worked. I enjoyed doing my bit to help.

By week three, she was well on the mend and back to normal walks. Rosie's input had been increased from one to two walks a day, so Colin just kept her out all day with him. Then another two dogs came on board the Ronnie Ronster's ever growing pack. Max the mongrel, was owned by Carla and well known to Colin and Ronnie. While Colin was still working, he would get up extra early to take Ronnie for a walk around the park every morning. He had met so many people and dogs at this time, and Max had been one of them. Carla had bumped into Colin in the park, and having heard through the grapevine of his new business, was looking to enrol Max.

Old Jack, the retriever, also began his walks that week. He lived in the same street as Gaile and Lola, and Colin had passed on a card one day when he met Rachel, Jack's owner. Now they required his services, and he too joined the gang.

Colin was managing all the extra dogs by having a morning walk with Millie, Rosie and Ronnie, then picking up Jack and leaving him back at our house with Ronnie and Rosie while he went to pick up Max, Jackson and Old Jack. We had discovered that if we put the seats down in the back of Cheeky, Ronnie, Jack and Rosie fitted quite comfortably. He would then come back for Ronnie, Jack and Rosie, and the six of them would head out to the park. I admired his courage immensely, as I sometimes struggled with just Ronnie, but he seemed to have it all under control.

Rosie

The last walk of the day would always be around the block with Lola, who was now used to this daily ritual owing to Colin's new tactics, and no longer resisted him.

At the end of month one, Colin and I sat down to review progress.

'Well, how do you feel it's gone then?' I questioned.

'Brilliantly! I've surpassed my target. I've got seven dogs and as Rosie is now a double walk, you could call it eight. I'm nearly where I wanted to be by month two!'

'I know, Colin. It's amazing how well it's all going. Are you enjoying it, though?'

'Lovin' it. It's hard work physically with all the walking. The picking up and dropping off of dogs takes longer that the actual walks! I think that'll get easier with time though. Time and practice ... and I'll get fitter too.'

'Well, just keep doing what you're doing, cos it's working.'

Colin's new clients were coming by him making friends with people and their dogs in the parks where he and Ronnie walked, as well as through personal recommendations from current clients. It was all happening so easily. So much so, that Colin expressed a little regret at not having done this sooner.

Because of Colin's years of experience in sales and his naturally pleasant disposition, I could see that promoting Ronnie Ronster's was going to be a breeze, and I had such a good feeling about it all. I loved to watch Colin head off to the park, being pulled along by this curious mixture of dogs of all shapes and sizes. It was progressing well.

We got ourselves into a wonderful routine. Every morning, I would get up and put the coffee on. I'd make Colin's sandwiches and a flask of tea, organise breakfast and then feed Ronnie. It felt great to be setting them both up for the day ahead, before I settled down into my own day.

Ronnie would follow Colin from bathroom to bedroom, to kitchen to living room, in and out, at his heels, staring at him with total concentration in anticipation of the day ahead. He'd be waiting for the moment Colin would say, 'Right, son, let's go. It's time to get to work', as he'd pick up the lead. Ronnie would go into his leaping and high-pitched shrieks of delight, dancing around the hall like it was his first adventure into the outside world. The sense of pride I felt as I watched the two of them heading out the door was colossal.

My own days were spent coaching individual clients, predominately over the phone, and working on building group-coaching clients. I would often be the holding ground for dogs too, as Colin dropped them off between walks, to make the pickup of other dogs a little easier. It was lovely getting to know all the dogs and having their positive energy around me as I worked.

Then one evening, Colin's phone rang and it was Anna, another dog walker. Colin had known Anna prior to Ronnie Ronster's, having met her and all her dogs in the park several times. Together they had chatted about the wonders of dog-walking, and it had been an inspiration for Colin to see how well Anna was doing. I listened with anticipation to one side of the conversation:

'Hi, Anna. How are you? Oh, how wonderful. Congratulations! I'd be delighted, Anna. Thanks so much for thinking of me. Yes, it will be a fantastic experience for me. Well, the most important thing is that you can enjoy your wedding and honeymoon. I'll do a good job for you, I don't want you to worry. Yes. Pop round next Tuesday, and we can have a chat about the dogs and owners, and I can get a feel for it all. Thanks again, Anna. See you soon.'

Colin's face was flushed with excitement. 'Can you believe it, Susan? Anna wants me to walk seven of her dogs!'

'Wow, that's amazing! So, she's getting married?'

'Yep, and she wants time off before the wedding to get organised, and then obviously there's the honeymoon. She's asked me to look after them for five weeks, starting the week after next!'

'Oh, my God! It'll be so great for you, Colin. It'll build your confidence and get you used to handling more dogs, and just get you out there. How do you feel about taking on that many dogs alongside your own so soon?'

'I'll be fine. It'll just need proper planning, and I'll need your help at home, if that's okay? It's fantastic. How lucky am I?'

'Of course I'll help. It's well-deserved, Colin. You're working hard and this is just another sign that you're doing the right thing.'

And I knew he would be fine. I'd seen him in action already and he had no fear with the dogs. He was able to keep them under control and would let them all off the lead in the proper surroundings, to burn off their energy, each dog returning to him when requested, with great ease.

'Oh my God!' Colin exclaimed. 'I never expected things to move this quickly. I need to get proper transport. I'll never manage all of the new dogs in Cheeky!'

Chapter Ten - The Grand Move

I trawled used car websites for days. Searching for the best deals had been one of my favourite hobbies for many years: from holidays to bathroom suites, there were bargains to be had.

And now I began the online process I so enjoyed, in search of suitable transport for Colin's new venture. We had made the decision to spend low initially, while we waited to see how the business would go. Setting ourselves a budget of £400, I was amazed at how many cars/vans were actually available at such a minimal cost. They may have been old, with high mileage, but they were out there and still roadworthy.

One in particular caught Colin's eye: a ten-year-old Daihatsu Grand Move, which resembled an early attempt at a people carrier. Colin liked the name as he felt it symbolised his new start, and he set off with Charlie, our brother-in-law, to view it. Charlie is good with cars, and this was his second shopping trip, having helped me select Cheeky the previous year.

A couple of hours later, the maroon Grand Move came chugging into our street as I ran out to meet it. To me, it looked like a heap of junk. There were scratches and bumps all over it, and rust around the wheel trims, but Colin looked so proud of himself that I didn't have the heart to say. Inside, there were shiny silver seat covers which looked like they'd been made out of an old Gary Glitter costume, but the interior was clean and fresh.

Charlie saw my expression and laughed.

'What do you think of your new car then, Susan?'

'Mmmm. Not sure what to say, Charlie.'

'It'll do you fine, but don't expect to get any more than a few months out of it. It won't last,' Charlie advised. In actual fact we got nearly a year out of the heap of junk and on trading it in got the money back we had spent. Not such a bad buy after all.

'I think it's great. The seats fold forward and I'll be able to get five or six dogs in the back,' Colin gushed.

'It's great, Colin. Well done. You're in business,' I reassured him.

Charlie headed home and we went for a coffee. I had a momentary flash of fear, a common emotion of the self-employed that comes in and out at the oddest of times. I shared my fears with Colin.

'We are doing the right thing, aren't we?'

'Of course we are, Susan. What's brought this on?'

'You've bought your car and are really going for this now, which is fantastic, but I'm just a bit scared. This is it now. We're both self-employed and relying entirely on our own ability to make money!'

'Hey, you! You're the one who's always saying "you can do anything you want". We've got to stand firm in this, and trust we can do it. You've got to keep reminding yourself why we're doing this. I'm teaching my granny how to suck eggs here.'

'I know. Even though I do this for a living, I still have doubts sometimes. I think I'm just having a wobble. I know how important it is for us to feel in control, and not be at the beck and call of others. I just get a little scared sometimes that it'll all go belly up!'

'You know as well as I do that whatever happens, we're resourceful, skilled people, who will find a way of making money, even if it does mean having to go back to work. But that's not going to happen, right?'

'I don't think I could work for someone else now. You're right though, hard work and perseverance, that's what it takes, and we've both got lots of that.'

Eighteen months previously, we had been in full-time jobs, driving top-of-the-range cars, enjoying regular holidays, and spending money without a second thought. Now, we found ourselves the proud owners of ten-year-old cars, facing an uncertain future without the security of the monthly pay cheque. We were totally responsible for earning our own money. Was this a step backwards, or was it about image and ego? I talked myself through this with, I felt, some measure of skill. I was becoming quite the effective life coach.

Of course it was scary that we were both now in the self-employed camp, and of course it was upsetting to let go of some of the material benefits of our old lives. Leaving the stress and strain of my old job had, however, been the most liberating thing I had ever done. It had brought a real sense of personal achievement that I just hadn't experienced in my previous role, and I now had such a keen sense of the value of money.

Spending time reassessing our expenditure and re-evaluating what was important to us had brought far greater satisfaction. It had reduced the previous emotional spending habits we had both formed as a result of the voids in our working lives. I remember going out regularly and buying things for the house, such as cushions or bedding, despite having an ample supply of perfectly good possessions already. Clothes and jewellery would bring on spending frenzies too, but the initial rush of pleasure was always followed by the depression of buyer's remorse. It was all so unnecessary, and looking back, the 'downs' that followed the purchasing were the lessons I had chosen to ignore.

On reflection, it was a reaction to unhappiness in my work. I didn't feel valued and so I tried to make myself feel better with the purchases I made. Added to the mix, was a long period of time when my mum was very ill, and this supplementary stress threw my spending into overdrive too. When money was readily available, in my experience, it became something that was very much taken for granted, and not appreciated in the way I now do.

There were costs and consequences to making the change from employee to self-employed. We gave up holidays together for over five years, but to be honest, we never wanted to leave Ronnie. Silly as that sounds, we both felt that with him being a rescue dog he needed lots of time to settle with us, before we could leave him with someone else. For several years, whenever we are away overnight, a friend or family member stayed at our home, so he could stay in his familiar environment. Pandering or what? Thankfully, we have now pushed the boundaries on this one, leaving him for a couple of nights then a long weekend and we've even managed holidays these last two years. He's been fine.

It is true to say, however, that neither of us feels the same need for the holidays. Making a living from what we love has removed the major stress from our lives, which brought on the demand for two or three holidays a year; another sign of emotional spending. Colin often tells me that he feels like he is on a permanent holiday, which just warms the cockles of my heart.

I stopped buying clothes, jewellery, make-up and things for the house on a whim. I just couldn't justify it anymore, and I had too many clothes, pieces of jewellery and cosmetics as it was. It was great to start wearing and using all the things I had taken for granted, or forgotten about, left lying in a drawer or cupboard, like the abandoned toys of a spoilt child.

We began thinking about what we put in our shopping trolley, instead of piling it high with no thought for the checkout bill. We'd have competitions on who could find the best bargains, or the most 'buy one get one free' offers, and marvelled at how much we'd saved on multi-buys. The Pound Shop became one of my favourite places to visit, and I couldn't believe how much I could get for a tenner.

Don't get me wrong. We were never in dire straits. There was always money in the bank to pay our bills and keep us going. It's a funny thing, however; the psychological switch that goes on when you leave a permanent job. Until you've come to terms with living with uncertainty — if that's ever possible — spending money on frivolous stuff just doesn't feel right. That feeling stayed with me for a couple of years into my business, and I think will always be with me to a lesser or greater extent.

Self-employment is not for the faint hearted, but the rewards are high: choosing with whom I work; being answerable ultimately only to myself; shopping at quieter times when everyone else is at work; being able to make appointments during the day, such as the dentist, workmen etc; working in my jammies; choosing when to work … I think I'll have a long lie this morning and work this evening instead; having a luxurious bubble bath in the middle of the day just because I felt like it; knowing that whatever money I bring in has been made through my own creativity, hard work and commitment to myself and my business; and the personal satisfaction that I grabbed all my courage in both hands and took a risk.

The trappings of employment are what had kept us stuck, and they are traps. I remember having endless conversations with my own coach about coping with the loss of salary, holiday pay, sick pay and my car. She told me calmly: 'Susan, it's so worth it', and she was so right.

Colin and I never looked back. He now had his car/van and Ronnie, his business partner, and was beginning to build up his client list. He took on Anna's dogs — Max, Holly and Millie the cross breads; Hamish the Airedale Terrier; Jacob the Cocker Spaniel; Bodie the Golden Retriever; and Scamp the wee Terrier — on top of his own dogs. The first couple of days were frantic, and he would come through the door looking bedraggled and exhausted. All the walking and checking of dogs was taking it out of him.

He would leave early in the morning and not get back until after seven at night. The additional dogs meant additional walks: two in the morning and two in the afternoon. It wasn't just the walking; it was the logistics of getting his head around where to pick up and drop off, and meeting new owners to ensure they were happy with the service. Coping with having more dogs in the new car, and getting them all in and out safely was also a new skill Colin had to learn … and fast. It was a lot to take on in one go, and he did share with me that it was downright scary at times.

However, with careful planning, repeated exits and entrances into the car with the extra dogs, and through building up a tolerance for the extended exercise, he got into his stride and began enjoying it. And Ronnie loved it: new pals and new walks.

Colin's confidence grew and he quickly picked up the tricks of the trade. We made journeys to pet stores to buy split harnesses which meant he could hold two leads in each hand, resulting in him being able to walk eight dogs. Each lead split off into two dogs so instead of having to hold four leads in each hand, he only had to hold two; clever and much more manageable. He bought a doggy first aid kit, and enough treats to stock his own shop, and on every shopping trip we purchased a healthy supply of poo bags; an absolute must. As time went on, his days shortened and his fitness level and tolerance for the extra work grew.

Then one afternoon I got a traumatic phone call from Colin:

'Susan, you need to come to Bellahouston Park now. I've lost my car keys and the dogs are locked in the car.'

'What?'

'Just come to the park and bring my spare set of keys, please … now! I'm at the side entrance.'

'Okay. I'm on my way.'

I jumped into Cheeky and arrived at the park twenty minutes later. I could see the Grand Move in the distance and Colin scouring the grass like one of the dogs when they get the scent of something. I ran up to him and got a glimpse of the heads of all the dogs popping up over the high-set windows, in-between the condensation being caused by all the internal panting. The dogs appeared a lot calmer than Colin.

'Here's the keys. What happened?'

'I had them in my hand when I brought the dogs back and I opened the door, got them all in the back and locked it. I had a poo bag that needed to go in the bin so somewhere between locking the door and walking to the bin I've dropped the keys. I've retraced my steps so many times, but I just can't find them.'

'Let's have another look together.'

Colin opened the door of the car with his spare keys, poured water into a couple of bowls for the dogs, and opened the windows. The search continued, but it was futile. However unbelievable it may seem that a set of keys could be lost in a radius of a few square feet, that's what had happened, and Colin couldn't spend any more time looking.

'You go and get on with your day, Colin. I'll stay and have another look.'

'Thanks for coming out with the keys, and sorry I've messed up your afternoon.'

'It's fine, Colin. We're a team, remember. There's no harm done, and the dogs are fine. You just got a fright, and these things are sent to try us!'

I continued looking for another ten minutes or so, then decided to give up the ghost. Where those keys went remains one of life's mysteries. On reflection they may well have ended up in the bin with the poo bag, but neither of us, in our state of panic, thought of that at the time.

Things were moving fast and it was now autumn. As it was a beautiful day, Colin suggested I come out on one of his walks. It was one of those days that looked like the middle of summer as the sky was so blue, without a cloud, but there was a chill in the air that cautioned the changing seasons. Ronnie, Colin and I hopped into the Grand Move, which now held a distinct *'odeur de chien'*. We followed a well-planned route to pick up all of Ronnie's pals, and it was great to see Colin in action. It felt a bit like being a helper on a school bus. My responsibility was to make sure there was no funny business, while Colin picked up the passengers.

Little Millie, who'd been our first pickup, had managed to make her way beneath the front seat to under my legs, and was nestled quietly at my feet. I would discover later that she had been chomping her way through an entire banana as we sped along, and was very pleased with herself.

Once everyone was on board we took the quickest route to the park. I thanked God, as the noise level in the car had been building gradually as each new dog arrived. There were barks coming from all directions and it was doing my head in.

'Is this what it's always like, Colin?'

'Yep, just till we get to the park. On the way there, there's always a lot of barking, but on the way back it's nice and peaceful.'

There were six dogs in the car and getting them all onto leads and out of the car was quite a challenge, though Colin was getting more skilled at this every day. I took two dogs, and Colin took the rest as we marched through the grass to an area that was safe, to let them all off their leads.

Autumn walks

What a beautiful sight that was. They all ran in different directions, but somehow still managed to form a pack. Little Rosie would run away then run back, leaping up and down with her frenzied greeting, while Ronnie just ran and ran and ran. He looked so happy and free, and I could see how much each and every dog was getting out of the experience. They were all so well-behaved, following us while still being far enough away to enjoy the freedom as we made our way through the park.

The colours were spectacular: reds, oranges and golds everywhere. Some trees were just a mass of red leaves, while others had a combination of all three. Each tree took on a unique hue as the sunlight danced its way between the contrast of the branches and foliage. Beautiful.

I loved the autumn and always have. I think it links into my love of all things Christmas. The colours of this season remind me that my

75

favourite time of the year is just around the corner, which fills me with excitement. It could also be down to the fact that I am a 'soft autumn'. I had had a session with a colour therapist many years ago, and that had been my diagnosis. Rich rusts and all shades of green, brown and red were recommended to me for my wardrobe, and I must say she got it spot on. Whenever I deviate from these colours it just doesn't work so well. Whatever the reason, I definitely have a connection with the warmth and cosiness of these rich colours, and on this sunny afternoon, I was revelling in them.

We had a fantastic walk and I discovered that all you really need to get dogs to come back to you is a pocketful of treats. At one point, I was surrounded by them all as they waited patiently to be handed a meaty morsel. We headed back to the car, and sure enough, the journey home was much more sedate. As we weaved our way through the streets, I realised that a big part of the job was about logistics, planning and timing. I had loved seeing how much Ronnie enjoyed his day, and remember thinking that we really had given him a good life.

It had been fun and enlightening to spend time with the Ronnie Ronster's pack. Colin was coping wonderfully and Ronnie was happy. I was so proud of my boys.

Chapter Eleven - The nights are cold, the sheets are thin

So what brought Colin to his love of dogs? It all began when he was ten. His father died when he was five, and his mother died when he was twelve. I often wonder how he ever became the wonderful man he is with such a sorrow-filled start in life. Then I remember how hard his sisters, Catriona and Chrisanna, and brother Murdo worked to keep Colin from the clutches of Social Services. It meant everything for the family to stay together, no matter how challenging it was.

They also had the support of extended family members, and together managed to build a life in the family home where Colin and I now live. And they did a really good job, despite what Catriona may sometimes believe, as she shares stories of extreme hardship after a few glasses of wine. Colin and Chrisanna were born in our bedroom, and until Colin met me, he had lived in the flat all his life, only moving out for three years to live with me when we first met.

The year before Colin's mum died, one day after coming home from school and walking through the enormous storm doors of the ground floor tenement flat, he got a huge surprise. This is how he described to me what happened next:

'As I walked into the hall, I could see the kitchen door straight ahead of me was closed. It was a sunny day and rays of light were shining through the gap at the bottom of the door. The rays were being interrupted by something. I could see little paws dancing around and I knew instantly it was a puppy. As I opened the door, there he was: Jasper, a little black ball of fur, clambering around the kitchen floor, becoming acquainted with his new home. I couldn't have been happier.'

From that day, Colin and Jasper became the best of friends, and Jasper is legendary in the many stories I heard about the years that followed. He would go from bed to bed at night, acting as a makeshift hot water bottle, with everyone getting their turn. He would drink coffee out of his own ashtray, with milk and one sugar, and be a part of every momentous occasion the family went through. Friends of Colin's from back then always speak of Jasper with great fondness. He truly was a blessing and a much loved dog.

Colin and Jasper

It is from building the bond with Jasper, and taking care of him as a young man, that Colin developed his love of dogs. This was to endure long after Jasper died, peacefully in his sleep, the night before Colin was due to take him to the vet to be put down … no lie.

Jasper was a rescue dog, and helped Colin through the immense pain of losing his mum to cancer the following year. He wasn't the first four-legged friend the family had rescued. The previous year, Catriona had brought home Sandie, a little fawn-coloured puppy from work. Sandie had been saved from execution by this act of kindness, and became a much loved family member. Tragedy struck only a few months later. Catriona was out walking with Sandie in the park when an Alsatian chased her. The terrified puppy had run away from Catriona and across the road only to be hit by a car. Everyone was devastated.

A neighbour had heard about the sad loss of Sandie and came to the door to tell Colin's mum that there was another little puppy in need of rescue. He too was about to be put down. And so Jasper joined the Campbell clan.

Colin's mum's death was, without doubt, the most challenging thing the family ever had to go through. Ironically, the year before his mum passed, Colin played the lead role in a school production of Oliver. He told me that there were tears galore from other parents in the audience who knew of his mum's battle with cancer and that the likelihood was that he was destined to become an orphan.

Colin as Oliver

Catriona was twenty and Murdo was twenty-two when their mum died. They were instantly propelled into the parental role for Chrisanna, who was sixteen, and Colin, then twelve. I can't even begin to imagine what this must have been like, but I sometimes get a glimpse of the horror and pain of it all in each of their eyes, when recalling past stories.

It was a huge financial strain to keep the house running. Catriona had to give up her dream of going to Art College, and worked alongside Murdo, as they became the main providers. I've heard many stories of the hardships they all faced, often told with the humour of hindsight, but I know there are some painful wounds that are slow to heal.

One by one, the family started moving on. Catriona met Charlie and moved into their new marital home, and Chrisanna bought a flat on the south side of Glasgow. Murdo bought the family home and continued sharing it with Colin for several years, before moving to Aberdeen to take up a new job.

Left to his own devices, Colin slipped into some bad habits. The flat became very run down and he spent most of his time in the pub next door, living on beer and carry-out dinners.

By the time I met him, he was in pretty bad shape; overweight and not taking care of himself or his home. Despite this, I was instantly attracted to him, even though it took me a bit of time to agree to go out with him. He had such an optimistic outlook on life and oozed positive energy. He never had a bad word to say about anyone, and lived very much in the moment. Looking back, I can see that, at that time, I was two-thirds of the way through a counselling course, and doing so much work on myself around positivity that it was no wonder I felt drawn to him.

Colin and I bought the flat from Murdo not long after we got married. It was in need of complete renovation, which we were able to carry out before we moved in, owing to Murdo's generosity in lowering the price of the flat. It really is a magnificent home, which we both cherish. The ceilings are so high that when we were getting a quote for curtains, the guy's measuring tape ran out about a foot before it hit the floor.

'I've never seen that before!' he cried. There are original fireplaces and cornicing, and the fact that it's a ground-floor, main-door flat makes it feel like a house. We even have our own small front garden, but the back court is shared with all of the other tenants in the building.

We are both so happy in our home and can't imagine living anywhere else, but I desperately want a private back garden. Every summer, when the sun comes out, I feel like I have cabin fever. I'd love to have our own space to sit in, dine in and enjoy leisurely evenings. We live opposite a beautiful park which we often use, but it's just not the same. Still, we have no plans to move at this time, as the flat and its location are just too good to give up, not to mention the enormous family history it holds.

Colin's family were chuffed with the renovation work and love to come back to the family home in its new glory. It's changed days indeed. There is a huge contrast between our over-the-top Christmases and the ones celebrated after Colin's mum died. Catriona jokes about the tiny silver tree that stood cheerlessly on top of the telly, with three baubles hanging from it.

They also talk about how cold the flat was. There was a zone in the living room between the sofa and the gas fire that was warm and cosy. Moving out of it, resulted in a coldness that felt like being outdoors. People would hold on as long as possible before running to the bathroom, and heading to bed was miserable. Colin and Jasper would sit on the floor, Colin leaning up against the sofa with Jasper lying in-between his legs providing extra warmth. This is one of his favourite memories of Jasper. Leaving the comfort and warmth of the zone was dreaded each night by all.

Now the flat is warm, thanks to central heating and draught-proofing of all windows and doors. I'm a hothouse plant that hates to be cold, and Charlie, my brother-in-law, often bemoans this fact, peeling layers off as he mops the sweat off his brow. I take great pleasure in reminding him about the zone, and he has to admit the new regime suits us all better.

Colin also tells stories of the one hot water bottle that would be shared between the four of them. It was one of the old stone ones you had to wrap in a towel to prevent initial body burns. Colin would get first shot and then when Chrisanna went to bed; it would be taken from him to heat her bed up. He would always hope that Jasper was snuggled beside him at the point of withdrawal, but if not, he told me about a little trick he'd learned to keep warm. He would pull the covers over his head and breathe heavily to create a vacuum of heat. I asked him how he didn't feel like he was suffocating, and he told me about his trick of sticking his arm out a little way at the top of the covers to create a chimney. On cold winter nights, when we hop into bed, he's also sung me a song they used to recite; 'The nights are cold, the sheets are thin. Snuggle in, snuggle in.' amusingly heart-breaking.

On a more macabre note, one Friday night, not long ago, as Colin and I enjoyed an end of week drink on our sofa, he began talking about his father's death. I had known that there had been several family members' coffins in our home overnight, before funerals, and to be honest, I just tried to push it to the back of my mind. Colin was casually recounting the fact that his dad's coffin had been but a few yards away from where we were sitting, as I felt the goose bumps pop up underneath my clothes. I wasn't prepared for what he told me next, however.

As a young, impressionable five year old, he was intrigued by the sight of his father lying in a coffin, a thing only children could get away with, and became fixated on his facial expression which held a crooked smile. His mum would find Colin in front of the mirror for hours after the funeral and eventually asked him what he was doing. 'I'm copying my dad's squinty smile,' was his blasé response. My jaw was hitting the floor as Colin recounted this story to me with the same casualness he'd shown as a child. He went on to tell me that this became his signature smile which can be seen in all of his old school photographs. Is it just me who thinks this story is heartbreaking and wonders what on earth social services would do with that kind of information these days? That's one of the wonders of long-term relationships; there's always more to find out.

Despite these hardships, Colin and his family are so well-adjusted and the nicest people you could meet. Jasper really did make a huge difference to Colin's life. They shared seventeen years together and Colin was his primary carer. He told me that he would buy Jasper a rubber ball every Christmas, and together they would head off to the park. Colin would throw the ball once, and Jasper would run and run and run, and bring the ball back. He would throw it a second time and Jasper would run and run and run, and bring the ball back. A third throw would ensue, and Jasper would look at Colin as if to say: 'Fuck it! That's not for me,' and head off in the opposite direction … every time.

He also told me about the time he took Jasper to a pet show at school. Despite Jasper misbehaving and pooing in the yard, he won third prize for having the shiniest coat. On looking back, Colin felt it had been a sympathy prize as he had gone alone; the only child there without his parents.

Caring for Jasper taught Colin responsibility at a young age, and began the lifelong love affair he now has with dogs. Who would have thought that, all these years later, the many lessons he learned from looking after Jasper would come into such good use in his new career?

Jasper

Chapter Twelve - Testing times

Ronnie has always been a live wire. From the moment he propelled his lithe body around that corner to make our first acquaintance, we knew he was a bright spark. Despite having had no intention of taking a high-energy dog (one of the reasons we had overlooked the Collie puppies in The Dogs Trust reception) he had melted our hearts that day and his exuberance only added to his ample charm. Still, high-energy dogs require high-energy training and lots of it.

During those early days, when Ronnie was still at the pound, Colin came home after one of his many visits proclaiming, 'He's really trainable you know.'

'Oh? How's that then?'

'I've been working on getting him to jump up on top of the table in the middle of the field, and then sit. He's getting it already. He'll do anything for a treat.'

The field where we had first walked Ronnie that dark December evening was a lot larger and more dog-friendly than either of us had been able to see. It was about the size of a football pitch with a ridge around the top that meant there were two paths, one at the top of the ridge and one running around the bottom. I think it was set up this way so that 'sticky' dogs didn't have to come face to face. A quick run up the ridge and they'd be separated, with canine war averted. In the middle, there was some basic agility training equipment, and it was there that Ronnie was being put through his paces. He loved it as much as Colin, and as the days progressed, his delightful personality began to show through.

Mixed in with this delightful personality, however, is also a strong will, coupled with selective hearing … unless there are treats on the go. He really will do anything for a Gravy Bone, but if asked without an indulgent reward, the outcome depends on his mood. Sometimes we get lucky; other times he completely ignores us, and goes in the opposite direction, with the look and attitude of a disobedient child.

And so the time had come for some proper training. We had both started the process through Pat's (the dog trainer) summer classes in the putting green, but Ronnie really needed something more structured, so Pat invited Ronnie and I to join his formal weekly training class in Bishopbriggs.

It was a very different set-up in the community hall, where the training took place, from the informality of the putting green. When we arrived, there were dogs and owners in the hallway, waiting to go in, and I could hear commands being shouted from the hall. A class was obviously just finishing. Ronnie and I stood together. I could see in his eyes that he was excited, but like me, a little unsure of these new surroundings. Suddenly, through one door, all the dogs and owners from the class burst out, and we were invited in through another door. It was all a bit chaotic, with dogs barking, some growling at each other as they passed, and a strong smell that reminded me of The Dogs Trust.

I walked in, nervous and apprehensive of what lay ahead. The room was like any other hall, with parquet flooring and a huge stage at the far end. There was a reception table just past the entrance door where Marilyn, the secretary, was ticking off all the dogs and owners as they arrived, and taking the fee. The cost of the classes seemed ridiculously cheap to me. It was only £25 for all the classes from September to May. Pat explained that it was run on a voluntary basis. The three trainers didn't take any money for their time and expertise. The secretary and other two committee members also gave their time voluntarily, and the fees were used to buy equipment and things like the t-shirts they were all wearing. Pat's had 'Head Trainer' on the back of it; very impressive.

There were long rubber mats all around the edges of the floor like a border, and Janis, the trainer of my class, stood in the middle as all of the dogs and owners grappled to find a place on the slightly sticky rubber. Ronnie and I took our position. There was a lot of noise coming from the trainers and helpers, as they made tea and talked and laughed at quite a volume. I would later find out that this was deliberate. The dogs need to be able to respond to your commands in everyday circumstances, with all the usual noises that go on in life. If the room was quiet and calm, it wouldn't reflect real conditions. This made perfect sense to me once I knew, but until then, I found the din really off-putting and irritating,

'Forward!' Janis shouted commands from the centre, and off we went, following the rectangle of the mats, the dogs walking to heel and then sitting when commanded. Ronnie responded well once he calmed down and got into it. We were both remembering what we'd learned over the summer, and the structure of the class was working for us. All our practice had paid off, as he even performed well on the recall task. Every now and then a dog would have an accident, and one of the committee members would appear with a mop and bucket, which explained the tackiness of the mats.

As the weeks progressed so did the level of training, and the expectations on the dogs and owners. By this time, we were asking our dogs to sit or lie, and walking to the other side of the hall where we were timed. The dogs had to sit for one minute and lie for two. Not long you may think, but as the dogs sat at one end of the hall and the owners stood at the other, all it took was for one dog to get up for most of the others to follow suit. Added to this, Ronnie had taken a serious shine to a springer spaniel, which, strangely enough, was male. If this dog was in the class I had absolutely no chance of getting Ronnie to stay anywhere. He would be off humping this poor unsuspecting dog who, just to make our misconduct even more shameful, was the star of the show.

Then one week, I got a call from Marilyn, the secretary, to say we were being moved up from the novice class to beginners. She told me this would mean coming along at a later time. So the following week we headed for the 9.30pm class, delighted at having been upgraded. When we got there, the class had started so we were plunged in with a group of strangers mid task. All of the dogs were walking to heel next to their owners without their leads on. What was going on? Surely the jump from novice to beginners wasn't this big? I dutifully took Ronnie's lead off, but unfortunately, his love interest had also been moved up so he was off like a rocket, to express his affection as only dogs can. As I prised Ronnie off the spaniel, his owner gave me such a stern look of disapproval it would have turned milk sour.

The next thing I knew, we were being told to sit our dogs, tell them to stay, then walk out of the room and leave them. I did as asked, but just knew there was as much hope of Ronnie staying put as there was of me seeing twenty-one again. As soon as my back was turned he was off towards his sweetheart. It was useless to even try, and Janis, seeing my exasperation told me to stay in the room with Ronnie, as he really wasn't going to comply. At the end of the disastrous class, I made my way to Pat.

'This isn't the right class for me, Pat. It's too advanced.'

'I know, Susan. This is the advanced class. You've jumped three levels!'

'But Marilyn phoned me and told me to come at this time.'

'There's been a mistake with a few of our classes. Don't worry about it. You're to come at 9.00 p.m. next week. That's the beginner's class.'

'Thank God for that! Well, it was certainly an experience!'

The beginner's class was a delight; just enough of a stretch to keep our interest without the humiliation of the advanced class. We worked our way through the many exercises we were given and practised dutifully between classes. Then test night arrived.

I'd been experiencing mixed feelings about it. I wanted the opportunity to show off all we had learned, but I was terrified it would all go belly-up and I'd lose my nerve. To make matters worse, we had to perform in front of all the class. Sitting in a row at the end of the hall, trying to keep our dogs calm, we waited like school kids about to be called into an exam. I watched with interest as the other dogs went through the test, some performing well, others not so well. This only added to my nervousness. How were my little friend and I going to do?

It was time to find out. Pat called us up. My palms were sweaty and my legs felt a little shaky. I'm really not good with tests. Ronnie, on the other hand, was just his usual self. He walked happily with me to the start of the rubber mat, tail wagging and mouth smiling widely.

'Forward!' and we were off. Ronnie was walking nicely beside me.

'Right turn!' We got to the end of the mat and made a beautiful right turn. We were on track.

'Right turn!' at the other end, we did the same. All was going well.

'About turn!' I tapped the side of my leg, while saying, 'In, Ronnie, in', and he followed my instructions to the letter. We walked back down the mat, Ronnie looking up at me with such concentration I thought my heart was going to burst.

'Left turn!' We made the turn with ease. 'Left turn!' and again, we were on the last leg. 'And halt!' Ronnie stopped and sat at my side as I bent down to give him the biggest hug I could in the short time there was until our next task.

My nerves were easing as I knew we had done well, and now it was time for the recall.

'Take your dog to the other end of the hall. Take his lead off, and get him sitting and settled.' I obeyed with all the conformity of an eager Girl Guide. 'Tell your dog to stay, then leave your dog and walk across the room.'

'Sit! Stay!' I placed my hand in front of his face as if making a "stop" sign as my words came out with great conviction. I walked to the opposite side of the room, praying with every step that he would stay put, and the little darling did. We faced each other for what seemed an eternity. 'Call your dog to you.'

'Come, Ronnie.' I gave it all the enthusiasm I could muster as he hurtled towards me. 'Sit, Ronnie.' As he made his approach, I clasped my hands together and brought them from his nose upwards along my body to my chest in the movement we had all been taught to get our dogs to sit and he did. 'Bring your dog to heel.'

'Heel, Ronnie.' I guided him around my legs with my hand, and tapped the side of my leg to bring him in, as he glided around me with ease and sat at my side obediently. I breathed a sigh of relief. We had done it.

Next it was time for the sit-stay, the trickiest task of them all, and the one we had had the most trouble with.

'Take your dog to the side of the mat, remove his lead and tell him to sit stay.' Done.

'Leave your dog and walk to the other side of the room.' Again, with every step I took, my back turned, so unable to see what he was up to, I was visualising Ronnie sitting beautifully … and he was.

'You will now be timed for one minute.' An eternity. I was sending telepathic vibes to Ronnie to stay put. I knew this was his biggest challenge as there were so many dogs, smells and distractions in the room. Then, with no warning, he stood up and casually walked away from his spot, making his way towards the other dogs. My heart sank. I had no idea how long he had sat, and my disappointment well outweighed the severity of the situation we found ourselves in. I had remembered Pat telling us that if the dog didn't stay for the full minute it was an automatic fail of the test.

'Retrieve your dog and bring him back, to do the down-stay exercise.' Despite my regret, the show had to go on, and I put Ronnie into the down-stay position as we went through the dance again.

'Leave your dog and walk to the other side of the room. You will now be timed for two minutes.' By now, my nerves were completely gone as we had failed the test, so the outcome of this exercise was irrelevant. Ronnie may just as well have done a full circuit of the room for all I cared. However, he lay there happily for the two minutes; so relaxed, in fact, that he rolled over onto his side for a wee snooze.

It was over and I made my way back to the other dogs and owners, heavy-hearted but relieved. We could sit the test again in April. We all watched nervously as Pat and the external adjudicator stood at the opposite end of the hall marking our papers. I couldn't quite believe that I was getting so worked up about a dog-training test. There were many other pressing priorities in my life, but at that moment, this just seemed so important. Pat made his way to each of us with our results, congratulating or commiserating owners as he passed them their test papers. I looked up at him with soulful eyes, the kind of look Ronnie gave us when he knew we were going out and he was being left behind.

'Well done. You passed. You both did really well.'

'What? I thought I was automatically failed because he didn't sit for the full minute.'

'He did sit for the full minute. You lost some points because he walked away, but he did sit for the allotted time. You should be really proud. You've got 53 points out of 60.'

'Wow, Pat. I'm delighted.' Again, my reaction to passing was very much an over-reaction, but I was just so proud of my boy and myself if I'm honest, for having the staying power with this. I hugged and kissed Ronnie like a proud parent after an exceptional parents' evening and we both bounced back to the car, with me waving my test paper like it was a winning lottery ticket. I couldn't wait to get home and tell Colin.

After passing the beginners class, we spent the next couple of months in the intermediate class, which was more challenging, but great fun. One night, Pat placed little jumps all around the mats, and two dogs and owners at a time had to run around with their dogs off the lead, and encourage them to jump over them. It was like being at Crufts, or the Horse of the Year Show if you used your imagination and blocked out the fact you were in a community hall. Ronnie did really well considering he'd never done anything like that before. Most of the time, he would clear the jumps, but in his usual manner, there were occasions when, for no reason at all, he'd just run around the side of them. It was the most fun night we had at the classes.

Before we knew it, it was May and the final night of training. This was the Awards Evening when all the dogs, at every level, were given their certificates, and there were a few special awards too for outstanding performances. Colin and I arrived at the hall and there was a real buzz about the place. Seats had been placed all around the edge of the rubber mats, and the room was full of dogs and friends and family. Gaile and Lola were there to support us, as were Neil and Lachie, another dog Colin walked, who were in a different class. There was a table full of raffle prizes so we bought a couple of strips.

Once everyone was settled, we were called class by class onto the floor to do a couple of rounds of the room with our dogs, showing off our new found skills. It was very exciting, if a little chaotic. Colin looked on with pride as Ronnie and I glided around the mat, both enjoying our moment in the spotlight. Then the awards began.

First up were the novices and everyone clapped as each dog and owner walked up to receive their certificates. Then it was our turn. When our name was called we walked proudly up to Pat as Colin took photos. Once the intermediate and advanced classes had been awarded their certificates it was time for the achievement awards.

'It's now time for the first place medal and shield for the beginners' class. This goes to a new dog and owner to the training this year, who've shown real commitment and perseverance throughout. The award goes to Susan Campbell and Ronnie.'

My jaw fell as Colin nudged me off my chair. As Ronnie and I walked towards Pat, I just felt disbelief. How had we managed this?

'Well done,' Pat said, beaming with nearly as much pride as me.

'I can't believe it, Pat. How amazing!'

'Well deserved, Susan.'

I felt really overwhelmed, not being one of those people who ever came first in anything. I could feel my face flushing and I was aware that people were talking to me, but I couldn't hear them because my mind was racing. The rest of the awards were given out to the other levels of classes and we sat, clapping the recipients politely.

Then came the progress award which was given to the dog that, in the opinion of the trainers, had made the most progress in the shortest time. Our names were called again. I nearly fell off my plastic chair and, for an instant, thought I had misheard. But no, it was us again, and we had to walk back up to receive another shield and certificate. My heart was bursting with pride for Ronnie and myself. It's so strange how much pleasure I got from not only passing the test, but then receiving these accolades.

'Well done, you,' Colin said as I sat down, trying to make space on the stage for another shield, while being aware that I didn't want to appear too showy.

'Colin, this is unbelievable. I just didn't expect all of this. What's going on?'

'Well, you came here every Monday night for nine months, and you and Ronnie worked your socks off, so I'd say you're reaping your just rewards, wouldn't you?'

'I thought I was just coming for my beginners certificate, not all this.'

'Enjoy your moment, Susan, and who's a clever boy then?' Colin lent down to pet Ronnie's head who, as usual, was completely oblivious to the stir he was causing.

Pat, Ronnie and Susan

The fruits of our labour

It was now time for the raffle. There was definitely something going on that evening, as time after time, our numbers kept coming in. We won some dog treats, a bottle of white wine, a bottle of red, and a bottle of fizz. It was getting embarrassing to keep walking up, so I sent Colin. We gave a bottle of wine away to Neil, but I just couldn't get over the luck I was having. I don't think I've ever had a night like it.

The formal part of the proceedings was over and Pat made his way towards us, to offer his congratulations. I was still in shock, but it was a really nice shock. Trestle tables were being dragged across the floor as the buffet was put out.

'Congratulations!' Other dog owners offered their good wishes, while Colin and I worked hard to distract Ronnie from the plate of goodies balanced precariously on the lap of the person next to us. His patience paid off, however, when they walked away to get a drink. Ronnie swiped a sausage roll off the plate with such speed and skill; we had no chance of stopping him. Thankfully, Pat didn't witness the theft.

'See, Susan, for someone who was afraid to even let Ronnie off the lead, you've come a long way in a short time,' Pat said.

'I know. I do feel a lot more confident with Ronnie now, and that'll help with other dogs too.'

'Just keep practising what you've learned. He's a great dog.'

We headed home, with Colin squeezing my hand and telling me how proud he was of us both. Going to the class was one of the best things I ever did. It cemented my relationship with Ronnie, and built my confidence in my everyday dealings with him. He obeys me far more often than he used to, and he still remembers all of the things we learned.

It also taught me that I'm a lot more competitive than I thought I was. I absolutely loved the recognition we received for our efforts. Maybe it's got something to do with working all those years in a profession that rarely rewarded me with praise for a job well done. In a funny kind of way, gaining the certificates and shields reiterated the fact that I had done the right thing in going my own way. It also proved to me that rewards in life can be found in the strangest and most unexpected places.

Chapter Thirteen - Introducing Ruby

We had just celebrated our second Christmas with Ronnie, and Colin was moving into his fifth month of his business. I was over the worst of my post-festive blues that early January Sunday afternoon. It was just like going back to work after a holiday: the first day was torturous, but three days into it was like you'd never been away. Not that I had experienced this for several years, having forsaken proper holidays for the self-employed lifestyle, but I could see the clear similarities with the passing of festive fun. It always amazed me that one day our home could be full of shiny baubles, sparkling lights and the smell of festive spice. The next, it was a poor shadow of itself, and the bay window in which the tree stood so majestically seemed so bare and cheerless. Then three days later, it's as if it had never happened, as everything went back to normal. Even though I love Christmas, I must admit to a sense of relief, as I finally feel I can breathe, once all the festive clutter has gone.

Colin cajoled me off the couch with the promise of coffee and cake at the end of a winter walk with Ronnie. We wrapped up and headed off to the park across the road. It was a crisp late afternoon, the kind that brings a slight mist to the air and everyone looks like they're smoking as they exhale white vapour with every breath. The park looked bleak. Trees were stripped of their foliage, and all of the summer and autumn rainbows of colour had deserted the area. January is a tough month. I comforted myself in the knowledge that in a matter of weeks the spring buds would be blossoming, and the regeneration of this season would breathe new life across the park once more.

As we walked, we bumped into several dogs and owners that Colin knew, and exchanged New Year greetings alongside the usual holiday stories. The light was fading as we made our way back. I was looking forward to a warm cup of coffee when I heard Colin say, 'Who's this then?'

I looked in the direction of his gaze and spotted a bundle of fluff bouncing around her owner's feet. 'Oh, Colin. She's beautiful. Let's go and say hello.'

As we made our way towards this little honey, she hid behind her owner's legs, sneaking the odd peek at Ronnie.

'Hi there. This is Ruby,' her owner said, and you could hear the pride in her voice.

'Hello, Ruby. You're a wee cracker, aren't you? How young is she?' Colin asked.

'She's four months.'

As I reached down to pet her, she came out for a few seconds and then retreated to the safe place she had created behind her owner. This was a gentle wee dog. As she got a bit more adventurous, she crept slowly towards Ronnie and they sniffed each other happily, both sets of tails wagging furiously.

'Oh, she likes him. I'm Elspeth by the way. It's so funny how all the dog owners know the names of all the dogs, but not the owners!'

'I know. I'm Colin and this is my wife, Susan, and this is Ronnie.'

'Oh, he's lovely. What kind is he?'

'He's a Lurcher-cross, a wee rescue dog from the Dog's Trust. We got very lucky. He's so good with other dogs,' I explained.

'I can see that. What unusual markings he has. Ruby's a Labradoodle.'

'She's beautiful,' I gushed as I leant down for another cuddle.

'You don't know any good dog-sitting services in the area, do you? I'm looking for doggy day-care for Ruby. My nephew has been looking after her while I work, but as of next month, he's not going to be able to. I need to find somewhere that she can be well looked after, all day.'

Colin sprang into life.

'Yes, I know a very good one. Here take my card.'

'You are not! How funny is that? Serendipity or what! Do you do day-care though? I'm not just looking for a walk. I really want her to be looked after all day.'

'Well that's something we can talk about. If you want to chat further, give me a call, and we can meet up and see what we can do. She really is a lovely dog.'

'She's my world. I just love her so much.'

'I know exactly what you mean, Elspeth. I feel exactly the same about Ronnie,' I concurred.

'Oh, that's great. I'm so glad I bumped into you all. I'll give you a call and we can chat about it then.'

'Great. Lovely to meet you both. Bye, Ruby. See you again soon,' Colin said.

We watched Ruby leap and skip her way along the path as only puppies can, and once again said, with a hint of sadness, how much we wished we had known Ronnie as a pup. I can only imagine that he was completely adorable with those floppy ears and gangly legs. We had missed the whole puppy experience, which can be a blessing in some ways, avoiding the house training and destruction. It will, however, remain a part of Ronnie's life we will never know. I saw a dog magazine one day with a picture of a puppy on the front page. He looked exactly how I imagined Ronnie would have been at that age, as this pup had a brindle coat, amber eyes and those famous ears. I bought it straightaway and still have it. I remember bringing it home to show to Colin.

'Look, look! It's Ronnie as a puppy!'

It was the nearest we were going to get.

'That was fortuitous,' Colin said as we passed the duck pond on our last leg home.

'I know, and what a lovely dog.'

'I would love to be able to help Elspeth. I think Ruby would be a great dog to work with.'

'Well, let's see how you get on when you meet them again. If it's meant to be, it will be.'

Elspeth phoned Colin a few days later, and arranged to come round to discuss Ruby's needs. Ruby seemed immediately comfortable in our home. She bounced around the couch from Colin to me, then back to Elspeth, in between jumping off and landing on Ronnie, who was taking it all in his stride. He was getting used to sharing his space with an endless stream of dogs.

So what did Ruby look like? She was a golden Labradoodle with masses of soft curly fur that cascaded over her body and face like shimmering silk. Her tail reminded me of a showgirl's feather, as it fanned everyone in her vicinity. She had the most comical expression, which always appeared to hold an element of surprise. A little smaller than standard Labradoodles, she was medium-size with a delicate frame under the oodles of fur, and gangly legs like Ronnie. Gorgeous brown button eyes, with the longest eyelashes I have ever seen, finished off the look of this exquisite dog. She was just beautiful.

Ruby

'So, Elspeth, tell me what it is you are looking for in terms of Ruby's care?' Colin asked, once I'd brought in the coffee and things had settled down a little.

'Well, I'm just looking at the options just now. I've spoken with another dog walker, but it would be really helpful to hear what you can offer. I really don't want to leave Ruby on her own during the day, as she's always had someone with her. She has separation anxiety, and gets really upset when she's left alone.'

'Do you leave her on her own at all?'

'Only when I absolutely have to and it breaks my heart as I know she cries after me.'

'I guess the thing is that there will be times when you do have to leave her, and from my experience, if you leave dogs in a warm, comfortable environment, they quickly get used to it, and learn that you do come back. Without Ruby learning this, you're going to be very restricted in what you can do.'

'I know you're right. I just don't feel comfortable leaving her.'

'I know exactly how you feel, Elspeth,' I said. 'The guilt I feel when we leave Ronnie is huge, but it's getting easier the more he gets used to it. We leave the radio on, and give him some treats when we leave, and he just sleeps until we get back.'

'When I've left Ruby, the neighbours have told me that she cries continually. I just can't do that to her.'

Elspeth was clearly an extremely conscientious dog owner, who didn't want to cause Ruby any distress. The difficulty was that her life was being seriously curtailed as a result.

'What sort of service could you offer Ruby? Do you do doggie day-care?'

'Well, at the moment, I generally just walk dogs, but let's have a think if there's anything we can do. Susan works mostly from home just now, so she would be in during the day. I could pick Ruby up in the morning, take her for a walk, and then drop her off here for the afternoon. How do you feel about that, Susan?'

'That's fine with me. The only thing to bear in mind is that there will be some days when I won't be here.'

'Well, I think on those days, I could take her out with me all day when possible, and we can also let her get used to staying on her own gradually. I could leave Ronnie with her for company.'

'That sounds like a good plan. She obviously feels comfortable here,' Elspeth replied, pointing to Ruby crashed out on the couch. 'Let me go away and think about it, and I'll get back to you in the next couple of day. Is that okay?'

'Of course. It's a big decision, so take your time. We're not going anywhere,' Colin reassured her.

True to her word, Elspeth phoned Colin a few days later and Ruby became another member of the pack. Little did we know at that time how close we were going to get to her. She came to us every day, and at first, she would follow me around from room to room, and lie by my feet as I worked. Then I noticed that she liked to sleep on the couch in the spare room. I put a comfy dog bed on top of it, and this became her favourite place to chill out of an afternoon. Every day she was becoming more and more independent, and soon we got to the point where I could leave her for short periods during the day, gradually building up to longer stretches, which she coped with admirably. She was growing up in front of us.

She also came to stay with us when Elspeth had to work away, and Ronnie and Ruby were becoming the best of friends. They would tear down the hall together tumbling and wrestling, or playing tug of war with favourite toys. It was lovely to watch the blossoming camaraderie. Bed times were becoming increasingly crowded, as everyone fought for their spot in an ever decreasing space.

'We need a bigger bedroom, Colin, so we can fit a king size bed in it,' I often said, as I tussled with the duvet. But we were cosy and happy, and Ruby was a warm addition to our lives.

Ruby and Susan

About three months into introducing Ruby to Ronnie Ronster's, Colin was out walking her with his other dogs when two police horses came into the park. Ronnie does not do well around these commanding beasts and immediately went into defence mode, barking and running up to them. Unfortunately, all of the dogs were off their leads at the time and Colin had to scramble around to ensure they were safe. But Ruby was off. The horses had put the fear of God in her, and she wasn't hanging around to make their acquaintance.

I got a frantic call from him. 'Susan, Ruby's run away. She got freaked by police horses in the park. Please come and help me look for her.'

My stomach flipped. Oh my God, where had she run to, and was she safe? All kinds of catastrophic outcomes were flooding my mind as I ran out the door to find Colin. What if she got into a fight with another dog? What if someone stole her? Being the beauty that she was, it wasn't out of the question. Labradoodles were not cheap either, and I remembered Pat, the dog trainer, telling us how dogs all over the West End were being stolen to be sold on; another dark side of the recession. Giving myself a shake in an attempt to disassociate myself from those black thoughts, like Ronnie when he had been caught in the rain, I ran out the door. I found Colin looking pale and fretful, marching around the park, shouting Ruby's name at the top of his voice.

'You go round the other way, and I'll keep looking in the direction she ran,' he urged.

'Listen, Colin, we'll find her. I've asked the Angels to help us and keep her safe. It'll be okay.'

He gave me a look, and I knew at that moment, the last thing he wanted to hear was my new-age 'let's put it out there to the Universe' stuff, so I shut up, and began walking in the opposite direction. It was starting to get dark, and I was beginning to feel uneasy walking alone. It's strange how a place that is so inviting during the day can become so threatening once night falls.

The shadows of the enormous trees made all kinds of menacing shapes across the paths. I could see the spindly fingers of witches pointing into the dark, as if showing me the way to my downfall. Monsters lurked behind each corner, and the bogey man could have leapt out in front of me at any time. The howls of distant foxes only added to the ridiculously scary situation I had put myself into. I carried on regardless. We had to find Ruby, but there was no sign of her at my end. My phone rang.

'She's been found.'

'Oh thank God. Thank God. Where is she?'

'She ran back to her flat. She was found just around the corner from it. I should have known, Susan. Pat's always told me that when dogs run away the first place they try to find is their home. They always try to get back home. I should have known. I should also have got Ruby onto the lead as soon as the horses came into the park. She's probably never seen a police horse before, and she's a nervous wee thing. I should have known.' Colin was giving himself such a hard time, and it was distressing to hear him thrash himself so severely.

'Colin, it's okay. She's been found, and she's safe.'

'It was Elspeth who phoned me. A woman found Ruby in the street behind her flat, and as it's Elspeth's number on her tag, she phoned her to let her know. Can you imagine what a fright she must have got being down in London, and getting a call like that?'

'Oh, Colin, how was she? What did she say?'

'She was shocked, of course, and wondering what the hell was going on. Anyway, I'm going to pick Ruby up just now. Can you come and get the other dogs from me?'

'Sure. I'll meet you at the fountain. Don't worry, Colin. It'll be okay.'

I'm not sure if I was trying to convince myself as well with my words. I had no idea if it was going to be okay. When we were working with the dogs I always put myself in the shoes of the owners, and thought about how I would feel. If this had happened to Ronnie, I don't know what my reaction would have been, or if I would want to continue using the service. While it had been completely out of Colin's control, Ruby had been in his care and he was responsible. His reputation could be seriously damaged by something like this, but the worst thing was the fear that something could have happened to Ruby. It didn't bear thinking about, and it really brought it home to me the huge responsibility of this business, as well as the pleasure.

Colin arrived home with Ruby, who seemed in much better shape from the ordeal than him. She was due to go to Elspeth's sister and brother-in-law, Sheila and Douglas, to stay for the weekend, so Colin got her things together and headed over to drop her off in Pollokshields. When he came back he told me that Douglas had been very kind and reassuring, telling him that dogs run away all the time, and not to worry about it. On leaving Colin had said, 'Bye bye, Ruby. See you on Monday, wee girl, if I'm not sacked!'

He wasn't sacked, and Elspeth forgave Colin for the nightmare we had all been through. Things got back to normal and Ruby remains a constant in our lives. When Elspeth moved house and was renovating her new home, Ruby stayed with us even more often, as her new place wasn't safe for her to be living in. At one point, when Elspeth lived in New York, she also moved in and we had some hysterical Skype calls, balancing Ruby on our laps so her mum could see all was well. She is always a welcomed guest. She's one of the family now, after all.

Chapter Fourteen - Night night, sleep tight

I love my bed, always have and always will. The regenerative function of sleep is unquestionable, but there's more to it than that. There's something so comforting, on a cold winter's night, about sliding beneath the warmth of a feather duvet, and settling down for some well-earned kip. It's equally attractive in the summer when the coolness of crisp white cotton softly caresses sunburned skin, and the worries of the day drift into the twilight sky as sleep gently takes over.

My bedroom has always been my sanctuary, sometimes too much so. Having experienced several bouts of depression when younger, it was my safe place. Shutting the world out became too easy, by just pulling the duvet tighter around my numb body and pretending I didn't exist. It's common for people experiencing depression to sleep more, as it prevents them from having to deal with their complete lack of participation in life, and the guilt and pain this brings. Looking back, I'm not sure I even slept that much. Dozing on and off would be my pattern, and the dead weight in the pit of my stomach would be the first thing I experienced on waking, to remind me I was still in this living hell. I know that, at that time, my bed provided a safety and security I did not experience anywhere else; like returning to the womb I guess.

I made it my mission to understand why I had experienced the blackness through reading, therapy and training in counselling and life coaching. I refused to accept the life limiting diagnosis I was given by the medical profession as they drew me diagrams of my mental health fluctuating for the rest of my life. They told me I would never be able to hold down a stressful job and would be on medication my entire life. How wrong they were. While I never want to go back there, it's made me who I am today and influenced my career choices massively. I have such a strong urge to support people to overcome their own demons, as I did, and help people to see that recovery is so possible.

Nowadays, my bedroom is a much happier place, and I have left those dark days well and truly behind. I have a passion for duvet covers, cushions and all soft furnishings, and I love adorning our wooden sleigh bed. I have little rituals which change with the seasons. April to September is crisp white duvet time. I've discovered Egyptian cotton, and boy do I love it; the higher the thread count, the softer the slumber. October sees the entrance of my rich gold and red duvets, marking the need to look out coats, hats and gloves, and these colours remain until the following March.

I do the same with my candles, burning white ones in spring and summer, and changing to red for autumn and winter. Somehow, it keeps me on track for the year, as I love the changing of the seasons and the unique experience each one brings. As I get older though, I notice how quickly each changeover comes around.

Since Ronnie has come into our lives, bedtimes have become very different from how they were. From night one, when he made his way so acrobatically onto our bed to this day, he has been a warm, furry presence. Some people will find this unnecessary and unhygienic I'm sure, while others will totally understand the bond between dog and owners. Whatever your take on it, it was our choice to allow Ronnie into our bedroom, and one we don't regret.

It has, however, meant that I haven't had an uninterrupted night's sleep in the last six years. Like me, Ronnie has a great love of bedtime alongside his own little rituals. He is often to be found on the bed before we retire, just warming it up for us. Jumping down when we climb in, he then taps the side of the duvet with his nose to let me know he wants to join us. I lift the duvet and he jumps up, climbs over me and settles down in-between Colin and I, nose pointing down towards the bottom of the bed. A few moments later, he flips over onto his back, looking very much like a kangaroo, with his front paws over his chest and his back ones splayed out in a most immodest pose. I then have to rub his back paws as we all go to sleep.

Not long into our slumber, however, Ronnie will get too hot, stand up taking the duvet and all the warmth with him, walk to the end of the bed and come out from under the covers. He then throws himself down on the bed — now on top of the duvet and still in-between each of us — while I try desperately to replace the duvet to its rightful position. Sleep resumes until, bless him, he gets cold. Up he walks to the top of the duvet, clawing at it to get back under, and the whole ritual starts again. The amount of times this happens in one night is dependent on the outside temperature. Interestingly, Colin rarely wakes up while all of these nightly shenanigans are taking place.

Why oh why would I put up with this, I hear people cry? While it has affected my sleep pattern, I can't describe the joy I experience when Ronnie nestles in beside us. It's so lovely that he sleeps between us, not favouring one over the other. I also like to think that he feels safe and happy with us, as we've provided him with ... well, pretty much the life of any dog's dreams. I've adapted to the changes and my body has got used to this different sleep pattern. Thankfully, I am one of those people who, when woken, can get straight back to sleep.

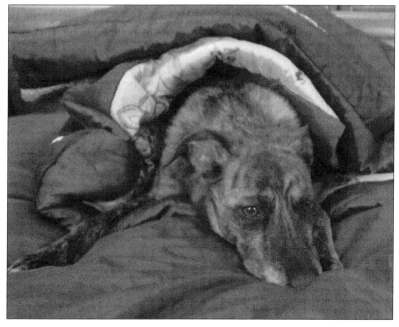

Favourite place

We always make sure he is clean before he gets into bed, and thankfully, one of the traits of Lurchers is that they don't smell (apart from their regular bouts of flatulence). Ronnie just doesn't have that strong doggy smell so many other dogs have, and this is a real blessing. I also don't mind that it means I have to change the sheets and duvet more often. It's a small price to pay for cosy nightly snuggles, and I particularly look forward to going to bed the night when fresh sheets have been laid. In my mind, one of life's great pleasures is taking a long soak in a bubble bath, slipping into clean pyjamas and then climbing into a freshly made bed; heaven.

Ruby has also become a regular in the bed now too. Elspeth takes such good care of Ruby, with regular trips to the groomers, that she smells delightful. On one occasion, Colin actually said he was going to ask Elspeth what perfume it was that they used on her so he could buy it for me. She started out sleeping curled up under Colin's arm on his side of the bed, not taking up much room and sticking to the same spot all night. I think this was because she was so grateful at having been invited into the bed that she feared any movement may result in her being tossed out again.

Such comfort

As she has settled in and become more confident all that has changed. Now Ruby will start off in her usual spot, looking every inch the angel. It won't be long though before she is clambering over Colin to nestle her way in-between us when a space become available from one of Ronnie's many exits. Often I will wake up in the morning to Ruby's head on my pillow, her soft pink tongue offering me a pre-shower face wash as her tail beats under the duvet.

As well as the dog-walking, we quickly began offering a sitting service, which is used regularly by Colin's clients. Some of the dogs are crate-trained, a practice which, when I first heard of it, I didn't like. I thought putting dogs into metal crates was cruel, as I felt they should have free reign of their home environment. However, having seen so many examples of dogs using them happily, I have to concur that they are a useful training aid. Dogs love having their own space, and feel safe and secure in their crates. Using them when dogs come to stay means they are bringing a little piece of their home to us, and it settles them in wonderfully.

They remind me a bit of playpens except they have a roof. Coming in different sizes, but all rectangular shaped, they're made of metal with plenty of gaps for the dogs to see out. Once the dog's bedding and toys are put inside, they become a little home from home. They're used mainly when dogs are puppies when their owners go out, and for sleeping in at night, though some dogs get so used to them they choose to sleep in them even when older. It really can prevent a lot of the destruction problems that painful teething mouths can cause, and it teaches dogs that they too have an area of the home that belongs just to them. I'm a convert.

Some of the dogs don't have crates, however, and to date, the highest count of dogs sleeping on the bed with us has been four: me, Colin and Ronnie, Noelle, the graceful Whippet, Rachel-Anne the cute-as-a-button Shitsu, and Jackson the majestic Lurcher. Ronnie was in his usual spot half-way down the bed. Noelle filled the remaining space in-between Colin and I at the top of the bed. Rachel-Anne was curled up under my arm on my side of the bed, and Jackson was at the bottom, stretched out over all of us.

We only managed one night like this as Jackson took up most of the space with his long frame and body. It was like sleeping in a sardine can. The following night, Jackson was far more comfortable sleeping on a soft blanket on the sofa; while we all stretched out, quickly filling the space he had left behind. Noelle came and went, as she found great comfort in the corner of our sofa with a blanket over her.

Colin and I do manage to get 'time for ourselves' amongst all of this mayhem. We've learned to be adaptable with our week-to-week schedules, to shut the dogs out and accept that things have changed. I'm sure all parents out there will relate to this too.

There was one unfortunate night when Ronnie was sick in the bed. This led to early hour cleaning and duvet changing, and a momentary re-think of our sleeping arrangements. But we just didn't have the heart to shut him out though and it's never happened since. I know it's not the same as having children, but there are parallels.

And so Ronnie has brought another side to my night times and love of my bed. Whether it's just him cuddling in or a combination of his pals too, our nights have never been the same.

Chapter Fifteen - The fight

It was a late January afternoon, five months into Colin's new business, as six dogs accompanied him around Bellahouston Park. The sun was shining, but it was bitterly cold. Colin preferred this to the rain, which drenched him and the dogs, and left the walls and rugs of our hall splattered with mud as Ronnie and his pals shook off the cold of the day. He'd once heard Billy Connolly say that there was no such thing as bad weather, only the wrong clothes. He would often quote this as he walked out the door, layered with insulation for the day ahead, and he also liked to remind me of this fact when I complained of the cold on any of our walks. Most annoying!

His afternoon was going well, with everyone running around in the frost, paws crunching, constantly on the move to keep them from freezing. Jackson, the majestic Lurcher, was on form, sweeping his way around the open spaces. The other dogs, especially Ronnie, would try to catch up, but were no contest for him. He was one of a kind. In the distance, Colin saw Nick, a guy he had met before, coming towards the pack with his English Bull Terrier. They exchanged pleasantries, and all was well as his dog sniffed his way through the pack.

I've never been a fan of English Bull Terriers. There's something about the look of their faces that makes me uncomfortable. I know I'm generalising, and the manager of the hairdressers I go to owns one. By all accounts, she's a gentle dog and wouldn't harm a fly. The photos she's shown me pay testament to this, and she really does look like a sweet dog. But there's just something about them. It could be a subconscious throwback to the film *Oliver*, and Bill Sykes' threatening character, who owned an English Bull Terrier called Bullseye. They both scared the life out of me.

I've got the same feeling about Airedale Terriers. I'll never forget opening my bedroom curtains one morning when I was eight and seeing a miniature Airedale with our neighbour's rabbit in his mouth. He was banging the rabbit off the ground and frantically shaking the life out of it. I ran in horror downstairs to tell my parents, but it was too late. The beautiful white rabbit was dead. The image of my neighbour desperately trying to console his son as he stood over the hutch crying and shaking his head is still fresh to me. I know it was completely instinctive for the dog to behave in this way, but I've never forgiven the breed for inflicting such a cruel sight on me at such a young age.

In saying that, Colin walks the most beautiful Airedale called Hamish. He's full size and a different colour to the one in question. Hamish is like a big teddy bear and very lovable. I've managed to detach him from the sad memory and bear no grudges against him.

Hamish

Getting back to the walk though and Jackson was behaving himself beautifully. He's the gentlest dog with humans, but can be a little temperamental with some dogs. He hadn't been neutered and some dogs show aggressive tendencies when this is the case. Because of this, he has a muzzle that he wears most of the time, but on this particular day, Colin

112

had left it off him. To get Jackson to really run and burn off his energy he needs to be muzzle-free. This is always a risky strategy though, as the park's a busy place, with lots of other dogs and owners passing at all times. However, Jackson was doing brilliantly, so much so that Colin got his phone out and began videoing the two dogs sniffing each other, their tails wagging happily. He was looking forward to showing Jen how well her boy was doing at the end of the day.

Best buds

Just as Colin was putting his phone away something changed; he heard growls, howls and that blood-chilling mishmash of sounds when dogs fight. Jackson and the Bull Terrier were at each other; tumbling and gasping, as each tried to dominate. Nick immediately grabbed his dog's collar, and pulled him off Jackson. Unfortunately, the dog was still attached to Jackson at the time. The skin on the side of his chest ripped away with him, as Nick battled desperately to get his dog to release his hold. Once he did, the damage was there for all to see; a huge gash in Jackson's side.

Both Colin and Nick stood in disbelief as they tried to make sense of what had just happened. It had started and ended in seconds. Nick's dog had a few puncture marks on his head, but nothing serious. Nick was

113

visibly upset about Jackson's injuries, but both he and Colin accepted that these things happen, and Colin now had to deal with getting Jackson to the vet, as quickly as possible. He got the poor fella onto his lead, rounded up the other dogs and headed back to the van. Before driving off, he had to make the dreaded call to Jen, who was at work.

'Jen, I'm so sorry, but Jackson has been in a fight.'

'Oh no. Is he okay?'

'He's got a substantial cut on his side. I'm going to take him straight to your vet just now.'

'You can't, Colin. It closes between 12.00 and 4.00 p.m.'

It was only 1.00 p.m.

'What happened, Colin? Did he have his muzzle on?'

'He was doing so well, Jen, with a Bull Terrier. I was really proud of him, and then it all just kicked off. No, he didn't have his muzzle on. I'm so sorry.'

'Oh, the poor thing. I can't get away from the school just now.'

'Don't worry. I'll take him back to our place. Susan's in and she can look after him. As soon as the vet opens, I'll take him there.'

Colin drove home, berating himself the entire way. What had he been thinking of, keeping Jackson without a muzzle with a new dog around? By the time he got home, he was in a terrible state.

'Susan, please take Jackson and look after him for me. He's been in a fight and I'll tell you about it later. I've got to get the other dogs home.'

Then he was out the door and I knew from the frantic look on his face that he was really upset; he darted in and out so quickly, ashen-faced and unable to yet talk about the incident, or make eye contact. I knew it was bad. As I examined Jackson, I realised why. The gash was large and looked painful. It was on his right side and roughly six centimetres long. Being so lean, Jackson didn't have thick fur and what little he had had been pulled off and the tear had produced a flap of skin that I knew would need stitches.

I made a bed up for him in the living room sofa and encouraged him to lie on it. This took a bit of logistical working out, as he kept trying to lie on the side with the gash. I turned him several times until we got there and he settled, head on my lap and we both stayed snuggled up for the rest of the afternoon. The wee soul never uttered a sound; not a whimper. He just lay there brave and stoic, as I soothed and petted him, wishing so much that dogs could understand the words of comfort I was administering. In between times, I flipped between wanting to see Colin and find out exactly what had happened and panicking about how Jen would react. I felt really bad for both of them, but most of all for Jackson.

Colin arrived back to take Jackson to the vet and off they went, two wounded soldiers. I kissed them both on the way out the door and attempted to reassure Colin, but could see he was in fix-it mode and on autopilot. There would be time later to dissect the day.

He arrived home about an hour later, pale and dishevelled. I put the kettle on and sat him down. 'So what happened?'

He recounted the sorry tale, first bowing his head, then shaking it, and then bowing again. I moved closer and gave him a much needed hug. 'I can't believe I left his muzzle off.'

'These things happen, Colin.'

'I know, but twelve staples, Susan. He must be in so much pain.'

'You're going to be tested, Colin. Ask anyone who's started their own business. Shit happens.'

'I'm only five months in, and already I've lost my car keys, Ruby's run away, and now this. I don't know if I'm cut out for this.'

'Of course you are. Remember my first year when, a few months into it, I spent all that money on that crap course? Remember all the conference calls to the company with the other students. So many of them became disillusioned and gave up. Some of them are still holding a grudge three years on. I made a mistake, and thankfully had a brilliant coach who walked me through it all, and helped me move on. I've made other mistakes since and will make more in the future, but I'm learning all the time. There's none of us perfect.'

'This is different, Susan. This is people's dogs. We know how precious they are to them, 'cause of Ronnie. It's not as straightforward as wasting money on something that didn't live up to its promises.'

'I know it's different, but I'm just trying to say that all businesses have their challenges, especially in the first year. The difference between the ones that survive and the ones that go under is persistence, not giving up, not matter what's thrown at you.'

'When people hear about this, my reputation will be shot. This is really bad, Susan.'

'You thought the same when Ruby ran away and that worked out. Look, you need to speak to Jen. She really values the service she gets from you. I'm sure we can get through this.'

'I don't know, Susan. I really need to think about what to do next.'

'For goodness sake, Colin, this isn't like you. You know how much you're enjoying your new found freedom, and overall, you're doing really well. Are you honestly saying you're thinking about giving all of this up, because of an accident? You're going to have to toughen up.'

I realised I was talking to the wall, and like Jackson, Colin needed time to lick his wounds. I gave him some space, and about an hour later the phone rang.

'It's Jen.' Colin had a look of panic in his eyes.

'Answer it and just talk it through with her.'

Twenty minutes later he came back into the kitchen looking like a mountain had been lifted from his shoulders. The relief on his face told me he was happy with how the conversation had gone. Jen had been so kind and even said that it could just have easily happened to her as she sometimes keeps the muzzle off to get Jackson to run. She had no intention of stopping using Ronnie Ronster's services and asked Colin to stop blaming himself.

Colin had insisted we pay for the vet bill so as not to affect her insurance premium and she reluctantly agreed to this. They both concurred that Ronnie and Jackson would never forgive them if they were parted and she had told Colin to put this behind him and enjoy his weekend. What amazing people Colin had as clients.

We smiled at each other as Colin said.

'As soon as Jackson's stitches heal, she's phoning the vet to get him neutered.'

'Well, that's good.'

'I'm sorry, I didn't handle this well.'

'You handled it as best you could. You got a real fright, but it'll never happen again, will it?'

'No chance.'

'Well then, lesson learned. Now go and get us a glass of wine and let's start our weekend.'

Jackson healed well, being the fit and healthy dog that he is. Colin got over the shock of the heart-stopping incident, and within a month, Jackson was neutered. This resulted in hardly any incidents of aggression with him in future, but Colin always kept his muzzle on around new dogs from that day on.

The fight had taught him some valuable lessons and shown us both that the journey wasn't always going to be an easy one. But then, anything worth having usually involves hard work and persistence, of which Colin, Ronnie and I have bucket loads.

Chapter Sixteen - Dalmallyfest

Colin and I share a love a music, which has had a significant impact on both our lives, pre- and post-meeting one another. Even though our musical tastes differ greatly — Colin being a total rocker, while I enjoy an extremely eclectic mix of music. The common importance this plays in our lives is what had brought us together.

Elizabeth, my sister, had joined a blues band called Sugar Man, and alongside Jim, my brother-in-law, on drums, she was singing and playing the keyboard with three other friends of mine, Bert, Lesley and Neil. Little did I know, but they were all friends of Colin's too. They were playing their first gig at The Bon Accord, an oldie worldie, real ale pub in the city centre, and myself and a group of friends headed out to offer our support.

It was a great night with the band performing brilliantly, and everyone dancing and enjoying themselves. My parents had even ventured into town to watch, with pride, their daughter's first performance. As I danced with my friend Grazia, I noticed a guy wearing jeans and a denim shirt moving towards us. He was having a great wee time to himself, enjoying the music and grinning widely as he came closer. Grazia took to him immediately and began dancing alongside him. We all enjoyed the music then headed back to our own tables and company.

Later, the same guy got up and gave a very impressive rendition of 'Mustang Sally' with the band, and it was then I realised he knew them all. I thought nothing of it other than that he was a good singer, and left.

The following weekend, I was at Elizabeth and Jim's, and my sister and I were sitting outside in their beautiful garden.

'You have an admirer,' she said, with a glint in her eye.

'What?'

'Yes. You made quite an impression on a friend of ours at the gig last Saturday.'

'What? Who?'

'Colin Campbell. Do you not know him?'

'No. Which one was he?'

'The guy that got up and sang with us. He was asking Neil all about you, and didn't realise we were sisters.'

'Oh, yes I remember him.' The memory of him dancing beside Grazia and me came flooding back, and I remembered how happy he had looked, like he didn't have a care in the world. 'But I'm not ready to start seeing anyone just now.'

I had ended a difficult relationship only a couple of months previously, and it had left me hurt and cautious. I felt I needed time alone. 'What's he like anyway?' I asked, obviously not that cautious.

'He's a great guy, but probably not long-term material; a bit arrogant. He used to be into am dram, so he's a bit of a luvvie, but I think he would be perfect to have a fling with. You know, Susan … someone to have some fun with and take your mind off all the stuff you've just been through.'

'Oh, I don't know, Liz. I don't think I could cope with a fling just now.'

'Well, just think about it. It could be just what you need.'

I didn't give it much thought, until I met Grazia for lunch a few weeks later. When I told her what Elizabeth had said she nearly fell off the bench we were sitting on, as we enjoyed our alfresco sandwiches.

'Susan, you have got to see this guy. I just feel he's right for you.'

'Grazia, I'm not ready to start dating again. It's too soon, and I don't want to mess him around.'

'I'm telling you, Susan, I got such a strong, positive energy off him. He's special, believe me. You've got to give it a try.'

What was going on here? I felt confused, but excited, jumping between throwing caution to the wind and retreating back to my shell. My sister had told me about a music festival called Dalmallyfest, which runs every year. She told me that Colin's band would be playing, as well as Sugar Man. As soon as Grazia got wind of this, a group of friends was rounded up, and we set off on our first experience of Dalmallyfest.

As the name suggests it took place in Dalmally, about two hours' drive from Glasgow, through the most breathtaking countryside. We pitched our three tents;-the domes creating a nice little community of their own amongst the other campers, all circling a mound of food. I have a vivid memory of those three days, as it was a food fest too. While food was included in the price of the ticket, Grazia, being of Italian descent, had brought enough additional food to feed the entire campsite. She could always be found poring over her wee stove, making sure we were all suitably fed, and she was in her element.

Colin's band, No Shame, were headlining on the Friday night, so we made our way up to the stage area to watch. Morvern hadn't seen Colin yet, so I pointed him out to her.

'Oh no, Susan, he's not your type.' These words were to become as infamous as my sister's 'He'd be perfect for a fling' line, as it later became clear that Colin and I were made for each other.

His band was fantastic and we danced through the entire set. Colin kept singing to me, which had me blushing and panicking in equal measures. When they finished, I made my way to the food tent, and Colin followed me. He took my hand and said, 'So, did you enjoy the set?'

'Yes, your band's brilliant. It was a great night.'

'A few of us are heading back to Bert's tent for a drink. Do you want to join us?'

I can still remember the alarm that set in as he asked me this. My body froze and the fight or flight instinct kicked in. I chose flight.

'I'm sorry, I've got to get back to my friends now,' I blurted out, as I turned on my tail and ran back towards the safety of the womb our tents had created.

What an idiot, but I just couldn't handle it.

Over the next two days, Colin made several attempts to speak to me, all resulting in the same ridiculous outcome. I was behaving like a teenager, not a thirty-five-year-old woman. We packed up, and as I was leaving, Elizabeth approached me.

'What's going on? I asked Colin how things are going and he told me you keep running away from him! Are you not interested, because that's what he thinks?'

'I don't know what's going on, Liz. I just don't seem to be able to hold it together long enough to have a conversation with him. I'm going home now, and I'm sorry it hasn't worked out, but that's the way things go sometimes.'

'He's not going to keep trying, you know.'

'I know and I don't blame him. The timing's just wrong, so let's leave it.'

Despite having continually run away from Colin all weekend, I couldn't stop thinking that I may have been too hasty. I kept remembering how brilliant his band had been, and the ease with which he had taken to the stage. He had also been the MC for the event, and was enthusiastic and kind about all of the bands, however they performed. This guy really did have something about him. Grazia and Liz certainly thought so, and even Morvern was coming round to the idea that this might be worth a punt. I found out that No Shame were playing in Glasgow, so again a crowd of us got together and went along. Take two.

This time, at the end of the night, when Colin asked for my number, I managed to stand in front of him long enough to pass it on. He called me the next day and we went on our first date the following week. The rest is history.

And so Dalmallyfest became an annual part of our lives together. I joined No Shame the year after I began my relationship with Colin. Initially, the plan was that I would sing and play keyboards, but my commitment to re-learning my long since departed piano skills just wasn't there. I enjoyed singing too much, so we all agreed this was an acceptable enough addition.

When Ronnie came into our lives, we couldn't wait to take him to Dalmallyfest. It's a very child and dog friendly environment, and we'd often watched all the dogs have a ball as they raced around the festival site, stealing dropped burgers and drinking beer from the glasses of

121

unsuspecting revellers. So we piled up the car and headed off down the M74. The old site of Dalmally had been changed, owing to complaints about noise from villagers, and it was now held in a YMCA site just outside Biggar. The name had been changed to 'Dalmallyfest in Exile', as 'Biggarfest' just didn't have the same ring to it.

The wonderful thing about the new site was that there were chalets for hire, and on this first trip with Ronnie we had booked one. There were two rooms in the chalet and, luxury of luxuries, a shower and toilet. We had camped for several years, and I was finding it increasingly challenging. I think you just get to an age when wading through a muddy field in the middle of the night to go to the loo becomes your idea of hell. Just getting out of the tent and into your wellies is an assault course in itself. And don't get me started on removing the bloody things on your return.

Morvern and Chrisanna took one side of the chalet and we took the other. Ronnie ran between each room not quite knowing what to make of it all. It was a new adventure for us all, and he seemed happy enough, though quite unsettled. Colin as ever, was the MC for the weekend, a role he was born to perform, so he got his cordless microphone out and headed up towards the stage to carry out his duties. We followed with our camping chairs, cool bag and Ronnie, straining at the lead to be with his dad.

The afternoon was pretty stressful to be honest. Ronnie just wouldn't settle. The noise and the smell of burgers and hot dogs from the food tent meant he was pulling constantly on his lead, resulting in choking fits that were distressing to watch. Morvern, Chrisanna and I decided to take him back to the chalet and sit outside, to try and calm him down. This didn't work either. He would hear Colin's voice from the stage and pull and haul to get to him. We were each taking turns at holding his lead, but all our hands were getting sore as he struggled to get free. When Colin returned to the chalet I told him what it had been like.

'Colin, this isn't working. He won't settle and we're all struggling to keep him calm.'

'I'll take him for a while. He'll settle down if I walk around the site with him. I've got to get back soon though, to introduce the next band.'

We welcomed the peace Ronnie's departure brought as we nursed our sore palms, and used the time to catch up and have a drink, then navigated our way through the rest of the afternoon and evening, each taking turns to look after Ronnie. As the night wore on, Morvern suggested we leave him in the chalet for a while to let him sleep. Reluctantly, I brought him in, and placed his bed on top of mine. Leaving some treats beside him, I left. The howls began almost instantaneously; heart-breaking and impossible to ignore.

'Leave him, Susan. He's absolutely exhausted. He'll just fall asleep,' Morvern advised. I knew she was right, but it felt so wrong.

As I walked away and the hollers became fainter I remember thinking this just wasn't fair on the wee guy. It was all too much for him, and was also spoiling our experience. When I walked back half an hour later, just to check he had stopped howling, all was quiet. Then I saw a head pop up from behind the chalet blind. He wasn't sleeping, and as soon as he saw me he was off again. I went in and brought him back up with me. I just couldn't leave him in there on his own.

It was getting near time for No Shame to perform, so we headed back to the chalet to get changed. It was so nice to be able to get ready standing upright. Wriggling into my dress in a tent had become wearing in previous years, and to have plug points for my hair straighteners, and a mirror to do my make-up was a welcome change. A buzz was building in the chalet as friends popped in and out. No Shame was the last act of the festival, so people expected a good set that was going to draw the proceedings to a close with a bang. We all took this very seriously, and planned and rehearsed the set several months in advance.

Another tradition that had grown over the years is me finding a glamorous dress to wear on stage. As Dalmallyfest always fell on or around our wedding anniversary, Colin and I bought each other our stage outfits as gifts. It was always fun in the weeks leading up to it to go out and trawl the charity shops for the best outfits we could find. I'd got some amazing designer dresses at a fraction of the price, which looked really good on stage; the glitzier the better. Colin loved to show off too, and always managed to find something a little different to wear. It was all part of the Dalmallyfest experience.

As we got ready I was trying to hide my dress from people coming in and out of the chalet. The band always went on and played two or three heavy rock songs first, and then I was introduced on stage. I walked around the back of the stage wearing my wellies and waterproofs over my dress. Morvern would be patiently waiting for me to help me slip out of my wellies and into my stellies as I was called on for the big reveal. Being much less of an extrovert than Colin, I was always nervous by this point. I didn't enjoy being in the spotlight nearly as much as he did, but it'd become a tradition and despite the nerves, I always got myself up there and put on a show. It was the only gig of the year where I felt my stomach flip.

Colin's costume this year was a particularly good one. He was wearing tight white jeans, sailor pumps, a white T-shirt and a cropped admiral's jacket, with tassels and gold buttons. From a distance, he could have been taken for a Freddy Mercury tribute act.

Morvern had agreed to watch Ronnie while we were performing, but I found his behaviour really distracting. Again, he wasn't settling and was pulling at Morvern, so she and Chrisanna were having a difficult time enjoying the show. The poor dog was tortured as there was just too much stimulation going on all around him, and it wasn't safe to let him off the lead in case he ran away.

The gig went well despite Ronnie, but when we came off stage I turned to Colin and with a heavy heart said:

'We tried, Colin, but this didn't work out. Ronnie isn't going to be able to come to Dalmallyfest again.' I saw the look of disappointment in his eyes, but he had to agree.

As it turned out, this wasn't the last time Ronnie enjoyed a taste of festival life. While he didn't join us at Dalmallyfest again, a couple of years after his torturous trip to Biggar, we were invited to a much smaller gathering of the Dalmallyfest crowd at the original site in Dalmally.

Bert, Lesley and Tony had decided to throw a one off reunion of stalwart supporters in the grounds of Bert's mum's cottage.

We packed up our tent (there would be no comforting chalets this time) and Ronnie's belongings and headed off through all of the beautiful scenery Argyll has to offer, stopping at the Rest and be Thankful for a doggie comfort break. It was September, the sun was shining and the trees were beginning to lose their summer vibrancy along with their leaves, but you could see that in a few weeks the place would be awash with red and golden blankets of colour.

Closing the show

When we arrived, we greeted friends and let Ronnie roam free amongst the revellers. Like most dogs he loved the outdoors and was happy to sniff his way around his new surroundings. We got a tour of the cottage, which was rustic to say the least, but had such a charm, even when pouring buckets of water down the loo to flush. I saw the same look in Colin's eyes I had seen when we visited my Aunty Trisha and Uncle Frank's cottage in Wexford. He was mesmerised by all of the nooks and crannies and the enormous character of the place. One day we will have one of these rickety wee cottages of our own and Ronnie will love it.

We pitched our two-person dome tent and headed to the campfire to join in the craic and enjoy some barbecue. Ronnie was roaming around, picking up discarded bits of burger and every now and then he would head down to the stream at the bottom of the field to enjoy a cooling drink of clear, fresh water. The smaller crowd was suiting him well as he coped so much better than at Dalmallyfest real. Colin got up to sing a few numbers during the acoustic set while Ronnie lay stretched out in front of the fire, keeping my toes warm. It was becoming chillier as the sun left us to our merriment.

Bedtime beckoned and I gathered myself, determined to remain optimistic despite having ended my love affair with camping several years previously. Before anything could be done, the trek to the cottage toilet had to be made, carrying the hope that the previous occupant had re-filled the bucket. I returned to the tent, trudging through the grass having followed the shapes of the many beautiful flowers, guiding me like lighthouses when the torch hit them, back to where I had come from. I could see Colin's silhouette in the tent comically struggling to get out of his clothes and into warm pjs.

'You're daft,' I mocked as I wriggled out of my wellies and felt my way in.

'Why?'

'I'm not even going to attempt to get out of my clothes. It's far too cold now. I'm just going to sleep in my jeans and put a fleece over my top.'

'Well I'm half way there now so I might as well see it through.'

Ronnie was still outside the tent, thoroughly enjoying this extended outdoor time. Once we were both settled we called him in, wiping wet paws with his old towel. We had a camping light tied to the roof of the tent so we could see all around it. Ronnie made his way to the end of the bed and crashed down. We had created a very cosy interior and were lying on top of an airbed covered with a duck down duvet and sheet with matching pillows and another duvet on top. It really was very comfy. We settled down for the night and it wasn't long before Ronnie's usual bedtime antics began as he clawed at the sheets to gain access in-between Colin and I. He was a very welcomed guest. That soft warm body kept Colin and I toasty all night as he didn't leave our side, shocked by the outside temperatures.

When I woke up in the morning, the sweat was dripping off me. Fully clothed with additional fleece layers on and sandwiched between Ronnie and the duvets, my body didn't know what had hit it. I was dressed for the Antarctic. Ronnie was up and bouncing about the confined area of the tent and Colin looked over at me.

'Colin, I can hardly breathe. I'm boiling!'

'You're looking a little flushed. Open the door of the tent a bit.'

I stretched over and pulled on the zip, drinking in the cool morning breeze that was coming in off the stream.

'Susan, that was a brilliant night. I just loved it, the three of us in the tent together. Did you not?'

'Yes it was lovely. I just need to get up and stretch a little. My legs have completely gone to sleep.'

'Yes but did you not love how much Ronnie enjoyed the tent and just being here?'

'Yes, Colin, I did but I think you're both a bit more suited to the outdoors than me. I've got to go and use that bloody toilet now. I won't be long then I'm going to have a wash in the stream. My mouth feels like Ronnie's slept in it.'

We got up and enjoyed a leisurely breakfast. I had thoroughly relished brushing my teeth in the stream as Ronnie paddled by and there is something to be said for getting a taste of the great outdoors once in a while. As we made our way along the winding roads back home, Colin was still waxing lyrical about our evening in the tent. We've never enjoyed a night under the stars since but, as I write and recall the immense joy it brought my boys, I think we should.

Chapter Seventeen - 1065 Ltd

I've never been good with numbers. It's just not something I'm interested in, or in any way drawn to. Words and conversation bring out so much more curiosity in me. In school, the only two subjects I showed any potential in were Music and English, and I was particularly good at composition. Maths and Arithmetic made no sense to me at all. In fact, I failed both O Grades spectacularly first time around. But thanks to a change of teacher I managed to pull my grades up to an 'A' in Maths and a 'B' in Arithmetic within a year. I even went on to get a Higher Maths the following year. Good teachers are so crucial to the success of pupils, and unfortunately, in my school experience, they were few and far between.

All of the jobs I held before starting my business had an element of budget management; something I avoided until the last minute, or delegated to a team member with a passion for numbers. It wasn't that I couldn't do it, I just didn't enjoy it. I would even leave my expenses for months on end and then have to spend a whole day working out mileage routes and hunting for receipts. Not good.

However, the thing about running your business is that you need to keep accurate and habitual records of your finances. It's an essential element of any company. There's so much to remember, and while a lot of it is transferrable from my previous budget experience, it somehow feels so much more important that I get it right because I don't have an HR or Finance Department keeping me straight. Without the support of Lorraine, our trusted accountant, I would have got lost down the black hole that is our tax system long ago.

My first year went by without any real problems. I started in the summer so my accounts didn't run for the whole financial year. I kept all the relevant receipts and invoices, and a note of all the mileage I had clocked up, in a folder with a printout of incomings and outgoings. When working from home you are also able to claim a percentage of your heating, electricity, council tax and insurances against tax too, and it all adds up so again it's important to file away any relevant documents. Not making a huge amount of money that first year, I actually got a tax rebate, which helped propel me into year two. By that time, Colin had made the jump to self-employed alongside me.

It then became my job to manage both our finances. As boring as I found this task, Colin was even more uninspired to execute it. He's also not the most organised of people and without my overseeing things, receipts would be lost and a fair proportion of our expenditure would go unclaimed. And so I run two folders and two envelopes full of our separate receipts while Colin keeps a spreadsheet of all the walks he does, and the associated income. When I say 'I run this', it's more a case of stuffing receipts into an envelope when I remember to do so, and piling up all of the relevant invoices and bills in a designated corner of our bookcase as they come in. Two or three times a year I pull it all out and spend a day getting it all in shape; just like the old days with my expenses! Old habits die hard.

There's always a big spurt of activity as the autumn approaches and I know we'll be meeting Lorraine to review the year and hand over our folders. Somehow, there's inevitably something I can't find, which sends me into a panic. Whether it is an essential receipt or several bank statements, I can guarantee something crucial will not be where it should be, resulting in us tearing our front room apart in search of it. I realise that this could all be avoided if I were more organised, and took time every month to sort things out. I promise myself every time I hand the folders to Lorraine that this will be the case, but it's just not in my nature. I'd rather spend a few days over the course of a year on it than have to assign time each month. Maybe this will be the year that's different.

We're pretty straightforward clients for Lorraine and have always got through the yearly review with ease, paying our tax and keeping everything above board. I couldn't sleep at night without this. One thing we are both guilty of is not taking Lorraine up on the year-round support she offers, and have only phoned her a handful of times in-between our annual meetings. However, in Colin's second year and my third year in business, we learned the hard way that keeping your accountant up to speed with your earnings is a crucial part of running a business.

Lorraine had come over to the flat and we'd dutifully handed over our folders, not thinking anything of the fact that we'd both just had very good year in terms of our income. She had a quick scan of our paperwork and told us she'd be back in a few weeks to go through our tax return. A couple of days later she called me.

'Hi, Susan. I hope you're sitting down.'

'What's wrong?'

'I didn't realise your income had grown quite so much this year. You do know you're going to have a substantial tax bill to pay in January.'

'Well, I knew I'd have tax to pay, but I didn't think it would be that much.'

'We're talking a lot of money here, Susan. I've not checked Colin's accounts fully yet, but he's going to be the same. I'm really sorry. If I'd known you'd both had such a good year, I would have warned you about this sooner.'

'It's not your fault, Lorraine. We're just so green when it comes to all of this and didn't think to let you know. It's our responsibility.'

'Look, I'll work on Colin's accounts now and come and see you both in a couple of days so we can discuss it more fully. I hope you've made some provision to pay this though, Susan. It's going to be a big bill.'

I put down my phone and burst into tears. How stupid had we been? I'd won several big contracts and Colin's business was just going from strength to strength, and while we both knew we had to make provision for tax we had no idea it would be so much. That's the thing with being self-employed. You get the full amount of your earnings, unlike a wage, which already has the tax deducted from it. It's really easy to forget that the money in your bank account is not all yours, and you feel really well off, which leads to spending more than you usually would. What a mess. I composed myself and phoned Colin.

'Lorraine's just been on the phone and we're in big trouble. Our tax bill this year is going to be huge.'

131

'What'd you mean? We've worked out our tax and it's manageable.'

'No, it's not, Colin. I didn't understand all of what Lorraine was saying, but it's something about having to pay the tax, then half again on top. We're going to be wiped out.'

'Susan, it'll be alright. How was it left?'

'She's coming to see us in a few days to talk it all through.'

'Okay then. Let's not panic until we know the facts. There will be a way around this.'

'No, there isn't. We've got to pay our tax. There's no way around it.'

'I'm in the middle of dropping dogs off, Susan. I can't talk now. I'll see you in an hour or so.'

I paced the kitchen, trying to calm myself down, but feeling an impending doom hanging over me. I just couldn't get over how stupid and naive we'd been: I, who prided myself on being so good with money, had let this one completely slip through my hands.

The four days between hearing our depressing tax news and meeting Lorraine were grim. I tossed and turned each night, running all kinds of desperate scenarios through my mind. First, there was the one of me having to go back to work; a situation I never wanted to be in. Then came the one where we couldn't afford to pay our bills anymore, which ran into the finale of us living under a bridge with only cardboard boxes and Ronnie to keep us warm. It never ceases to amaze me where my mind will take me when fear comes in. I guess we all have an ultimate terror of becoming destitute.

There are currently so many stories doing the rounds about successful people losing everything to the recession, and don't even start me on the television programmes that shamelessly scare the life out of us. There's a current trend of Panorama-style documentaries, which follow families from riches to rags. They seem to revel in exposing how redundancy can result so easily in desperate attempts to stay afloat, which inevitably lead to the loss of homes, marriages, and everything people have worked their entire lives to build up. Despite knowing these programmes are not good for my mental health, I am drawn to them in a twisted, voyeuristic way. During those long nights of 'Taxgate' I reran these shows in my head, imagining the television cameras coming to visit Colin, Ronnie and I under our bridge, to film our shameful story. Colin just slept peacefully beside me.

Throughout the days, I would carry on with things as best as I could. It was now my priority to bring in as much work as possible to help pay the tax bill. I knew, however, that whatever extra I brought it would need to be carefully calculated regarding the tax for next year. It was almost enough to make me want to earn less, but there was no real logic in this. I would swing from anger to feelings of foolishness, then onto despair as I tried to get my head around the blow we had received, as a result of complete inexperience. I kept hearing in my mind that ignorance was no defence, as a judge lorded over us, ready to throw us into the cells. And then what would happen to Ronnie? Colin just kept walking the dogs.

Then there was the Internet: a wonderful invention when in a positive state of mind and searching for a holiday or the next great bargain; dangerous, however, when in a state of panic. Of course, I went on to search for stories of others who had found themselves in a similar situation, and there were plenty: from businesses that had gone bust to people who swore they would never run their own company again. The stories were there infesting my already heightened state of panic.

I know it's never a good idea to go Googling when all is not well, having learned this in the past from looking up medical symptoms. I've privately declared myself dying several times, after self-diagnosing simple ailments that cleared up themselves, but which, according to the Internet, were terminal illnesses. I know I'm not alone in this, but I also now know that it's a futile way of finding solutions, and one I have learned to limit.

Eventually, Lorraine arrived at our door. As she walked in she had a look of pity which threw my exhausted body into a spin of panic again.

'Okay,' she said, as she took our folders out of her big black bag. 'I'm so sorry again for all of this. I know it must have caused you a lot of stress and worry over the last few days.'

'Lorraine, please don't apologise. Like we said, it's our fault for not keeping you in the loop. How bad is it?' Colin asked.

She came to sit beside us and showed us the figure she had worked out, based on both our incomes.

'Oh my God! How can it be that much? We calculated it at about half of that for the two of us,' I gasped.

'You haven't taken into consideration some extra national insurance or the additional half you have to pay on top of what you're already paying.'

'But I don't understand. We pay our national insurance every month. What additional half is this?' I said, perplexed by this piece of information that no business advisor or business owner had ever informed me of.

'You're always a year behind with your tax, so this bill is for the year before. But you can't wait until the following tax bill to pay what you owe on this year. You have to pay half in January and the next half in July so you are contributing to the current tax year. The national insurance you pay doesn't cover everything, so there are additional costs at the end of the financial year to make this up.'

'I've never heard of this anywhere,' I exclaimed. 'How on earth does that encourage small businesses to be successful, if they have to pay out some much of their earnings in advance tax?'

'It's just the system, Susan. Everyone has to do it. The reason you're getting caught out is because this is your first really profitable year, but it will balance itself out next year.'

'But it doesn't encourage people to be successful. We'd be so much better off if we hadn't earned as much.'

'No. It will balance out. It's just a big blow in year one. It's because you're so used to your tax coming off when you earn it, rather than all at once.'

'Yes, but people who are earning don't have to pay half again in a oner.'

'But they are paying tax continually so it's completely different. I know it's a shock, but we can look at another option which, given your earnings, is probably the best way to go.'

'Great, Lorraine. Tell us about that then,' Colin said, in an attempt to defuse my indignation.

'Well, I think the best thing is for you to combine both your businesses into a limited company.'

'Okay and what's involved in that?'

'You would chose a company name and this would be the overarching company, with Ronnie Ronster's Dog Walking Service and Inspire Community Coaching both as trading arms of it. You would both become Directors of the company, and rather than drawing a salary, you claim dividends and pay Corporation Tax rather than Income Tax.'

'How does that work then?'

'You can both take out money up to the value of the tax allowance then after that, any drawings are taken as dividends. You would need to register your business with Companies House and open a business bank account, so you put all of your business dealings through this account, no personal transactions.'

'So would you say this is the best way to go for us?'

'In these circumstances, yes. It makes sense given the way both your businesses are now going. It's about doing what is best for your companies at this time.'

'Okay. What do you think, Susan?'

'It sounds like a good option to me. There are obvious benefits to our businesses and it'll make us more organised with our finances. But what shall we call the new business?'

'What about 1065 Ltd?' Colin said, with a sparkle in his eye.

'I like it. I don't know why, but I do.'

'Well, it's where it all started, and it's got quite a ring to it.'

'Okay, Lorraine. Looks like we're going down the limited company road. Can you take this forward for us?' I asked, relieved that we had found a solution of sorts.

'Yes, that's no bother. I'll contact Companies House with your new business name and they'll send you out all the information you need, along with your unique company number and certificate which you need to keep safe. Are you both okay?'

'I feel better than I did and quite excited about this new venture,' I said.

'The way I look at it is we want to have big tax bills every year, because that means both our businesses are successful,' Colin said. God how did he do it? How did he always manage to see the positive in things when I had crumbled like stale biscuit? Much as I love this about Colin, sometimes it can really irritate me, as it constantly shows up my 'half-empty' attitude.

'I think it's also taught us that we need to keep in touch with you far more, Lorraine. I hope you realise we're going to be on the phone to you non-stop now.'

'That's fine by me. You know you can call me any time.'

As Lorraine left, we flopped onto the sofa with a sigh of relief. We had learned so much from the experience and paid our hefty, but a little lighter tax bill, as required at the end of January. What a crap time though, just after Christmas. It has made us more organised as a result, and now that we know what we're dealing with, we can make sure there is always enough put away to cover the additional tax requirements.

It had been a very stressful week and one where I had considered, as I do in times of tension, if it was worthwhile continuing with my business. Despite this, something has always kept me going, and it's more than just a stubborn pride in refusing to fail. The down days are more than compensated for by the up ones: those days, when a new contract comes in, or a client has a massive breakthrough, or days when I have the freedom to see a friend for lunch, or visit my parents because my workload allows it; those days when I wake up and remember again that I don't have to rush into an unhealthy office, and face a barrage of problems that were making me ill. I know these things are priceless and we're learning all the time.

Chapter Eighteen - A life well-lived

'Colin, Peggy was hit by a car on Kelvin Way tonight. She's dead. Please don't call me. I don't want to talk, but please let folk know. I can't bear having to tell people. Thanks.'

From the look of shock on Colin's face as he read his screen, I just knew something really bad had happened to one of the dogs. We were sitting at our kitchen table eating dinner as he passed the phone over to me. 'No, no. Oh my God! No, not wee Peggy.' I couldn't find the words and just kept repeating 'no' as my eyes filled with tears.

'I need to reply to Kathryn's text, Susan. Help me, please.'

We struggled to pull something together, though nothing we could have written would have brought any comfort to Kathryn as she grappled with her grief.

'You must be devastated. Of course we will do everything we can to help you through this. I would like to speak to you as soon as you're ready. She will be sadly missed by everyone. All our love, Colin and Susan.'

Colin phoned Gaile and told her the sad news. She was with Neil who owned Lachie, a playful Collie that was also part of the pack. Gaile said she would let Chris and Pat know. We welcomed the help. Elspeth was next on the list, and Colin's hands shook as he searched for her number, his voice cracking when recounting the story again. All I could do was rub his arm, as he made the necessary calls to all the other dog owners who knew and loved Peggy. My tears just kept flowing, but Colin was in autopilot, doing what he had to do to help Kathryn.

Ronnie was under the table, quiet and aware that something difficult was going on. I couldn't finish my pasta, and it went into his bowl in an attempt to ease the tension in the room.

'Oh, Colin. Poor Peggy, and poor, poor Kathryn. She must be heartbroken.'

'I know. It's just so sad. She was such a fantastic wee dog.'

'We need to go and see Kathryn when she feels ready.'

'I know. I'll sort it when she gets in touch.'

'You seem to be taking this really well. I can't stop crying thinking about her, and how we'll never see her again.'

'I think I'm in shock. I just need a bit of time to get my head round it.'

I left him alone as he looked through old videos and photos of Peggy on his laptop, and his laughter came travelling through to me as I sat on our sofa. That was the thing about Peggy; she just made you laugh. Ronnie was curled up beside me, trying to comfort me, and every now and then he would lick away my tears. I held him tightly, so grateful to have him by my side.

This wasn't the first time one of Colin's dogs had died. Not long into his business a beautiful greyhound called Annie had passed away. Her owner, Lesley had been packing her car in preparation for her holiday when Annie had got out of the close, run into the road and been knocked down. She wasn't that badly hurt and Lesley had rushed her to the vet. She needed an operation, but her injuries weren't life-threatening. Sadly, Annie died under anaesthetic. It was so awful as if she hadn't needed the operation, she would have made a full recovery. She wasn't an old dog, but there was always a risk with an anaesthetic. You just didn't expect it in a young, fit and healthy dog like Annie.

I remember the morning Lesley had phoned Colin to tell him. He went straight round to see her, to offer his support. He was visibly shaken on his return and it made me think of the many sides there were to this job.

The next morning, Kathryn called, and Colin did all he could to console her. I could hear her tears through the phone as she recounted Peggy's last moments. I had to battle really hard not to start crying again. Colin was visibly upset when he came off the phone.

'She was in the putting green and got distracted by something. She ran the length of the fence then got through a gap at the end, straight onto the road and under a car. She died right away.'

'Awful, but at least that's a blessing. I know it's a cliché, but she didn't suffer. That'll be a little comfort to Kathryn later.'

'This is something we're going to have to get used to, Susan.'

'I know. It's a part of life, but it just feels so unfair. How old was she?'

'She had just turned two at the beginning of this month.'

'Oh God, that's so terrible. What a short life she had.'

'I know. Kathryn wants us to go round tonight. Is that okay?'

'Of course.'

I knew death was something we would encounter in this venture. Anyone who owns a dog knows the chances are that they will outlive their canine companion. In some of my darker moments, I consider how I will cope when Ronnie dies, and I know Colin has his moments too. I think the trick is to enjoy as much of the present you have with your dog, and not focus on the future. I know people who have never got over the loss of their dog, and the intense pain of that loss has prevented them from ever getting another one.

My dad is a case in point. He can't talk about the passing of our beloved Ben — the family dog we had for fourteen years when I was growing up — without filling up. He recounts the story of Ben's last day and the look he gave my dad when he put him in the car to take him to the vet.

'He knew something was going on and I felt like I was betraying him. I never want to go through something like that again.'

That was nearly twenty years ago, yet the memory is still raw for my dad. Despite many happy memories of Ben, neither he nor my mum will entertain the idea of getting another dog. He's irreplaceable to them. I know non-dog lovers will find this kind of thing ridiculous, but dogs really do become an enormous part of any family, and their loss needs to be mourned as such. I would like to think that dogs will always be a part of our lives, and that when Ronnie does eventually go to his putting green in the sky, we will acquire another furry friend: not to take his place, but to give a new rescue dog a loving home, and continue to enjoy the many pleasures of dog ownership.

Dad and Ben

Colin and I were now experiencing the sad loss of a much-loved dog in the Ronnie Ronster's pack. He had to carry on, get out there and walk all of the other dogs in his care, and I had to get on with my working day too. The words of Paul McCartney's *Another Day* kept playing over in my head all morning: 'So sad, so sad, sometimes you feel so sad'.

We got through our day and braced ourselves for the visit to Kathryn. She and her partner Skip answered the door, both looking tired and bewildered. Kathryn had black mascara smudged around her eyes. It had obviously been a tough day. Passing her flowers and a card (Colin and I had struggled with what to bring), we sat down to a cup of tea and sympathy.

An hour later, we left feeling quite uplifted. We'd spent the time recounting happy memories and funny stories about Peggy. Kathryn spoke about the time she got the call from a charity shop to say Peggy was wandering around inside. While with Colin's pack, she had managed to get under the fence, across the road and into the shop at such speed that he hadn't even noticed she was gone. A rather embarrassed and relieved Colin ran across the road to retrieve her quickly. Skip spoke about the immense impact she had had on him in such a short time, and they both recounted with great love how Peggy had woken them in the mornings, with her exuberant bouncing onto the bed and face-licking antics. Colin had so many memories to share about all of the dogs Peggy played with, and how much fun she was to have in the pack. Our stories left us all feeling less at a loss.

There were a few tears, but not nearly as many as I had anticipated and Kathryn was holding up really well. I was so glad she had Skip beside her. They would be flying out to Australia for a month the following week, and this was just what they needed. Colin explained that he wanted to do a tribute to Peggy on Facebook, compiling some of the photos and videos of her. Kathryn agreed to this, and said how much it had helped to hear people say they loved Peggy, and to just talk about her.

They both looked shattered and were in need of a good night's sleep. As we walked back to the car, Colin put a protective arm around me and pulled me in tight to him. We all knew it could have been any of the dogs, as so many of us have experienced our canines running away. Ronnie had had several narrow escapes, running away twice and on the second occasion, crossing several busy roads to make his way home. He'd also nearly drowned in the river the day he got stuck too far out, but he's still with us. Peggy was just unlucky. It struck me as being the same as for we humans. Our time on this planet was always unknown and could change in a heartbeat; a true lesson in living in the moment and valuing what we have now.

Peggy had joined the pack just after Ruby, and was only four months old. I'd never seen a Cockerpoo before, which is a mixture of a cocker spaniel and a poodle. Looking like a cut-down version of Ruby, they were often taken for sisters, or mother and daughter, both sharing beautiful golden coats of cascading curls. She had brown button eyes and the cheekiest of expressions. Never had I come across a happier dog, and you always got her the same way; bouncy and full of fun. She was a little ray of sunshine.

Everybody loved Peggy because of this and as well as being a regular on Colin's walks, she often stayed with us. Kathryn was a self-employed television producer and would regularly have to go on location for several days, or be called down to London. Peggy and her bag of tricks would arrive, and there was always much fun on her visits. She was never any bother, and having been crate-trained, would settle easily at night. In the evenings she loved to walk along the top of our sofa, pop her head in-between Colin and me and nibble our ears.

She also had a passion for footwear, slippers and socks, in particular. We were always reminded that Peggy was staying when we would have to hunt for our slippers on returning home. The comical sight of her with one of Colin's slippers in her mouth, nearly the size of her, will always stay with me. It was one of her favourite games, and she would tear off down the hall, stopping to look back and see if you were following her as she ran between rooms, loving the attention. Kathryn told us that she only stole from people she really liked, and we had felt very privileged to be on her list of preferred footwear providers.

She also loved her food, and despite being fed at her regular meal times, would often demand more. Her little paw would tap her bowl and she could frequently be found with her head and paws lying on top of it, looking up at us like Orphan Oliver. If she was ignored, she would continue to bang furiously on her bowl until it completely overturned. You couldn't disregard this little dog. Colin had so many photos and videos of her taken over the entire time we looked after her, as she was so comical. How lovely that she would be forever captured on these.

We had several visits to a dog-friendly pub around the corner from us with Kathryn, Peggy and other friends, and she was always the star of the show. Everyone wanted to pet Peggy, from staff and customers to passers-by. Despite being fully grown, she was still tiny, so had the permanent look of a puppy. People would gasp with delight when they saw her, and many a time I heard customers say they wanted a dog just like Peggy.

And now she was gone.

Peggy

It really brought home how fragile we all were. She had been in our home only a few days previously. I had returned from a meeting to be greeted in her usual way, bouncing up and down, trying to reach me and lick my face, jumping on Ronnie in a desperate attempt to get him to play. He would miss her too. Colin had, on occasion, managed to get her to jump up into his arms, which demonstrated just how high she could jump. Our home was always such a fun place with Peggy around, and I still couldn't believe that this little bundle of fur would never come running down our hall again.

Chapter Nineteen - Do your duty

Jury duty is not something I had a great deal of experience with until I became self-employed. I was called once about twenty years ago when I was working in Paisley as a Community Worker but not chosen as a juror. It had resulted in an interesting morning off work as I witnessed several of our local accused offenders being slapped down by a very stoic judge despite every effort by their lawyers to plead their innocence. All were repeat offenders and the judge was having none of it.

That was my only time inside a court until five years ago when being summoned for jury duty became a regular event for both Colin and I. The first time it happened for me, I was given an excusal by sending a letter and explaining that my work situation was such that it would cause a great deal of stress to take time off. The second time I was subpoenaed, I had to go in the morning of the stint and speak to the Clerk of Court. I pleaded my case and he let me away stating I would be called again within the six months.

It's really stressful when you work for yourself and this comes up. Colin and I are not ones to avoid our civic responsibilities, but that week I had a diary full of meetings and a good few of them were for potential new work. While most people in employment look forward to getting a wee break with jury duty, it's a completely different story when you're self-employed.

The third time it happened I bit the bullet, realising that this wasn't going to go away and I may as well clear my diary and get it over with. The Clerk of Court had told me the last time that in the Sheriff's Court, most cases only last a couple of days and that it shouldn't impact too much on my work. It was time to get this monkey off my back.

It was mid-summer and the weather was glorious so I walked down to the Sheriff's Court in Glasgow, enjoying the stroll along the Clyde and the warmth on my face. Once inside there was a lot of waiting about until we were eventually told to go home and come back at 2.00pm. I walked home and then back again, and by the time I returned my feet were pretty sore. It was quite a distance. The Clerk of Court then took over stating that she was now ready to call names from a bowl to make up the fifteen jurors. An excruciating few minutes followed as my heart raced and my palms began to sweat. One by one people stood up and took their seats in the court room and finally we were at fifteen and my name hadn't been called. I couldn't believe my luck and was happily putting my book back into my bag, ready to skip out the door, when she said,

'You are free to leave now but please turn up again at court tomorrow at 9.30am. We have a real shortage of jurors and you will be allocated another court room to go through this procedure again.'

I wasn't off the hook yet and dutifully made my way back again the next day. After lots of hanging around, we all entered nervously into a new courtroom. The same Clerk of Court greeted us and set out the stall for the day.

'Thank you for your patience. We are now ready to choose the jurors for this trial. Please be aware that this case is a complex one that is likely to go on until at least the middle of next week. If you are unable to commit this time, please come and speak to me now.'

I sat shocked and not quite knowing what to do. It was a gamble. If I asked to be excused I would be back here again in six months' time. But if I was chosen I was going way over the couple of days I had set aside in my diary for this. Twitching in my chair as I grappled with the dilemma and watched several people scrambled up to plead their case for freedom, I decided to wait it out. My nerves were shattered as one by one she picked the white pieces of paper out of the glass bowl. You'd have thought I was the one going into the dock. On it went for what felt like an eternity, some people happily making their way to the sitting area, (they don't like their job, I thought to myself) while others dragged themselves up, sighing heavily (self-employed, I thought).

Miraculously, for a second time my name wasn't called and I could have thrown my arms around the Clerk. Then one of the jurors realised he knew someone involved in the case and had to come off the jury. Good grief, would this never end? I was on high alert as the bowl was placed back in the Clerk's hands, but I skipped it again. Someone was looking out for me that day and I danced out of the cool court room into the wonderful warmth of the sun.

I got the next day off after calling the jurors' phone line but was called back again on the Thursday. Thankfully the case was dropped and that was the end of my jury duty. I haven't been called back in the last two years and I think showing willing paid off and hopefully it will be another twenty years before I'm called again.

Colin has had to endure similar jury duty ordeals. The first time he was called, despite sending a letter, he was told he had to report to court as requested. This resulted in a mammoth amount of organisation on our part. The date he had to go was in early January so we had to tell all of his clients well before Christmas that he would be taking that Monday off. What was scarier about Colin's summons was that it was for the High Court. Any juror for these cases could be cited for weeks, even months, depending on the case. This was going to be a stressful few weeks.

We decided that my friend Tina and I would cover the dog walking for the Monday to see what would happen. Colin requested that his clients find an alternative where possible, explaining that if this couldn't be found, Tina and I were on hand to take this on. While several of his clients were able to accommodate this request, eight dogs still required a walk.

Tina arrived at our home early that Monday morning, wrapped up like an Eskimo, all fur and water proofed. I too resembled someone from Scott's great Antarctic adventure as it was one of the coldest days of the year so far. I had made a flask of warm coffee and sandwiches to sustain us on our expedition and we headed out to scrape the van of its thick ice. Ronnie was looking a little bemused as to why his aunty Tina and I were taking him to work but he hopped into the van as obediently as ever.

Our first pickup was Rosie the Jack Russell, just a short drive away. I parked up outside her flat searching for the keys in Colin's bum bag which he had colour coded alongside a helpful list. I think I must have been a little too enthusiastic in my approach to the close as before I reached it I lost my footing on the sheet of ice that had replaced the pavement.

My body when straight up into the air and I landed flat out on my back, banging my head sharply on the ground. There ensued a ridiculous scramble on my part to get back up on my feet as quickly as possible but the sheer ice was making this impossible. I was sliding around all over the pavement with nothing to grasp onto to help me up. I eventually slid my way to the side of the pavement on hands and knees and managed to push myself back onto my feet with the aid of a parked car. Looking around for any witnesses, mortified by my predicament, I slowly made my way to the close door. Tina was sitting happily in the warmth of the van and had missed the show. This wasn't a good start.

Rosie made up for it though, giving her spectacular welcome as I opened the door to her flat. She leapt off the floor, high enough to lick my nose several times and was giving welcoming squeals of delight. We headed downstairs and I made my way back to the van very gingerly and nursing a sore head.

We then went on to pick up Ruby the Doodle and Max and Millie the Cross Breeds. Max was a medium sized black mix of Lab and Collie and Millie was a big black teddy bear of a dog, a German Sheppard, Collie and Lab cross. She pulled me so fast down her steps towards the van I nearly landed on my backside again.

Big Millie

Off we all headed towards Bellahouston Park. I was feeling a little hot and sweaty after all of the running up and down stairs to pick up the dogs and realised just how much of the job is taken up with the collecting and dropping off part of the process. Still, my multiple layers would stand me in good stead once we got to the park.

As Tina and I chatted away in the front of the van, things took a nasty turn in the back. I could hear growling and snarling and suddenly a fight broke out. I had no idea who it was between and a few sharp words from Tina and it was over. Ruby however was having none of it and began pushing her way through the small gap at my side of the grate that kept the dogs from getting into the front of the van. I felt a wet nose in my ear and her soft fur at the side of my face as I drove along and began encouraging her back to where she should be. Ruby is a determined dog however and was not about to go back into any more potential future fights. The next thing I knew, her front paws were on my shoulders and she was half way onto my lap. I panicked as I was still driving at this point and she was just about to land on my lap, obscuring my vision. Tina grabbed the wheel and between us we managed to manoeuvre the car to the side of the road and stop it safely just as she plopped into my lap like a new born lamb.

'Ruby, you gave me the fright of my life there! Come on now, you need to get into the back. The fight was over before it even began,' I said as I coaxed her out of the driver's door and back in with the other dogs who were all sitting well-behaved now.

'Are you okay, Susan?' Tina asked as we both started laughing.

'I'm fine, just a little shaken. We've only been out an hour and I've managed to give myself concussion and nearly crashed the van. This isn't for me!'

Once we arrived at the park, we had to negotiate our way the short distance from the van to the enclosed dog area which in normal circumstances would be a breeze. With the snow and the ice it was treacherous under foot and it took us a good ten minutes just to reach the gate with many scary wobbles along the way. Once in the area, however, it was wonderful to watch the dogs running around in the snow. Ronnie particularly likes it and loves to roll in it, eat it, dance in it and generally just make the most of the occasional treat. We threw the ball back and forth for an hour as the dogs burned off all of their energy not even noticing how cold it was. Tina and I on the other hand were blue. My hands and feet felt like they were going to drop off.

Making our way back to the van was as challenging as our previous journey out and we were so pleased to get back in, sip on some hot coffee and blast the heater. It was now time to drop off some of these dogs and pick up the afternoon group.

'God, Susan, I can't believe we have to do it all again! How does Colin do this? It's really hard work.'

'I know, but I think we have been unlucky with the weather too, Tina. This is a particularly bad day.'

'I really hope he gets off jury duty or we're going to be exhausted doing this all week.'

'Fingers crossed.'

Ruby and Rosie were staying out all day alongside Ronnie so we dropped off Milly and Max and headed for the new arrivals. First we picked up Iggy, a lovely black Cross Breed, then graceful Jackson, the Lurcher and finally Zak, the Westie. I had to do all of the picking up and dropping off as Tina wasn't insured for the business, so I was getting a real workout. We made our way back to the dog park and repeated the ball throwing and careful journeys to and from the van. The dogs just loved it and we couldn't help but get caught up in their joy of the day, despite our coldness.

Once we had dropped the last of the dogs off, we looked at each other with relief.

'I'll say it again, Susan. How does he do it? We had half the dogs he usually has and there were two of us!'

'It takes practice and a building up of tolerance. I remember when Colin first started, he would come home absolutely exhausted and he only had a few dogs back then. He's been doing this for years now so he's built up his fitness level and confidence. We did well, Tina.'

When we arrived home, Colin was curled up on the couch.

'So what happened? Did you get excused?' I asked anxiously.

'Yes. They told me straight away just to go home.'

'What so you've been home all day?'

'Yep, it's been great having a wee day off.'

'You could have let us know and done the afternoon shift! We're shattered and frozen.'

'Sorry, I just really fancied the break and I knew you would get on fine with Tina. It's good practice in case you have to do it again. Now you know what to expect!'

'Bloody cheek. Ok, we'll let you off with it if you make us a nice cup of coffee.'

'I'll do better than that, I think you deserve something nice to eat with it too, a reward for all of your efforts.'

As Tina and I thawed out in the kitchen, Colin made us French toast with cheese melted on top. It was the best French toast I'd ever tasted and the coffee really hit the mark too. It had been an interesting, enlightening and exhausting day and Tina and I had had a laugh as we always do while Colin enjoyed a rare day off.

Chapter Twenty - Different paths

I've often wondered how different my life would have been if I'd had children. Never having made a conscious decision *not* to have a family, I think I always believed that one day it would just happen. But it didn't. I'd always had a challenging time with my cycle, but in my thirties it got worse. The pain would reduce me to tears at times, but when I woke up one morning on my bathroom floor realising I had passed out, I knew it was time to seek help.

My doctor referred me to the hospital for a laparoscopy, a minor exploratory operation to find out what was going on. As I was coming round from the surgery, the consultant approached me and stated: 'Let's make this quick, shall we. It's nearly lunchtime. You have extensive endometriosis. I've been doing this a long time and have never seen such a bad case. It's everywhere, and certainly explains why you've been experiencing so much pain. It's going to be extremely difficult, if not impossible, for you to have children. We'll talk more at your consultation in six weeks.'

And then he was gone.

Even in my groggy state, I knew this had been a particularly insensitive diagnosis. Thank goodness for the kind nurse, who gently lifted the duvet under which I had hidden myself, and brought me hankies and words of comfort. In some ways, it was reassuring to find out what was wrong, and to know that it wasn't all in my mind. I think most women put up with an amazing amount of pain on a regular basis, just because they thought it was par for the course. I know I did. But on the other hand, I was suddenly faced with the reality that I may never have children.

Ironically, one of the best treatments for endometriosis is to get pregnant and that is what I was advised to do, and as quickly as possible. My ticking time-bomb of a biological clock was forever being pointed out to me by the medical profession, and with the mess 'my bits' were obviously in, it seemed a tall order. I was now thirty-five, well over the conception hill in their eyes. Not only that, Colin and I had only been together three months, and he had just been made redundant. It was a recipe for disaster.

'You heard what the consultant said, Colin. I'm supposed to try and get pregnant now!'

Colin had stared into space with a look of panic in his eyes.

'Please don't worry. It's not what I want either, and I've no intention of trying to trap you with this. We've only know each other five minutes, and now you're unemployed. It's not exactly the best start for our relationship, or the best environment to bring a child into.'

'I'm sorry, Susan, but I'm just not ready for all this. It's freaking me out.'

'I've just told you: neither am I. Let's carry on getting to know each other and see how things pan out. I think the thing you really need to think about though, is whether you want children in the future. There's a pretty good chance you won't be able to have them with me, so you need to be sure you're okay with that. Now's the time to make that decision, before we get any further down the road.'

'Susan, I know I want to be with you, and make a real go of this. If we can't have kids, then we can't have kids. I'm not going to end the relationship because of it. I'm really happy with you. Neither of us knows what the future will bring, but I think we could make a really good life together, kids or no kids, and that's good enough for me.'

And so we carried on and didn't start trying for a baby for the first few years of our relationship. Once we had got married, moved into a bigger home and felt settled in ourselves, we felt the time was right. Unfortunately, time was not on my side. I was now in my late thirties, and while remaining optimistic, I would swing between a certainty that I would get pregnant to a feeling of there was not a chance in the world it would happen. I put it in the hands of the Angels. Colin remained consistent in his love for me and the life we now shared, and never seemed up nor down about it.

That's the thing, though. I knew it was my body that was letting us down, so the guilt of not bearing him a child lay firmly at my door. He would always say it didn't matter, but what else could he say? Having seen Colin with Ronnie, and with children of our friends, I knew he would make a fantastic dad. He'd definitely be the fun parent, being a big kid himself. I knew he would have loved a daughter, a wee daddy's girl, but it just never happened.

Sometimes, I wonder what a child of ours would have looked like. What bits of Colin would they have had, and what would they have inherited from me? What personality traits would they have grown into, and how good would we have been at imparting our beliefs and values to a child? I would always have wanted him or her to have grown up as a kind-hearted, principled and well-rounded human being, but could I really have achieved that? I'll never know what kind of mother I would have made. It's one of those major life experiences for which I have absolutely no reference points.

I can't bear to be around those mother earth types who thrive on telling you: 'You'll never experience true love until you give birth to a child. That feeling you get when you first see them is like nothing you'll ever go through in your life again: pure love that's so different from other types of love.'

I'm sure it's true, but how cruel to brag about something like that to someone who knows they will never experience it.

But there's something to be said for *not* having children too. Without a doubt, Colin and I would not be able to live the lives we do now had we experienced the many pressures of parenthood. We wouldn't have taken the brave decision to start our businesses. Neither of us would have risked not having a steady salary each month. In fact, I had held onto my job far longer than I'd wanted to, for fear of losing maternity benefits if I had fallen pregnant. We also wouldn't have had all of the freedom we now enjoyed, and Ronnie certainly wouldn't have had all of the attention he received from us on a daily basis. The time and energy this took just wouldn't have been available to him. The chances are we wouldn't even have got a dog with all pressures of children, and the need to continue in full-time jobs.

So, while there is sadness in never knowing the many joys children bring, at times I also have, if I'm truly honest, a slight sense of relief. Life is so demanding as it is. How on earth could I ever have juggled babies too? I'm old enough to know that things happen (or don't happen) for a reason, and life brings other opportunities to make up for the losses we experience. My counselling and life coaching training has also greatly helped me come to terms with this. I'm able to name the feelings of loss and sadness I experience when they come up and accept that they will always be there to a lesser or greater extent. We all have our stories.

Ronnie is certainly one of our greatest gifts, and he's given both Colin and I the opportunity to test out our parenting skills on him. The maternal instinct I experience towards him is so strong, that sometimes I feel my heart will burst with love for him. I'm overprotective at times and often worry about his well-being. I'm sure this is similar to the emotions parents feel, though I'm also sure some would belittle such a strong reaction to a dog.

A mum to the dogs

Colin and I both call each other 'Mum' and 'Dad' when referring to our relationship to Ronnie, as do all our doggie friends with their own canines. There is actually a definition for this behaviour known as Anthropomorphism – *the attribution of human form or other*

155

characteristics to anything other than a human being. Pat, the dog trainer, can often be found tutting and shaking his head when he hears us speaking to our animals in this way.

'It's a dog, for God's sake. Stop treating him like a human being!' will be his impatient response, but on occasion, I have heard him refer to one of the dog's owners as 'so and so's mum'. Even he falls foul of these terms of endearment.

Another strange thing — though I think just a sign of our changing times — is that I have more friends without children than with them. Maybe this is just because we don't have a family and so are naturally drawn to others in the same boat. I know my friends who have children now also have a whole new set of friends they met at antenatal clinics or playgroups etc., and they have become a really important support network for them. We, on the other hand, have remained out of that whole circle, and even in our forties are still living a relatively young lifestyle. Our childless friends still love to party, as do we (though definitely not to the extent we all did when younger), and our weekends are often filled with dinner parties, trips to restaurants and bars, and general catching up with the people we love to spend time with. The effect this is having on our now ageing bodies will catch up with us at some point, I'm sure, but we're enjoying life to the full and I wouldn't want it any other way.

Most of my friends with children wouldn't change this for the world. Some however who are brave enough to be honest with me, have said that if they had their time again they would choose not to procreate. The stress, worry and financial burden children bring has just been too much for them. While they completely adore their offspring, and follow up their candour with reassurances of not wanting it any other way, there is an obvious envy of the lifestyle Colin and I enjoy.

One friend told me that she was so impressed that Colin and I had not bought into the whole having children thing. She has two wonderful children, but admits that she had her family because she felt the pressure of society to do so, it was about fitting in, and to see Colin and I not bowing to this pressure impressed her greatly. The reality is, however, as I pointed out to her, we had not made a radical non-conformist decision not to have children. It just didn't happen.

Then there's another friend who also has two beautiful children … I'll never forget the day she phoned me with the news.

'I'm pregnant.'

'Oh my God. That's wonderful news.'

Silence. Not a sound came back from my friend for what seemed like an eternity.

'What's wrong? Are you not happy about this?'

'I don't know how I feel, Susan. I think I'm in shock. I didn't want kids, so it's come as a real surprise to me.'

'Oh sweetheart. You'll be fine, honestly. It's bound to be a shock if that's how you felt, but once the baby's born, you'll feel differently. I'm sure you will.'

My words were falling on deaf ears as she grappled with this uninvited guest. Throughout her pregnancy, which was a tough one, she told me how she felt her body had been invaded by an alien, and just couldn't get her head round the whole new experience. Then I got the call to say her son had been born; the most straightforward birth in history. She had only been in labour for two hours when he made his entrance into the world. The minute I saw her holding her new love in her arms in that hospital bed, I knew all was well.

Both her children are now her life. She talks with such passion about them and is a wonderful mother, dedicating her time to making them the best people they can be. She tells me how sad she is that I don't have children, and can't imagine her life without them now. We're all different and I guess that's what makes life interesting.

I remember an acquaintance once telling me about a friend of hers being horrified at the fact that she didn't have children.

'But whose going to look after you when you're old?' she said, perplexed by the situation. At the time, I remember thinking that this was one of the most ridiculous reasons for having a baby, and I still don't think it's a good foundation on which to build a family. I must admit, however, that as I and my parent's age, and I see how much more they need me, I sometimes feel a sense of fear for the future.

What if Colin died first? Let's face it, in most cases the men do. Who will look after me when I'm old? Then I shake the fear off and remind myself that I'll make a pact with my childless friends, to share a home, look after each other and thoroughly enjoy our twilight years. What's the point of worrying about it now?

I am aware though that my poor mother has been left without grandchildren from either of her daughters. She never makes a fuss about it, but I see the disappointment in her eyes when she hears about another friend whose son or daughter has just had a baby. All of her siblings have grandchildren, and it must be hard for her not to experience and enjoy what is seen as one of the great rewards of having children: being able to spoil the grandchildren.

She is prone to depression, particularly in her later years, and I wonder if the distraction of grandchildren would have kept her more focused and well, but what can you do? My dad is neither up nor down about it. He's told me often that grandchildren would be bad for his image.

I'm also aware of the terrible heartache that has befallen friends and family when they have miscarried or had to endure the roller coaster that is IVF treatment. Colin and I chose not to go down that path, believing that if it was meant to be, it would be.

Any gap that may have been there for us has been well and truly filled by Ronnie, and by all of the many dogs that are now in our lives. Our home has become a safe place for dogs of all shapes and sizes to visit, stay and just have lots of fun. They do feel like an extended family, and caring for them all brings such a sense of satisfaction to us both. Maybe, in this life, I just wasn't meant to be a mother.

We all take different paths and I certainly have many opportunities to flex my maternal instincts. It's sad, but it's certainly not the worst thing that could happen to someone.

Chapter Twenty-one - Marathon man

I'm aware I keep on promoting the many benefits of dog ownership as I wax lyrical about the changes Ronnie has brought to us over the years. But one of the most fantastic benefits has been watching Colin's transformation into a fit and health-obsessed man, something I would never have believed on meeting him. Thirteen years ago, he was overweight and not taking any form of regular exercise. His diet consisted of carry out meals and beer and while he was the same beautiful person, he wasn't taking care of himself at all.

To be honest, it wasn't long into our relationship before he started making some changes. I know from my own experience of living alone that it can be hard at times to motivate yourself to cook a dinner for one. Shopping can feel like a sad affair, especially if you get to the checkout with a trolley load of dinners for one: a reinforcement of being alone. Sometimes I would dine on bowls of cornflakes and slices of toast, not being able to face cooking and I know Colin's many trips to the Indian, Chinese and Pizza takeaway shops were for the same reason.

I realise I'm painting a black picture here and many people live very happily on their own, and there are indeed many benefits to only having to think about yourself. I had a lot of happy memories of the single life as had Colin, but I always knew I wanted to share my life with that one special person and that didn't come into play until I met him.

So our eating habits began to improve. I ate cornflakes at the right time of the day and the take away shops near Colin mourned his loss. He started to lose weight and began enjoying five-a-side football twice a week. Long-term, however, the football wasn't for him. Colin enters into everything he does with great abandon and he was suffering too many injuries. He would arrive home sporting yet another enormous bruise or limping from an ankle or knee twist and so after a couple of years, this came to an end.

It was Ronnie's arrival that really propelled his fitness to a new level as the amount of exercise our new family member required meant we were both walking far greater distances than ever before. Then with the launch of the dog walking, Colin was out all day, physically active from start to finish. With the business being in the West End of Glasgow, most of his clients lived in tenement flats so on top of walking the dogs, there were the many trips up and down close stairs to collect and drop off his pack members. He was shrinking before my eyes.

Then came the running. He began dabbling in this three years ago. At the start of his first year he made a proclamation: "I'm going to run three 10K races this year". I applauded his dedication as I lay on the couch munching through the remnants of my selection boxes.

True to his word, he began running more frequently. Then he joined a running club organised by Achilles Heel in Glasgow. I believe this was the turning point. The group organisers were so passionate about running and helping people to be their best that this positivity and support pushed Colin forward in his training. Other participants proved to be invaluable too in offering advice and healthy competition. Everyone was chasing their personal best but it also helped to have people around you to measure your progress.

I watched Colin go from running a couple of kilometres to several miles in a matter of weeks. He'd come bouncing back into the house, breathless, flushed and not smelling his best, but beaming as the adrenalin pumped around his body. I could see how much he was enjoying it.

He ran a 10K within months of joining the group then a few other charity races and by late Spring he announced that he wanted to run the half marathon in October - The Great Scottish Run. I was fully behind him as I could see how easily this was coming to him. I say "easily" but I know this wasn't easy at all. He was running four times a week, building up his stamina and strength. It was the fact that he was enjoying it so much that made it look easy. It wasn't a chore. He couldn't wait to get his trainers on and sprint out the door. One of the key teachings of life coaching is about doing things that you love in life –work, hobbies, sports etc. - as you'll then be fully motivated to do them.

October was approaching and Colin had received his running pack and was in full training mode. I was so sick of eating pasta. He decided to run for Macmillan Cancer Support in memory of our two friends Sharon and Torhild. We were on countdown and Colin was following a strict training regime to optimise his chances of making it around the course in one piece. Achilles Heel continued to offer amazing support and encouragement too.

The morning of the race arrived. Colin had been awake since six and I was up not long after. He put his green MacMillan top on with his running number attached and left the house to cries of support from me. I followed on with Ronnie and when I got to George Square, somehow managing to find Colin amongst the thousands of runners, my heart was racing and bursting with pride. There was an amazing atmosphere around the place with music blaring, motivational warm ups and loved ones hugging and kissing their runners.

Colin was buzzing and when the gun went and they were off, I had goose bumps all over. A sea of people were running up St Vincent Street to the sound of The Proclaimers *Letter from America*. It was magical. My friend Morvern (our photographer for the day) found Ronnie and I and we made our way to Glasgow Green to wait for the victorious finish. Meeting up with Catriona and Chrisanna too, my sisters in-law, the day was turning into quite a party. We stood near the finish line watching flashes of colour pass us as cheers and claps went out and I just knew I had to look out for Colin earlier than he was expected. He was due at 1 hour 50 minutes but he came thundering past us at 1 hour 43 minutes. I was jumping up and down and screaming "Go Colin!" when he passed. He gave me an exhausted smile as he made his last steps across the finish line.

What a performance and what a day. I had watched Colin make a decision to do something and take all of the necessary steps (literally) to make it happen, then go and do it. He was a perfect life coaching client, so proud of his finishing time and keen to make future plans for further runs and so began his quest to complete a marathon.

The training became longer and more gruelling as I watched him leave our home right through the winter to follow the plan Paul from Achilles

Heel had produced for him. Following it to the letter like a teacher's pet, he would be away for hours at a time, arriving home exhausted and famished. Ronnie and I would be waiting with encouraging hugs, warm towels and plenty of food. I couldn't believe his commitment.

Half Marathon

This continued for six months and as the time drew near he began final preparations. You never actually run twenty-six miles in marathon training. The most he had travelled was twenty-three, which was incomprehensible enough to me. This was something to do with it being too much for the body to handle before the race but it unnerved me slightly to know he'd not met this milestone before the race. The weeks leading up to it he began reducing the number of miles to give his body a break before the huge, final push it would require.

He was also living the life of a monk, rarely drinking and eating foods that fuel. Who was this man? In saying that I'm perhaps giving him a little too much credit here. A motivating factor for Colin's running was the fact he could eat whatever he wanted and I would see packets of biscuits continually evaporating from our treat cupboard and find chocolate bar wrappers all over the house. On the rare occasions I travelled in his whiffy dog van, there would be sweet packets and Greggs bags strewn all over the place. He was having a great wee time to himself.

The day before the race arrived and I could see his tension mounting. We had decided that it would be best to leave Ronnie at home this time so he stayed with Charlie. Colin began organising his running gear, ironing it within an inch of its life and laying out his personal number over his top to be attached with safety pins. Neither of us slept well that night as we had to be up and away by 7.30am. The race was in Edinburgh, starting at 10am and Colin wanted to get the 8.00am train through from Glasgow. I can't remember the last time I saw this hour on a Sunday morning, enjoying weekend long lies as I do. Colin later confessed that he'd woken at 4am and not been able to get back to sleep. What a long day it was going to be for him.

We got to Queen Street Station which was full of excited runners. There was a 10k and half marathon on that day too, so the place was a sea of trainers and florescent running gear. Grabbing a coffee, we made our way to the train and spent an uncomfortable journey wedged between competitors and I was glad to step out into the fresh air of Edinburgh Waverley station. It was May but the weather was very changeable, perfect really for the race as running in blistering heat is not pleasant. As we made our way towards the starting line the rain began to spit on us and the air was electric. We could hear the sound of the warm up blasting in the distance as motivational music blared through the traffic.

All of the competitors were put into different coloured starting areas on the street depending on their expected finish time. Colin was in the white zone and I watching him stretching and limbering up for a good ten minutes before running over to wish him luck as the starting gun rang out. I raced along beside him for several blocks, pointing my phone at him only to discover it hadn't been videoing: pesky new phone that I wasn't up to speed with yet. It wasn't quite as an impressive a sight as the Glasgow half marathon, as the road was straight as opposed to St Vincent Street being uphill, but it still looked magnificent. Thousands of heads on multi-coloured running bodies coursing up the street as they pushed themselves to their limits.

I made my way back towards Waverley Station to meet my sisters-in-law. Catriona and Chrisanna had kindly volunteered to keep me company during the several hours it would be until I saw Colin again, hopefully victorious. We decided to make our way to Musselburgh and pass our time there. It really shouldn't be called the Edinburgh Marathon as it only starts there and then goes everywhere but, passing through Portobello, Preston Pans, Port Seton and ending in Musselburgh.

Arriving off the train at Musselburgh station we walked out into a housing estate with no idea of where we were. I spotted a sign further on so we made our way towards it. It said "Town Centre – 1.5 miles". None of us were too happy with this news, but we quickly corrected ourselves and plodded our way towards the town when we remembered what Colin was in the process of doing. Musselburgh is a lovely little place and having walked along the main street we stopped off at a coffee shop and sat outside enjoying the sun which had made a welcomed appearance. I had purchased a large gold chocolate medal that was hanging on the counter. That would make a nice touch and some welcomed sustenance for Colin, I remembered thinking. The time was moving fast and I was continually looking at my watch trying to work out how far into the race Colin would now be. We decided to make our way to the finish line and see how things were going.

The race end was just along the road in a school sports field and there were people six deep right along the barriers, so seeing anything was going to be tricky. Catriona insisted I leave the two of them and push my way into the crowds and I managed to squeeze myself two deep into a spot where, if I stood on my tip toes, I could just see the runners pass.

The sun continued to shine but about fifteen minutes before I spotted Colin sprinting towards the finish line, all sweat and endorphins, the heavens opened. There I was, on tippy toes, desperately trying to catch his historical passing and drenched to the skin. But it was worth it, a split second sighting, never to be forgotten. I was yelling at the top of my voice through umbrellas and Kagools, followed by a squelching trek to the finish line to search for our hero.

He was proudly wearing his medal and I presented him with the chocolate one too. He looked incredibly fresh considering and I couldn't believe how well he had done: three hours and forty minutes. What an achievement for a first marathon. All was going swimmingly until his brother, Murdo, turned up and the enormity of the day and many months of training caught up with him. He broke down and sobbed on his big bro's capable shoulders, experiencing the much needed release of all those racing emotions.

We made our way to one of the catering tents and ordered burgers and beers to enjoy in the now returning sunshine. Neil and Woody, other friends, arrived to congratulate Colin and join in the festivities. Not only did Colin achieve his goal in such a short period of time, he also made over £1,200 for the Lilias Graham Trust, a small charity who do fantastic work with families when there is significant risk of the children being taken into care. Win win. Our friends and family had been so generous with their donations and we'll always be grateful for that.

Colin could feel himself begin to seize up a little and so we decided to make our way back to Edinburgh. Little did he know that having just run twenty-six miles, he was now going to have to walk another one and a half back to the train station. There wasn't an available taxi in sight and buses were moving more slowly than we were. This small town was bursting at the seams. We made it back to the station in one piece and by this time we were all exhausted. It had been an exciting day for us all but now it was time to get home, pick up Ronnie and hit the sofa for some much needed R & R.

Having gone from 'I want to achieve running one marathon in my life time,' Colin then went on to run a second in Barcelona and achieved an even better time of 3 hours 35 minutes, knocking six full minutes off his previous marathon. He hadn't had the best of run ups to it as his training plan had gone a little awry with an injury and dose of a horrible virus that was doing the rounds and had floored him all over the Christmas holidays. Despite this, as I meandered my way through the streets of Barcelona to meet him at the finish line, something once again told me to be there before his anticipated arrival and once again I was right. Just by chance, I had squeezed myself into a space about 500 meters from the end of the race and within seconds, he was in sight. What was now becoming my signature response to the end of his races, went into overdrive as I jumped up and down, yelling his name at the top of my voice. He caught my eye and let out a huge smile of satisfaction as he ran on towards Nirvana. As we met, under the orange tree we had agreed before the race, his sense of pride was bursting out of every sweaty pore of his body. What a day and what a guy.

There was a whole crew of people from Achilles Heel in Barcelona that weekend and we shared some lovely meals and memories as runner and supporters all revelled in the excitement of it all. As we sat in Playa Royal, just around the corner from our hotel, with Gemma and Fiona, two lovely young women Colin had spent many pre-marathon training sessions with, they were all excitedly talking about the many other beautiful European cities that host marathons. Perhaps being a running widow wasn't going to be so bad after all.

Chapter Twenty-two - Coping alone

'You work really hard don't you, Susan?' Colin asked me, as he settled down on one of our kitchen chairs to take off his boots.

'Yes.'

'And you haven't had a holiday in a long time?'

'No.'

'And you miss the sun and seeing new places?'

'Yes. For God's sake tell me what you're getting at!'

'How do you fancy a trip to Cape Town?'

'Ah! Murdo and Laura-Anne.'

Before I go any further, I feel I need to explain Colin's confusing family names. Murdo features heavily in the Western Isles where Colin's family came from originally. There's Cousin Murdo, who is getting married, and is known as Murdo Angus. His father is Murdo Alex, known as Murdo A. Colin's brother is also Murdo Angus, named after his father and Colin's middle name is Murdo. But my own personal favourite has to be Colin's aunt, who is called Murdina and married to Alex Murdo (Colin's dad Murdo's wee brother not Murdo Alex, cousin Murdo Angus' father – got that? No neither have I). Colin's speech at our wedding caused quite an uproar, as he completely confused our guests, while paying homage to all the Murdos.

'Yes, [Cousin] Murdo phoned today. He's tying the knot in South Africa.'

'Wow. How exciting. When?'

'12th December this year.'

'Colin, that's only a few months away and right before Christmas. I thought you were going to say next summer or something.'

'I know, but just imagine, Susan … the weather's fantastic at that time of year and you'd come home for Christmas all relaxed and tanned. Think about it. We should go.'

I thought about nothing else for days. Things were going well for both of us work wise, but the old self-employed mentality kicked right in. The contracts I had were only up until the end of the year. What if no new work came in? It was just before Christmas, an expensive time, and then … what about Ronnie? We had never left him for more than one night. How would he cope being away from us for all that time? It was too soon to land that on him, although in reality we had now had Ronnie for almost two years, and were just avoiding leaving him.

I caught myself mid-internal dialogue and couldn't believe how many barriers I had placed in front of the trip. Where was my sense of adventure? I have to admit that I am not the most adventurous of people. Don't get me wrong, I love going on holiday, but I also love coming home. I'm the ultimate home bird, who enjoys all of the comfort and familiarity of her own surroundings. What a cheap date.

Another shameful admission is that I don't like flying. This strange change of heart occurred in my early thirties. Up until then, I had always considered the whole airport experience and journey to be part of the holiday. Then I took a flight to Gran Canaria and suddenly had a mammoth panic attack. My palms became sweaty, I couldn't get a breath, and the feeling of claustrophobia was all-consuming. If I could have opened the emergency exit and leapt into the clouds I would have done so.

Managing to get myself to the toilet on shaky legs, I stayed in the confined, whiffy box for a good fifteen minutes, breathing deeply and trying to compose myself. The contradiction of this escape plan was not lost on me, as why would I put myself into an even smaller space while feeling claustrophobic? I can only think that I needed to be alone in my panic and the thought of becoming completely out of control in front of a plane full of people was adding to my distress. I think at that time, there were a lot of changes going on in my life that I wasn't dealing with very well and this is how it decided to manifest itself. If we don't deal with things, they will find a way of letting us know.

Unfortunately, it scared me for future trips. While I have taken many flights since, it's not something I enjoy. It's completely a hit or a miss as to whether I'll get through them panic-free, which is what causes my pre-flight anxiety. It remains a work in progress.

However, add this to the mix of *the reasons why Susan couldn't go to South Africa* such as leaving Ronnie and my business responsibilities, and the scales began tipping in the wrong direction. And so the many conversations started about the pros and cons of my overcoming these irrational fears. My friend Morvern, a born explorer who has travelled to most corners of the world, spent hours talking me through the countless journeys she had endured to create the most amazing memories. Another friend and fellow counsellor, Lee, worked her way gently through my psyche in an attempt to get to the root of my trepidation. Both came up with fantastic action plans to get me through the twelve-hour flight to Cape Town, but my heart just wasn't in it.

Murdo, the groom to be, is a close cousin of Colin's. They'd spent summers together in Stornoway as children and have a wonderful relationship, both sharing a witty sense of humour and the storytelling gift. Laura-Anne is from South Africa, but Murdo and Laura-Anne now live in Edinburgh. The wedding was intended to be a family affair, with all of Colin's siblings invited. As time went on, it became apparent that the trip was not going to be practical for most of us. Charlie, Catriona and Chrisanna couldn't go, and Julie, (brother) Murdo's wife was unable to get the time off work too.

It appeared that the only ones able to make the trip were Colin and (brother) Murdo. In all honesty, it's likely I would have gone had the rest of the family been jetting off too. The distraction that comes from travelling in an excited group often keeps my panic at bay. With the numbers dwindling, it was time to raise my concerns with Colin.

'I think you and [brother] Murdo should go to South Africa together, Colin.'

'Really? Is that what you really want?'

'Yes. I'm getting myself in a state about the journey, and the fact that none of the rest of the family can make it tells me it should be a boy's trip. I can stay here and look after Ronnie. You know Scotty has offered to keep your business ticking over while you're away, so I would be here to support him as well.'

'You know I'd much rather you were coming with me, Susan, but I understand why it feels too much just now. It won't be the same without you though.'

'I'm really sorry, Colin, but I think this is the best solution all round. It'll cut the cost in half too, so I won't be worrying about enjoying Christmas.'

'Okay. Agreed then. Go do your stuff on the Internet and get me a great deal to Cape Town.'

And I did. Sipping coffee in the airport café, Colin suddenly pointed his phone at me. 'Say something. Send a good luck message to the happy couple.' I bumbled my way through a self-conscious video greeting, which Colin would play later, much to the delight of (cousin) Murdo and Laura-Anne. It was a thoughtful touch.

The weeks leading up to Colin's departure had been a mixture of excitement and trepidation. As the time came nearer, it was actually Colin who was experiencing more anxiety than me. The day before he travelled was particularly difficult for him.

'Susan, I don't want to go.'

'What? Oh, Colin. You know you'll have a fantastic time once you get there. We'll be fine, honest.'

'I know you will, but I hate leaving you. You know how I get when I go away. I'm really scared something will happen and I won't make it back. I've so much to lose now. The thought of leaving you and Ronnie terrifies me.'

'Darlin', everything's going to be fine. Flying is so safe and before you know it, you'll be home. Please, just enjoy this wonderful trip. I don't want you to spoil it by fretting about everything.'

We had a long hug as Ronnie jumped up in between us, and an apprehensive Colin went into the bedroom to finish his last-minute packing.

As I watched him walk through the departure gates, I suddenly felt a rush of fear and great sadness. I hated being apart from him too, and I was worrying about how I would cope with Ronnie on my own. Driving home, the first flakes of snow began to fall. By the time I reached home, there was a light dusting on all the trees, and the short walk from the car to the flat left my coat covered in little white sparkles of ice.

Ronnie gave me his usual greeting when I walked through the door. It always lacked the gusto of his welcomes when Colin was with me. He jumped up and was happy to see me, but he then immediately looked behind me for Colin. The look of disappointment on his face when he realised he was not there could have been really offensive to me if I hadn't become so accustomed to it.

'You'd better get used to it, Ronnie. You're stuck with just me for the next ten days.'

I actually ended up being alone in the house for all of four hours. Our friend Karin had kindly agreed to come and stay for the first few days, to keep me company and help with Ronnie. I was anxious about letting him off the lead when I took him out myself. Somehow having someone with me greatly eased this anxiety, and I knew I was going to have to set him free. There was no way he could go ten days on the lead.

We settled down with food and wine and had a lovely wee night catching up. The snow was falling as fast as the temperature, and I had the heating up full. After rather a lot of wine, it was time to take Ronnie for his last walk, so Karin and I wrapped up against the elements and headed across to the Art Galleries. Everywhere was covered with thick snow and looked so beautiful. The ground was glistening and the trees sparkled as their branches drooped with the weight of the snow.

We crunched our way around the familiar last walk of the day, and Ronnie dutifully did his business. It was lovely to be out in the crisp frosty air. As we approached the flat en route home, a wave of panic came over me.

'My keys. Oh my God! I don't have my keys!'

'Don't panic, Susan. We'll retrace our steps and find them.'

With a flamboyant about-turn, we made our way back to the deep footprints we'd just left, scouring the paths like the police tracing clues for a missing person.

'Maybe you accidently threw them in the bin with the poo bag.'

'Yes, Karin, that could be what happened. Let's go.'

Thankfully, we could both remember which bin I had used and waded our way through the snow towards it. Ronnie was blissfully unaware of the panic that was going on around him. He was just so delighted to be getting a bonus walk. We got to the bin and without even thinking about what we were doing began picking out rubbish (the majority of which was poo bags), in an effort to find the keys. What a sight we must have been, two tipsy middle-aged women raking through a bin full of shit. It could have been worse. The low temperatures had resulted in frozen shit, which was somehow more palatable to us.

About halfway through emptying the bin, I had a sudden flash of inspiration, turned on my heels and was off, leaving a bemused Karin, poo bags in hand, wondering what on earth was going on. I made my way to the spot where Ronnie had relieved himself. There, under a large oak tree, glistening in the snow, were my keys. The relief that shot through my body was immense. We weren't going to be locked out on one of the coldest nights of the year. I ran back to Karin waving the keys and squealing with delight. Ronnie was dancing about, enjoying the show. We laughed the whole way home and for several hours later, whenever we remembered what we'd actually been doing in that bin.

The worst part of it all for me was the thought of having to tell Colin that within a few hours of him leaving, I had managed to lock us all out of the house. Thankfully, it never came to that and every time I take Ronnie out now, I secure my keys in a zipped jacket pocket. Lesson learned.

When we woke up the next morning it looked like Siberia outside.

The snow had been falling heavily right through the early hours and the radio traffic reports were struggling to keep up with amount of accidents and blocked routes. Today was the first day that our friend Scotty was due to take over Colin's business in his absence, but it wasn't looking good.

Before Colin headed off, Scotty had spent the day with him, meeting the dogs, owners and learning the routes Colin took, and the best parks for stress-free walks. Colin had written everything down for Scotty in the minutest detail: addresses and phone numbers for all the clients; the order in which to pick up and drop off the dogs; each dog's temperament; their likes and dislikes; and how to handle any issues that might arise. He had told all of his clients about his trip, and had been able to considerably scale down the number of dogs that needed to be walked, but there were still dogs that needed to be taken out that day.

Scotty had headed off early to take his step-son to school. Mistake number one. This twenty-minute journey had taken two hours, and on arriving, he had discovered that the school was closed. He called me when halfway through the return journey in a frenzy. Not realising it was going to take so long he had thought he would be able to drop Finn then return home for the directions and keys. Mistake number two. He was now stuck in snowbound traffic and barely moving.

'Susan, I'm so sorry. I don't know what to do,' Scotty's voiced sounded frantic.

'Let me think, Scotty. Don't panic. I'll go and pick up the local dogs and get them out on foot. Oh God no, I can't. You've got the keys at your place!'

'This is an absolute disaster. I'm just not moving and haven't for the last hour. The poor dogs!'

'Listen, Scotty, this can't be helped. We're just going to have to keep calm and wait and see what time you get home. As soon as you get there, phone everyone and let them know what's happened. With any luck, people won't have been able to get to work either, and will be home by the time you get there.'

I was attempting to stay calm, but inside my guts were churning. What the hell were we going to do? Karin and I sat holed up in our kitchen. The heating was on full blast and we were wearing several layers, but the cold was still chilling our bones.

'Oh my God, Karin. Scotty is stuck in the snow and none of the dogs have been walked yet.'

'Bloody hell! Well, we can't do anything about it, so let's just sit tight and wait to hear from him.'

I sat tight and tense well into the afternoon, all the while knowing that the dogs would be so uncomfortable, and that Colin's business and reputation was on the line. It was only the first day, and already it was all going pear-shaped. Scotty phoned with an update. He hadn't managed to walk any of the dogs. It had just proved impossible and dangerous to navigate the roads. He had however phoned all of the clients and explained the situation. Everyone had understood the circumstances, having been caught up in wild weather themselves.

Only one dog had not been able to hold on until his owner got home. I fielded the phone call, working hard to sustain the positive relationship Colin had built up. It had been an extremely stressful day for both Scotty and me, and no one's fault, just freak weather. It appeared that this storm had taken everyone by surprise, resulting in complete chaos as the gritters ran out of salt, and the highways clogged up. We had actually got off lightly in comparison to the many poor souls who had been stranded on motorways overnight. Many people were without electricity too. It was a mess.

Colin phoned that night from 26-degree Cape Town.

'How are you?' he asked.

'Oh, doing fine. No problems at all.'

What was the point in telling him the truth? Two days into his holiday and two crises averted, I felt it only fair to keep those details to myself for now.

Over the next few days the weather didn't improve, but the council's road-clearing tactics did, enabling Scotty to get to some of the dogs and alleviate the tension. Several of the owners had been through such horrific travel experiences the previous day that they were working from home, so no walks were required. Karin and I battled on regardless with Ronnie. He still had to be walked, and we were doing a grand job of looking after him. Apart from the extreme cold, I was really enjoying watching Ronnie prance and leap about in the snow.

It was during this time that I had enrolled in Pat, the dog trainer's, obedience class at Bishopbriggs Community Hall, and I was taking my training role very seriously, practising what I had learned each week, in-between classes. Now, despite the snow being nearly up to my knees in the putting green, I was putting Ronnie regularly through his paces. The poor dog was almost submerged in the snow, but he dutifully walked to heel, turned and sat when commanded. He was doing brilliantly. This was small comfort, however, when the call came in from Colin to say 'Tomorrow, Murdo is taking us all out for the day on a yacht!' Jammy so and so.

I was never so happy to see Colin walk through the arrival gate, tanned and tired, his eyes full of love for me and his heart aching to see his boy. Ronnie leapt so high in the air when his dad walked through the door he nearly hit the chandelier.

Thanks to Karin and her unwavering support, and Scotty's help with the dog walking, we had coped alone, but were so happy as our little family was reunited. There were some tall tales to tell from both of us that night.

Chapter Twenty-three - No … Not his ear!

I was going about my usual day, sorting a bit of housework here and there in-between working on my business. My days were now becoming more balanced in that I wasn't only coaching individual clients, but was also working on specific projects which took me away from the flat on a regular basis. I was offering coaching and community work consultancy to organisations in the public and voluntary sector, and loving it. Thankfully, on this day, I was home.

My phone rang around eleven o'clock and I saw the familiar contact of "Hubby" flash up on the screen.

'Susan, you need to come to the park now!'

'What's wrong?' I could hear the terror in his voice.

'Ronnie's had part of his ear bitten off by one of the dogs. I need to you to come and take him to the vet.'

'Oh my God! How did it happen?'

'Can you just come now? I don't have time to go into it, just get here please.'

Once again, I hung up the phone, panic stricken and planning a trip into goodness knows what. It took me a few minutes to compose myself as I raced from room to room searching for appropriate shoes, bag and my phone, which I had put down after my conversation with Colin and now couldn't find. During my drive across to Bellahouston Park on the Southside of Glasgow, my mind was flooded with images of Ronnie, blood soaked and in desperate pain. He wasn't the bravest of dogs. Colin had come home several times from walks saying Ronnie had broken his leg again with a wry smile. This was usually the result of him taking a tumble or running into another dog then limping to Colin while howling at the top of his voice. Within seconds and after the administering of the magical healing properties of a treat, he would be running, limp free, after the ball again.

I parked up and ran the short distance from car park to the enclosed dog walking area. I could see a number of people all huddled around the dogs with Colin in the middle of them. Not interested in anything but finding Ronnie, I pushed my way through to see him sitting on the grass looking very sorry for himself. And who wouldn't? Moving closer there was blood all down his neck and back and the full extent of the injury was plain to see.

The top of his left ear had been severed and the fur around it looked ragged and uneven, similar to some of the many awful fringe cuts my mum had given me as a child. There were large droplets of blood at the edge of his ear dripping profusely onto his coat and the grass. Colin approached me.

'Here, take this. The vet may be able to do something with it.'

In his hand, on top of a bloody tissue, was the detached part of Ronnie's ear. Colin had scoured the grass to find it and this gruesome sight was now being waved in front of me.

'God, Colin, what on earth happened here? That's a big bit of ear!'

'The dogs were running around as usual chasing the ball and Rocco just swept past, catching Ronnie's ear as he ran. It wasn't malicious, just high jinks, but look at the result!' He pushed the blood-splattered hanky towards me again as I pulled back, grimacing.

'Right, I need to get him to the vet now. We can talk about this later.' I took the gruesome bit of cartilage and placed it tentatively in my bag.

Colin got all of the dogs back on their leads, thanking the kind people who had been supporting him through his trauma as I gently encouraged Ronnie up and out of the park. When we got back to my car, I covered the back seat with several throws and Ronnie jumped in obediently. Colin was a couple of spaces along from me, encouraging the other dogs into his van. I got my phone out and searched for the vet's number. Anne, the head nurse answered. We knew Anne well from our annual trips to the vet for booster jabs and check-ups. It was always an ordeal as, like so many dogs, Ronnie has a great dislike for the vet.

When we had first brought Ronnie home, one of the things the Dogs Trust had told us to do was to register with a vet and take him for a check-up. The first vet we registered with during those very early days with Ronnie just didn't work out for any of us. Dogs seem to have a sixth sense when it comes to vets and on our initial visit to this unfamiliar territory, Ronnie became nervous and was pulling in the opposite direction as we approached the building. Dragging him over the door, he began barking at the receptionist and everyone else in the waiting room. I was mortified.

He wouldn't settle at all as we anxiously awaited our turn and by the time we were called in he resembled a rabid dog, panting and drooling as his claws scraped along the vinyl floor. Once in the consulting room it quickly became clear that the vet was not used to dogs like this. She was either a student or very newly qualified, but either way she had no idea how to handle the situation and neither did we.

Several times Colin tried to lift Ronnie up onto the table and succeeded twice, only to have him leap off as soon as the vet came near him.

'You're going to have to muzzle him,' she said, her voice full of trepidation.

'Do you have any muzzles?' I asked 'This is our first time bringing him to the vet and we weren't expecting this reaction.'

'Here you are.'

She handed me a hessian basket full of muzzles of all shapes and sizes. I picked one out that looked a suitable size, but when I attempted to slip it over Ronnie's snout he up and turned, placing himself securely in the farthest corner of the room. Moving slowly towards him, I bent down and gently tried to place it over his heavily panting mouth but he was becoming more and more distressed, as was I. Colin was trying to hold him steady, but it was no use.

At this point another vet entered the room.

'What's going on here?' she asked looking perplexed at the sight of me curled up in the corner with Ronnie, vacant muzzle in hand.

'The dog's not co-operating so I've suggested we muzzle him.'

She picked up the notes we had brought from the Dogs Trust.

'Ronnie is a rescue dog. You should *never* corner a rescue dog as you don't know how they will react. I would suggest we leave it for today and you make another appointment and we can try again. This has all been too much for him.'

Both Colin and I looked at each other with huge relief as I put Ronnie's lead back on and was dragged out of the door and into the street with great force. He was in full agreement with the more experienced vet. We walked home in shock. I had experienced my first dog Ben's reaction to the vet while growing up which was always one of disgust, but he had conformed once in the consulting room and gone through the motions, like a sullen teenager. Ronnie on the other hand had morphed into "devil dog" and not even the simplest of health checks had been carried out during this fateful first visit.

'We'll need to find another vet. I'm not taking him back there!' I vowed as we approached our flat.

'I know. We can have a look when we get home.'

And that's how we came to meet Anne. Working in another local vet that was recommended to us, Anne is an expert in helping with "sticky dogs". She takes no nonsense and keeps Ronnie held in an arm lock for his entire consultation, but it works. He's getting to know the vets now and Anne gives him lots of treats after the humiliation of being so unceremoniously retrained. While it's still a distressing experience for all, they seem to "get" Ronnie far more than the initial surgery.

'Anne, it's Susan Campbell, Ronnie's owner. He's been in an accident and had a big chunk of his ear bitten off by another dog.'

'Bring him in right away. I'll take a look at him and let the vet know.'

I told Colin what was happening, gave him a big kiss and cuddle then sped off into the distance. Driving as carefully as I could while trying to ensure I got there as quickly as I could, I glanced back often at my wounded soldier. He was sitting so quietly not making a sound, but his soulful eyes were heart breaking. I think he must have been in shock.

When we arrived at the vets, Anne was waiting for us and urged us into the consulting room.

'Oh dear, Ronnie, what's happened to you then?'

I opened my bag and took out the macabre piece of skin and fur, shocked again at the sight of it now under the strong lights of the room. It was about two and a half inches by two inches and looked even bigger than when Colin had initially showed it to me.

'Sorry to be so graphic but we thought you may be able to do something with this?' I presented it to Anne.

'Goodness me. That's a fair bit of ear he's lost, but I'm afraid we won't be able to do anything with it. Skin grafts don't take on animals like they do on humans. Let me get rid of it for you.'

By this time Ronnie had shaken himself several times and there was blood all over the walls and floor. It had the look of a massacre and my poor boy was now cowering in the corner. Once again my heart was breaking for him as I knelt down and gently kissed his head.

'Okay, we're going to have to get this little chap into surgery today.'

'What? Oh, I wasn't expecting that.'

'I'm afraid this isn't just a case of a few stitches. He's going to need reconstruction surgery to even off his tear and he needs it quickly. The ear is such a vascular part of a dog's body that it won't stop bleeding easily, so we need to get it sorted now. He'll be operated on this afternoon and you should be able to take him home tonight. I'll get him downstairs and settled now. If you could wait for me, we need to go through some paperwork.'

I had to pull all of my courage up so as not to burst into tears there and then. The last thing I wanted to do was walk away from Ronnie when he was in such distress and leave him in the place he hates most. It had to be done though and I ripped myself away from him after one last, over lingering hug as I watched him being taken downstairs to the "cells".

Anne returned with a pile of papers for me to read and sign, similar to when a human is going through an operation.

'Do you want the extra health checks that we can do before we give him the anaesthetic?' she questioned.

'What's it for? I've never heard of that before.'

'To be honest, the basic checks will be fine for Ronnie. He's a fit dog with no health problems. These advanced checks are for older dogs or dogs with lots of health issues.'

'Do you really think he will be okay without them? I don't mind paying the extra if you think he needs it?'

'It's your decision, but I don't think it's needed.'

'Okay, I'll leave it then. One thing you could do though is clean his teeth and cut his claws while he's under. I know that won't be covered by the insurance but it would be great to get it done.' And with that and the signing of all the necessary paperwork, I left.

Sitting outside in the car, I let a couple of tears fall then prepared myself for the call to Colin.

'He's got to have an operation this afternoon.'

'Oh my God. I didn't realise it was that bad.'

'No, neither did I, but he'll be fine. We should be able to bring him home later tonight.'

'Did you pay for the extra health checks?' Oh shit, how did Colin know about these?

'Er … no. Anne said they weren't needed as Ronnie's fit and healthy.'

'No, Susan, you should have paid for them. Remember what happened to Annie?'

'Annie was just a one off, one of those awful things that sometimes happens, Colin. I think you're over-reacting. He'll be fine.'

'I just want to make sure we've checked everything. Anaesthetics can kill the healthiest of dogs just like Annie.'

'Look, Colin, do you want me to go back in and tell Anne to do the checks?' There was a long pause.

'No, you're right, Susan. I'm being over cautious. He'll be fine.'

'Colin, I mean it. You're getting me in a panic now and I'm happy to pay for this if it will make you feel better. The last thing I want is something happening and you blame me.'

'I promise I won't. I'm just scared, Susan, and want everything to be okay.'

'I know, me too. It will be okay. He's a strong wee boy. They're going to phone after four to let us know how he is.'

'You know I didn't take him seriously when he first came over. I thought he was doing his usual and playing up for a treat. I feel so awful as he must have been in so much pain and I was just telling him to go away and play.'

'Oh, Colin. Well he has had many moments of over-reacting to injuries – the dog that cried wolf too many times! Let it go and get on with your day. I'll keep in touch.'

We both had an unsettled and taxing afternoon. My mind kept going back to the conversation with Colin. What if something did happen? I'd never forgive myself. Then I would remember Ronnie and the looks of complete anguish he kept giving me with those stunning amber eyes. What if that was the last memory I had, betraying him as I walked away? This was followed on by laments of his injury. Why did it have to be his ear? I had fallen in love with those ears at first sight and they were an ongoing source of amusement. Always changing direction; standing up straight, then out to the side and at the most unexpected times. Even the sound of them flapping as he ran or shook himself had become so familiar to us.

I wrestled with my thoughts for the four hours in-between leaving Ronnie and getting the call, while begging the Angels to keep him safe.

'Hi, Susan, it's Anne. He's fine. Woken up and coming around nicely.'

'Oh thank God. Thank you so much.'

'You can come and pick him up at eight. He should be more awake by then, but he'll be groggy most of tonight and I've got a list of things for you to do that we can go through when you come in.'

My relief was all consuming, like a wave of heat moving through

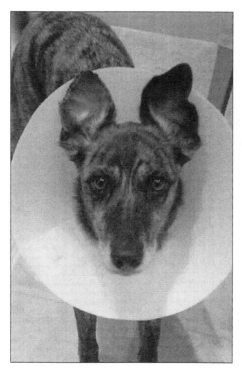

Heartbreaking

my body from top to bottom mixed with the excitement that Ronnie would soon be coming home. I could tell by Colin's reaction that he had experienced a similar response as we both marvelled at our wonderful dog.

8pm finally came. From the time Colin arrived home from work till then, he was like a wee boy waiting for a play date with his best pal. He kept looking at the clock and commenting on how slow the hands were moving. I was glad to get him in the car and on our way.

Ronnie came scrambling up the stairs looking remarkably spritely for a dog that had just been through surgery. He was wearing the "Cone of Shame" also known as the lampshade or bucket collar, and he looked appalled at the indignity of it all. His wound was open and I could see blood and lots of stitches. It had a real rawness about it. That curly tail was wagging ... a good sign. Hopefully he had forgiven us.

We were given a piece of paper with a list of do's and don'ts for the next ten days. Most of these were around not taking the bucket off, and giving Ronnie his painkillers and anti-inflammatory meds. We also had to ensure he didn't eat anything heavy for the first 24 hours and check the wound regularly for signs of infection.

'We've put dissolving stitches in the wound. We felt this would be better for Ronnie. All you need to do is bring him in to get his wound checked in ten days and he won't have to go through any stitch removal. Only short walks I'm afraid, on the lead until you bring him back in,' Anne advised. Colin and I looked at each other in horror. How on earth would he cope with that?

We brought him home and settled him down. It was torture watching him trying to snuggle in with the plastic contraption creating a massive barrier between us. He also kept banging into door frames, the coffee table, walls: you name it, and he banged into it. He was finding his way and the anaesthetic was still affecting his balance and this did get easier with time. What didn't get easier was witnessing him catching his ear in the lampshade collar if he moved a certain way. I could have cried for him every time I heard him squeal, knowing there was nothing I could do to stop it happening, but ever on hand with an awkward cuddle.

He still managed to sleep in the bed with us, bucket and all. Each night he would burrow his way down under the duvet like a bulldozer. The plastic cone would flatten slightly under the weight of the duvet but it did still look very odd and I received a few bumps and scratches from that lampshade.

The day after the ordeal, Colin sat me down to have a serious talk.

'Susan, I need to have a horrible conversation with Mary.'

'I know. What are you going to say?'

'I'm going to have to tell her that I can't walk Rocco anymore. I can't take the risk of him doing that to another dog in the pack. It's bad enough it was Ronnie, but could you imagine if it had been one of the other dogs?'

'Is there no way you can work around it? You said it wasn't malicious. Could he not be muzzled?'

'I thought about that, but Rocco loves to play fetch. He's obsessed with the ball and would be demented with a muzzle on. It's not going to work, Susan. I'm going to phone her now.'

He came back into the kitchen ten minutes later.

'That was awful,' he whispered, ashen faced.

'Tell me.'

'She took it really badly, saying Rocco has never done anything like that before so it's unfair to stop walking him for a one off incident.'

'What did you say?'

'I said that I couldn't take the risk and muzzling him wouldn't work. I didn't tell her it was Ronnie, I said it was one of the other dogs in the pack.'

'Wasn't she bothered about what he'd done?'

'To be honest, no. She was more concerned about who was going to walk Rocco now. She didn't offer to make any contribution to the vet bill.'

'Terrible, really awful. We're just going to have to let this one go and this is why we have insurance. You've done the right thing.'

'Oh I know I have, but it was horrible.'

The whole thing had been difficult and one of those experiences life throws at you that you just have to get through. I do feel we both benefit so much from the tools and techniques I use in my life coaching when things like this happen. Everyone has to deal with setbacks and challenges

185

and it's not about what happens to you, it's about how you react to it. It's fine to spend a bit of time letting the painful emotions come up; in fact it's a necessary, healthy part of the healing process. There has to come a point, however, when you let these go and learn from what you've been through. Getting stuck in the negativity, or giving up, results is a lost opportunity for growth.

Ronnie recovered beautifully. The ten days of restricted exercise had been torturous to watch. He was still, despite the lampshade, bashing his way around every room at Colin's heel as he got ready for work every morning and sitting with him as he counted the keys and planned his day. Leaving the flat without his business partner was just all wrong and Ronnie would lie in the hall, cone flattened, staring at the door all day. He didn't understand.

The vet had done an excellent job on his reconstructed ear. While it may be half the size of his other one, I'm delighted to say it's still as animated, sometimes more so. It will often stick up of its own accord in a way it couldn't before because it was too heavy, so we get double the ear action. The main thing was Ronnie got through his operation, Colin got through a tough time in his business, and together we became an even stronger unit. And I still adore his ears.

Chapter Twenty-four - Puppies

I guess there must be some people in the world who don't like puppies, but I've yet to come across them. There's just something so magical about those little bundles of fur whose paws are often too big for their bodies as they tumble and somersault their way across a room. Like toddlers, they find such joy in the new discoveries we take for granted and have an exhausting boundless energy which quickly converts into contented snoozes as they recharge, ready for the next assault.

I have had the pleasure of providing the "puppy snuggling" service at Ronnie Ronster's since very early on in the business. It all began with Milly, Colin's first client, followed by Ruby Doodle who needed initial day care, and it expanded from there.

We had all been devastated by the loss of Peggy, but then Kathryn got a call from the breeder, two months after Peggy's death. Peggy's parents, a Cocker Spaniel and Miniature Poodle, had been bred again and she was expecting a litter any day. She wanted to know if Kathryn and Skip would like one of the puppies. After much soul-searching and mind wrestling about the pros and cons, they went for it. Who could resist, especially when the photos started coming through after the pups were born?

Eight weeks later, Betty was picked up from Fife and on a crisp and sunny February afternoon, Colin and I went to make her acquaintance. As Kathryn opened the door to their beautiful flat we heard the sound of little claws on wooden floors, scrambling to meet us. I actually squealed in delight as this wad of golden fur ran in-between my legs then was off down the length of the long hall, crashing into the table leg then racing back to do a repeat performance with Colin. It was as if she was saying 'Hello, hello, how exciting, more new people to meet!'

She was like a teddy bear and very similar to Peggy, though with a darker coat. Peggy was blonde while Betty was more dark golden, but they had the same button eyes and manic energy. Kathryn scooped her easily into her arms and formally introduced her.

'This is Betty.'

'Hello, Betty,' we cooed over her like a new born baby. 'Oh you're just beautiful,' I gushed.

'She's a little scamp, really putting us through our paces but we adore her already.' Kathryn opened the door to the decking area of outside space off their living room and Betty sniffed her way around. She was already responding well to her name and came running over for a pat when called. At one point she stopped to do a piddle to rapturous applause and praise from the proud new parents.

We headed back inside for coffee and homemade flapjacks and Betty crashed out on my lap, exhausted from all of the excitement. Her warm little body felt wonderful after the chill of the outdoors and her little pink tummy was moving rapidly up and down under my cold hand.

'So are you up for looking after her a couple of days a week?' Kathryn asked.

'What do you think?' I responded with glee.

'She's learning fast and we've nearly got her toilet trained. We just let her out every hour,' Skip said.

'That's the way to do it. I'm sure she'll be no bother and she's crate trained?' Colin asked.

'Yes, she's quite content to sleep in the crate and we're just getting her used to being left on her own.'

'Okay, when do you want to start?'

'How does next week sound?' Kathryn requested.

'How does that suit you, Susan? You're the one who will be puppy snuggling?' Colin enquired.

'That should be fine. If you can just let me know in advance what days, I can plan my diary around it.'

And with that, we made our goodbyes and headed home to our own four-legged friend.

Betty became a constant, twice a week presence in my life for the next six months. She scrambled down our hall every morning to greet me as I picked her up and got my face washed again. Together we would get through our days, me stopping whatever I was doing every hour on the hour to let her out the back. She would run around, do her duties and we'd play for a while until returning to the safety of her crate where she would soundly sleep until the next toilet break. She was a joy.

As the months flew by it was soon time for her to join the grown-ups and venture out into the real world. I would miss her, but the videos Colin brought home of her tearing up the park with her antics let me know all was well. What a confident puppy she was, showing no fear for other dogs. She would jump up on their backs, run under their legs and generally just run and run and run. Colin took so many videos of her that he edited them all together into a short film with the classic eighties song "Betty Boo" playing in the background. I would often hear the song booming out of his laptop and him chuckling loudly. It was impossible not to be cheered up by it.

One year she spent a few days with us between Christmas and New Year and experienced our annual Hogmanay party. Everyone was so taken with her as she raced around the flat leaping from person to person. Her favourite game is fetch, just like Ronnie, but she prefers a Frisbee to a ball and her favourite one had been carefully packed in her holiday bag. There were so many people willing to play with her that night that every time I went into the hall I had to be careful not to fall over the flash of golden fur tearing down it either towards the Frisbee or bringing it back. The party went on late that year and Betty never stopped the entire night. Oh, to have that amount of energy.

No sooner had Betty left me to join the pack than Colin arrived home to tell me of another puppy in need of snuggling.

'Susan, do you remember Jane that you used to work with?'

'Yes, why?'

'She phoned me today. Your friend Mary passed my number onto her. She needs someone to look after her King Charles Cavalier puppy. What

189

do you think?'

'How old is he and how often would it be?'

'They've just got him, so he's very young and it would be four days a week. He sounds adorable.'

'Well I can fit it around my work as best I can, but I am getting busier.'

'We'll work around it, I'm sure. He's crate trained and it will only be until he's big enough to come on proper walks.'

Oscar first came to visit the Sunday before he was due to start with us. When Colin carried him into the living room, I gave out my usual squeal. What a cute puppy. He was tiny with beautiful rust coloured markings and huge ears. I think the journey from his familiar surroundings to his new territory had been overwhelming as he spent most of the afternoon curled up on my lap, sleeping and very contented. Colin had taken a video of him leaving Jane's house and the wee fella looked so tiny standing in the door frame of the van waiting to be transported to meet me. Jane had left a message on the video pleading with me to take good care of her beloved puppy. Having spent the afternoon with the little guy, I told Colin to reassure her all would be well.

Once again I experienced the joy of a puppy tearing down our hall to greet me four mornings a week. Oscar quickly settled in and even more quickly recognised where he was being taken each day. I always knew when he was about to arrive as I could hear him long before I saw him. He barked continually from the van to the door, little high pitched puppy barks, until he was let off the lead to run at me. Once he reached me the barks would change to squeals and he would jump up, willing me to pick him up, and I always did.

We rubbed along nicely together each day, me following the same routine as with Betty as I supported him with his toilet training. His recall wasn't the best as he was just learning, and together we worked on it. He just loved to be chased and quite exhausted me on occasions as I tried desperately to get him back into the flat. It must have been an amusing sight for our neighbours to watch this puppy run rings around me as he darted in-between my legs as I got so close but never close enough.

Oscar was less happy in the crate. He was a puppy who really did expect to be snuggled the entire visit. When placed back in, he would howl at the top of his voice, desperate to be on my lap. I capitulated often but also recognised that he had to learn, so together we worked on lengthening the time he would spend in the crate and he did, in time, get used to it.

Oscar and Tiny

Breagha, the beautiful black Labrador, also used our services as a pup. It was on a more informal, as and when required, basis, and her visits were as welcome as all our furry friends. She was around four months, so a little older and wiser and a whole lot bigger than I was used to. Her paws were enormous, a sign of what was to come and Alison, her owner, was training her well. Crate trained, she would obediently go in by herself whenever requested and I loved to watch her sleeping, her sleek black coat glistening as the sun from the window danced over it. She was a beauty and has grown into a magnificent dog.

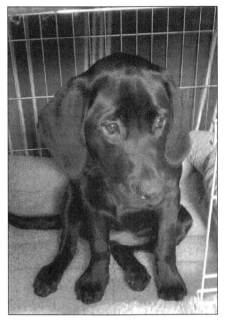

Breagha

One little dog who wasn't technically a puppy, but was smaller than most of the puppies I snuggled, was Raja, the teacup Pomeranian. He was actually an old boy but you would never have known it. All fluff and bluster, this rust coloured pompom on legs would come marching down the hall making the most curious little barks of delight. Pomeranians often have problems with their limbs and this little guy was no exception. He had been through an operation to have steel pins in his forelegs resulting in them sticking straight out as he walked as if he was performing the Can Can … very endearing and thankfully he wasn't in any pain.

Once again I would spend my days with a warm bundle on my knees as I went about my business. He truly was a lap dog and we loved each other dearly. His owner moved to London about a year after he joined us and it was with a heavy heart that we parted company.

There were accidents galore in the early days of looking after the puppies and I could always be found with a cloth and bottle of anti-bacterial spray by my side. It's to be expected while they learn and we purchased several steam cleaners, some more effective than others, hence several, to mop up little messes.

One puppy that came to stay with us for the day was a regular pint-sized shitting machine. Cosmo, a Lhasa Apso, was just a ball of fur. My friend, Morvern, came over to meet him and spent the day hysterically laughing as he walked all over her, ferociously licking her face and neck and arms and hands and anything he could get close to. He was a real character and brought much merriment to our home that day. I never had the anti-bacterial spray out of my hands though. His daughter, Tiny, also spent some time with us a few years later and she had the best time playing with Oscar.

The puppy that really made its mark on us though, has to be Frankie. We were walking in Kelvingrove Park on a beautiful summer's day when we had to stop and do a double take. Running up and down a hill, chasing a ball was a miniature version of Ronnie. All ears and legs, with the same brindle markings, we just had to go and say hello.

'Oh my goodness, sorry, but we had to come over. He looks like a puppy version of our dog,' Colin exclaimed

'So he does. What's your dog's name?'

'This is Ronnie and we got him from the Dog's Trust when he was eighteen months old so we never got to see him as a puppy, but looking at this wee fella, I think we just have! I'm Colin, by the way, and this is my wife, Susan.'

'Hi, I'm Joanna and that's Frankie. He's a Whippet. Look at the two of them running together after the ball, that's adorable.'

Ronnie and Frankie ran up and down that hill together for the next twenty minutes, both displaying the same love of fetch. How divine it had been to see a young version of Ronnie. We so often talked about what he must have looked like as a puppy and now we were getting a glimpse. Frankie joined the pack too and often stayed with us as well as coming on walks, and he's turned into a fine dog, full of fun. One night, we were enjoying a drink in The Ubiquitous Chip, a fine establishment in the West End of Glasgow, when I spotted Joanna and Frankie. The welcome we got from him when he realised we were there was spectacular. He knocked me off my feet at one point so I was lying on the floor being walked all over by him. Colin's face was washed for a good five minutes and it was so lovely to be greeted with such love and enthusiasm. He's a cracking dog.

Frankie

I'm not in a position now to puppy snuggle like I used to. My business takes me more and more away from the flat. I miss it but I love what I do and we haven't had as many requests for the service since I've not been available. Life gives you what you need when you need it. When I was able to offer these little bundles of joy the care and attention they required, I was able to do my work from home and I'll always be grateful for that. I highly recommend snuggling a puppy every opportunity you get.

Chapter Twenty-five - Welcome abroad

Holidays were something we had learned to live without for a number of years after setting up the businesses and adopting Ronnie. It wasn't that we didn't have the opportunity. To be honest, we just didn't want to leave Ronnie those first few years, and we were also learning how to juggle self-employment and taking time off. Having both left behind the stress of working for someone else too, we had less of an urge to escape our home lives, feeling more than contented with our lot.

The rejuvenating benefits of holidays cannot be argued against however and while we both struggled to leave Ronnie, we also acknowledged that we wanted holidays back on the agenda and would learn to manage the guilt.

We adopted Ronnie at the end of 2008 and it was late 2010 when Colin took his trip to South Africa for his cousin's wedding. I had to wait until May 2012 for my first break and even then, it wasn't with Colin. My best friend, Morvern, and I flew out to Majorca for a week while Colin kept the home fires burning. It had been wonderful to get a break and some sunshine, but oh how I missed my boys.

Our first holiday together wasn't until May 2013, over five years since our last break, which seems implausible on reflection given that we were so used to taking holidays at least twice a year prior to this. And yet I hadn't felt any real adverse effects. Sure, I'd missed the sunshine, given the kind of summers we *enjoy* in Glasgow and the special moments holidays bring, but Colin and I now had much more time together. Living in the West End, we were blessed with restaurants and bars on our doorstep and our lives had much more of a holiday feel to them.

In saying that, it was with great excitement that I booked up our *first in five year's* holiday. Enjoying my usual trawl through websites to find the perfect accommodation, the hours slipped past. We had decided to revisit one of our favourite spots, Nerja, on the Costa del Sol and I had found us a wonderful apartment in Capsitrano Playa, just along the bay. The race was now on to organise everything around this. Who would look after Ronnie?

Having only left him for one or two nights at a time in the last four and a half years, this was going to be the challenge. Thankfully, Catriona and Charlie were able to offer their services and as Ronnie had stayed with them several times, never looking back as he raced through their front door, this lessened our anxiety. An extended break from the wee fella was still going to be tough, but I just kept telling myself that this holiday was ridiculously overdue.

We packed Ronnie's holiday bag once our own suitcases had been dusted off and filled with clothes that hadn't seen the light of day in quite a while, you know the kind of things you only wear abroad. His bed was filled with toys, treats and ball chucker, alongside poo bags and enough food for a week. I bent down to give him a last kiss and cuddle before he was out the door with his dad and I was left standing in the hall not quite knowing what to do next. I couldn't bear the thought of going with them as leaving him would have been too traumatic – for me, you understand, not him. As it turned out he had run straight into Catriona and Charlie's back garden and was having a lovely time to himself, not even noticing Colin slip away through the front door.

As we were getting an early morning flight, we had dropped Ronnie off the night before. A strange silence shrouded the flat that evening as I did my last minute packing. Finally falling onto the couch with an exhausted flop, my hand automatically reached out for the warm furry companion who always flopped down beside me. His absence was everywhere. No bed in the hall, or dishes in the kitchen and I wasn't tripping over toys as I made my way from room to room. Getting into bed without our usual night time snuggle left me feeling empty. Once again I was taken to that dark place of … that very sad day in the future … so I jumped into bed and cuddled into Colin as we had an interrupted sleep that comes with having to get up at 4am.

I endured the flight to Malaga as I stoically endure every flight we take, not being a comfortable flyer. When we arrived at our apartment and threw open the balcony doors, I gasped at the perfect view over the sea. All of my hours online had paid off again. This was going to be a fantastic holiday. And it was. We enjoyed lazy days and chilled evenings sampling the finest Spanish cuisine and to be honest, Ronnie was remembered but not nearly as often as I thought he would be. At one point I heard Colin's phone ring, but he didn't recognise the number so let it ring out. I didn't think much more of it until later that evening when we were out having dinner by the sea.

'Susan, I know you're going to think this is really silly, but I'm worried about something.'

'What is it?'

'The phone call earlier.'

'Yes, what about it? Did they leave a message?'

'No message, but it was a Lanarkshire code.'

'So?'

'Well the Dog's Trust is in Uddingston. I know I'm being ridiculous but what if Ronnie has run away or something's happened to him and they're trying to get hold of me?'

'Oh, sweetheart, I'm sure it's not that at all.'

'I've been worrying about it all day.'

'Why didn't you say something? Look, this is easily solved. Text Catriona and ask how he's doing.'

'Okay. I'll do it now.'

Catriona replied to say Ronnie was doing just fine and had just enjoyed a bowl full of sausages. Colin's face relaxed into a broad grin as he read the text and then he started to laugh.

'What an idiot!'

'You're not an idiot. You were just concerned something had happened to him. That's natural, but he's fine so let's enjoy the rest of the night, eh?'

'Yes, I can relax now.'

One of the major highlights of the holiday was visiting the Nerja

197

donkey sanctuary just along from where we were staying. It was an amazing place, staffed entirely by volunteers and offering a safe haven to horses, donkeys, mules, cats and a rescue dog. The animals had come from all over Spain and were now enjoying the love and care that had been sadly missing in their previous lives. The donkeys were just beautiful and there were five cheeky foals all sticking their heads out over the pens to snatch the apples and carrots we were holding. I was in heaven. Colin then disappeared as I continued to pet and preen the babies.

Nerja Donkey Sanctuary

A little while later, I found Colin lying down on the ground in another pen and I could just see a black snout peeking out from under a hutch. It was the rescue dog, timid and cowering, but desperate to come out and say hello. Brian, one of the volunteers, came over.

'He's a wee beauty isn't he?' he said with great pride.

'He sure is. What's his name and how long has he been here?' Colin replied.

'He's called Chocky and he's been with us a few months now. He's very wary of humans and will only sleep under the caravan at the gate at night despite us trying to get him to come indoors. You're doing well with him though.'

'We have a rescue dog of our own who looks a bit like Chocky.'

'If you like, you can try taking him for a walk.'

'Oh, I'd love to.'

'I'll just get his lead.'

Colin and Chocky

Colin stood up and gently brushed off all of the dust from his clothes. When Brian came back and handed him the lead, Colin lent down to slowly attach it to Chocky's collar and with some tender persuasion, Chocky gradually began easing his way out from his safe space. He did have a look of Ronnie yet he was a little stockier. Tan in colour with the most beautiful eyes and smile, though I think this was just him panting from the heat rather than being happy to see us, he had a commanding presence. We walked through the gate to a grassy area just outside and Colin began to work his magic. He ran up and down the lawn encouraging Chocky loudly and they both looked like they were having a great time. It reminded me of the first time I stood in the Dog's Trust field watching Colin and Ronnie run up and down, though the weather was far more favourable.

'This is a bit of a busman's holiday for you is it not?' I joked.

'I know but isn't he great.'

We took lots of photos of Chocky as he sat obediently just before we took him back. What a lovely way to spend an afternoon. We couldn't resist going back to the donkey sanctuary before we went home. This time we stocked up on lots of bags of apples and carrots and a big box of biscuits for the volunteers. They relied heavily on donations and having been so impressed with the setup, we wanted to contribute something for all of their efforts. I also bought some lovely key rings and bookmarks from the shop which made for special gifts back home. I was so sad to read on their website last year that they were having to close due to a lack of funds. What a shame that such a valuable service would no longer be available to all of these animals in need. They were, however, ensuring that all of their current animals found new homes.

On our return to Glasgow our bags were dumped in the hall and we sped back out the door to go and pick up our boy. He gave us a lovely welcome and by all accounts had had a charming holiday too. Catriona and Charlie are real dog lovers, having had several Collies, but being between dogs just now, they enjoy looking after Ronnie and we don't have to worry about him whenever we go away. The only trouble is they too love their holidays so our time away often clashed with their own breaks.

The important thing was we had enjoyed a week away from Ronnie without any major incidents or concerns. He had been well looked after and according to Charlie, was a credit to us and there had been no issues with either of our businesses. Colin had given all of his clients plenty of notice of his absence and offered alternative cover from local dog walkers he had befriended. I had just blocked the week out of any appointments in my diary months previously, so all had been well and we arrived home, safe in the knowledge that holidays were now back on the agenda.

The following year, Morvern told me she had booked a villa in Majorca for herself, her uncle, her cousin and her husband, and she kindly invited us along too. I spoke to Colin about it who was a little less enthusiastic with the idea than me. It wasn't that he didn't appreciate the generous offer; it was just that our holidays were so precious to us only having taken one in five years and we realistically would only be taking one that year too. It had to be right.

We weren't demanding in terms of our expectations of a holiday, just somewhere nice to sunbathe during the day, a good market for gifts and nick-nacks to bring home, and local restaurants to enjoy leisurely dinners each evening. The most important thing was having quality time together. Morvern's family were lovely people, but Colin didn't know them well and going on holiday with virtual strangers could be a recipe for disaster. He was concerned that our one holiday of the year may not go to plan.

I was stuck in the middle. Morvern had booked the holiday as a treat for her special birthday that year and I wanted to go and share this with her, but I also fully understood Colin's concerns. In the end we agreed to go and, with some trepidation, I booked our flights to Palma. While they were spending two weeks in the sun we opted for one, joining them in week two.

The villa was beautiful, with its own private pool and glorious views of the sea and across to Palma. Being only five minutes from the airport, I was in my element watching the planes fly overhead carrying holiday makers to and from the many resorts of this beautiful Balearic Island. Despite having some issues with flying, I have a passion for planes and marvel at the miracle of engineering of these graceful machines. Colin calls me "Herbert" when teasing me about my plane spotting tendencies.

We had already had the heads up from Morvern that her uncle had been taken into hospital for a couple of days before we got there. His blood pressure had been very high and the heat had dehydrated him, causing him to feel unwell. As we reached the villa, minutes later, he arrived back from hospital too, thankfully better, but looking wary and we enjoyed a warm welcome as they showed us around our temporary accommodation with great pride. We had a lovely en-suite room at the front of the villa taking in that perfect vista.

It soon became apparent that Morvern was unwell too. Before we had come away, she had been hit with a virus which was exhausting her, but she had felt much better the week before leaving. However, while away, it had made an unwelcomed return and she just wasn't herself. I could see her trying to put a face on things and push through it, but it was too much for her. We were so disappointed that she felt unable to do all of the things she had planned to. Being an epic explorer, she loved to research the places she visited and make a plan of trips to see as much as she could, but she just wasn't fit to go anywhere further than into the town along the bay.

Added to this was the fact that we had come into the holiday a week later than everyone else. Routines were set, food was bought and it felt a little like staying in someone else's home rather than us all sharing. This wasn't anyone's fault; it was just the interesting psychology of situations like this. A schedule of going out to dinner one night then staying in the next had been established in the first week and we fell into this too. Morvern kept telling us to do our own thing, but I didn't want to seem rude by leaving the company every night. We did go out alone one evening for dinner and had a wonderful meal by the sea.

The weather was fabulous and sunbathing by the pool each day was very relaxing. We also had a lovely day in Palma with Morvern's cousins, but, unfortunately, Morvern hadn't felt up to joining us. A couple of nights before we came away as we sat on the terrace looking out to sea, Colin looked deflated and spoke to me.

'I don't think I can wait until next year for another holiday, Susan. Next June seems such a long way away. I really feel we need to get away again before then.'

'I feel so bad for Morvern. She was so looking forward to this and she's had a shit time. I don't know what to say.'

'It's not your fault. We both agreed to come here. I'm not blaming you. I just feel like it's ages away till our next holiday.'

'I know. I'm really sorry.'

'Stop apologising. I'm not meaning to sound ungrateful for this holiday. It's a lovely place and they're great people. It just hasn't turned out like we had planned, has it? There isn't even a beer in the fridge!'

'Oh God. We should have bought some on the way up the road. People are just not feeling well, so they're taking it easy.'

'I know, I get that and it's not like we drink that much on holiday, but I'd have liked a beer after my dinner!'

'Do you want to go out for one?'

'No, it's okay. Just leave it.'

I felt awful; torn once again between my husband and best friend. Morvern had been planning this break for months, well years really, as it had been a goal of hers and she'd spoken to me many times about her birthday plans and I could see how much she was struggling. Now Colin was on a downer as our holiday was drawing to a close and I was beginning to long for home and snuggles with Ronnie. Then I had a flash of inspiration.

'Look, why don't we go away again in September?'

'Do you mean it?'

'Yes I do. We need our holidays and we're both doing well workwise, so let's sort that out when we get home.'

I saw Colin's face soften at the prospect of a further break in a few months' time. In a couple of days we would be home and I would start to make plans. It gave us both something to look forward too. Morvern's family had enjoyed the holiday, despite her uncle's illness, so all had not been lost and they really were good company in a beautiful place.

Ronnie had taken his vacation with my friend Tina this time. She had offered many times to look after him and, with Catriona and Charlie being away too, it made sense given her love of dogs. It had all gone well though she did look a little frazzled on our return. I could fully relate to this as Ronnie is a lot of work. I have the benefit of him being out every day with Colin and the pack so he burns off a lot of his energy. Without this daily routine, I'm sure Tina had her hands full keeping that vigour at bay, but she gracefully told us all had been well.

On returning, our friends Karin and Peter were home for a visit from Abu Dhabi. Peter, the Polish pilot, had been living in Glasgow for many years where he met Karin, but then lost his job when Globe Span went bust. Securing another job in the Middle East, Karin had joined him, they married and would return fairly regularly to see family and friends. We were telling them about our holiday and that we were now looking into another one in September, when Peter said,

'Come to us. We'd love to see you.'

'Yes,' Karin echoed. 'We've been asking you to come out and visit for ages. Why don't you make that your holiday?'

'Wow, what do you think, Colin?' I asked in anticipation.

'You know me, I'll go anywhere. It's a long way to go though. How do you feel about the flight?'

'I'll put you on my "friends and family" list. They're business stand-by tickets and there's a really good chance you'll get upgraded to business, plus you'll get the tickets at 10% of the price,' Peter offered.

'Oh my God, Peter, that is so kind of you. I don't know what to say. I think I could cope with the flight in business class!' I laughed.

'Well think about it and let us know. We'd love to have you and we could show you all around Abu Dhabi,' Karin suggested.

'Thank you so much for the offer,' I said as we all went on to catch up on other news.

We did think about it and decided to go for it. Despite my trepidation about the journey, I knew this was the chance of a lifetime and I made a promise to myself to deal with the anxiety. The journey there was going to be mammoth. A flight to Dublin at 2.45pm (on a silly wee propeller job plane) followed by a 5 hour wait for the flight to Abu Dhabi at 8.45pm that evening, arriving at 7.30am the following morning, 4.30am our time.

Again, Catriona and Charlie were going to be away at the same time as us, heading up to Stornoway to see family. I didn't want to ask Tina again, so soon after her last Ronnie sitting duties, so we had to get our thinking caps on. Colin suggested Chris, our dog walking friend and photographer who had taken the beautiful photos of Ronnie when we had first adopted him. He was now doing a bit of dog sitting and as he was local and Ronnie knew him and his gorgeous black Lab, Harvey, it made perfect sense. Chris was delighted to help out so plans were made and that was one thing I wouldn't have to worry about.

While I was delighted that we were now getting back into a holiday routine, I was still carrying a little worry about leaving our businesses again so soon. We had worked so hard to build them up, but I also knew that time away was essential to rejuvenate and I've had some of my best creative moments while lying in the sun.

As the holiday drew nearer, my anxiety levels rose. How was I going to cope with these flights? One of the reasons I booked early morning flights whenever we went away was so I just got up and out without having too much time to think about it. This time we would have the whole morning before heading to the airport for 1.30pm and then five hours at Dublin. I was also feeling very guilty as I had family in Dublin and I hadn't let them know we would be at the airport. I knew my Aunty Trisha and Uncle Frank and my many cousins would have loved to have met up, as would we, not to mention Aunty Mary and Uncle Noel, even if just for a quick coffee, but I also knew Trisha and Frank were going on a cruise the next day and I didn't want to put that pressure on them. Equally, I had no idea how I would be once we reached Dublin as one of the ways I cope before a flight is to go into myself with my iPod and meditations, and poor Colin hardly gets a word out of me.

It was too late now. We were on our way so I would just have to

205

handle the guilt and as Morvern dropped us at Glasgow airport, telling me I would be fine and to have a wonderful time, I worked hard to let it go. It was a glorious autumnal day but the wind was gusting wildly. As we walked onto the tarmac towards the small plane, my heart was racing. How would this tiny, elastic band plane cope with these high winds? As it turned out, the flight was easy; a few bumps on the way up then smooth all the way with the softest landing I'd ever experienced. It felt very wrong to be walking around the airport, hearing all of the Dublin accents and not seeing my family, but that's the way it was.

We followed the instructions Karin had sent us, making our way to the Etihad Airline's desk and met with a smiling ground staff member very willing to help.

'Where are you off to today?' she asked.

'Abu Dhabi. We've got these staff stand-by tickets we've been told to show you,' Colin gushed. She took the papers off us and read them carefully.

'That flight's full.' She looked at us straight on while both our jaws dropped to the ground and an eternity passed in a matter of seconds. Then we saw one corner of her mouth start to twitch as she said,

'Your faces were an absolute picture. I'm only messing with you.'

We all burst out laughing, our merriment rising to a heighted pitch caused by the total relief of this news.

'You're a bad one, you! You really had us going. Have you been sitting there a while feeling a little bored?' Colin joked.

'Since one o'clock. I'm really sorry, I just couldn't resist. You'll get into business no bother. There are more than ten seats left. The check-in desk is just about to open, so just take your bags over and they'll sort you out.'

'Thank you, that's wonderful,' I said, swinging between emotions. My heart was racing at the prospect of actually flying business class.

"If anyone asks, my name's Mary,' she said with a wink as she covered her name badge. We walked towards the check-in desk still chuckling.

Sure enough, we were upgraded but there was a wobbly moment at the desk. Peter had told us that there was a dress code when travelling on a staff ticket: no jeans, trainers or t-shirts and we had dressed accordingly. Just before we had left the house, Colin had put a hoody on. I remember at the time asking if he was taking a jacket with him but, he said that the hoody would be enough for him. The woman who was checking us in left us for a couple of minutes to go and speak to her manager. I didn't witness what happened, but Colin had seen them looking us up and down before she returned to the desk.

'Do you have another jacket with you?' she inquired to Colin.

'No, sorry. Is that a problem?'

'I'm afraid there's a strict dress code and you will need a jacket.'

"No problem at all. We've got five hours until the flight. I'll get a jacket!'

We turned tail and made our way upstairs to the information stand to find out what shops were at the airport beyond the security gate. The very helpful woman told us that while there were some shops, there wasn't a great choice and we would be better off going to a shopping centre, a ten minute taxi ride away. We jumped in a taxi and made our way there. It was a blessing in disguise. The distraction of going to the shops and seeking a suitable jacket was just what I needed and we turned it into an adventure, having something to eat there too.

Colin got a lovely suit jacket in the sale and looked the part. He was so taken with it he decided to go back and buy the trousers. I had been outside on the phone excitedly telling Morvern we would be travelling in style when he proudly presented me with the trousers saying.

'What do you think?'

'Very nice. Let me have a closer look.'

'Are they the same colour?'

'No, Colin, they're darker and they're a different pattern. Your colour blindness strikes again!'

'See what happens when I go shopping on my own! Thank goodness I checked them. Come on, I'll take them back.'

Unfortunately, there were no trousers that actually did match the charming jacket so they were handed back with refund received.

Before we knew it, it was time to get back to the airport. We found our way to a taxi rank then made our way through the departure gates and headed for our flight. Just as well I hadn't arranged to meet my family. We entered the plane through a separate door avoiding the long queue. While this was welcomed, I had a real sense of uneasiness about it and it somehow felt wrong. Money really does talk in our society. I resolved to just enjoy this experience and push my socialist beliefs to the background for once.

We were shown to our seats; well they were more private booths than seats. I was at the window and Colin was across from me in the aisle. We had only sat down when a member of the cabin crew brought us a hot towel infused with the scent of lavender and a glass of champagne … champagne socialist right enough. She then asked what I wanted for dinner and from an extensive list of delights I chose the mezzi platter to start followed by salmon trout on a bed of sautéed potatoes with asparagus and marbled cheesecake to finish off my feast in the sky. Receiving a further glass of Champagne just after we had taken off, I realised this was going to be an experience never to be forgotten.

We played with the remote controls at the side of our seats to move the chairs up and down from upright to the full bed position and then into massage mode. Switching lights on and off from all directions and choosing our in-flight entertainment, we must have looked so uncool as we marvelled at every new treat that came our way. The pillows and blankets were so soft and I was already deciding how I was going to recycle the pretty complimentary bags with socks, flight mask and toiletries we were handed.

The flight was a breeze and although neither of us slept, despite the comfort, we enjoyed every minute of it which is probably why we didn't sleep. A couple of hours from Abu Dhabi, I lifted up the window screen to reveal the most beautiful sunrise on the horizon. The red and orange colours of the sky were breath taking. Colin was just about to get stuck into his full breakfast when he turned round to me and said, 'This is just like being in a hotel!' his eyes shining brightly. I had to agree. We were very well looked after and revelling in this new experience.

Savouring every moment

As we walked through the arrivals lounge at the airport, bleary eyed but still buzzing from the flight, we saw Karin and Peter waiting for us. I hugged them both and just kept saying "Thank you, thank you, thank you." as we made our way into the blistering heat towards their air conditioned car.

Abu Dhabi was quite an experience. We stayed at Karin and Peter's beautiful apartment in an ex-pat community about twenty minutes outside the city. Spending our days lying by one of the many pools or on the beach five minutes from their flat and our evenings enjoying good food and company, the holiday was exactly what we both needed. Peter, who is a fantastic cook, spoiled us with his culinary delights and on the first night we all laughed as Colin re-told the tale about his jacket.

'I've never been asked to wear a jacket. That's ridiculous!' Peter exclaimed.

'I think it was because Colin was wearing a hoody, Peter. We should have thought to take it off and put it in his bag as I'm sure that would have been fine. It doesn't matter though, honestly. It was a good laugh and really passed the time for us,' I explained.

'Peter and I both said when we saw Colin coming through arrivals in his suit jacket he was taking the dress code a bit seriously, especially with the hankie in the pocket!' Karin laughed.

We also had many conversations about Thandi, the gorgeous Boxer puppy that Karin and Peter now owned who was still in Scotland, waiting to be old enough to travel to them. We had been lucky enough to meet her before the holiday when Karin and Peter were home and she was a beauty. It had been a long term dream of Karin's to own a Boxer again; having had them when younger. They both talked excitedly about all of the things they would do together once their new family member arrived, while we reminisced about how we felt when we first had Ronnie and how wonderful their lives would be with a dog in it.

Thandi

I sat and marvelled at how much our lives had moved on since adopted Ronnie and that the goals I had set myself were all coming true. We were both also coping so much better without Ronnie than our first holiday away from him. Despite missing our fury companion, the benefits of a full night's sleep were only adding to the chill out factor of our break.

We spent a lovely day in Abu Dhabi with its impressive sky scrapers and decadent shops and visited a heritage centre with magical stalls full of local delights where I fell in love with a camel I called "Cammy" as he cuddled into me in the blistering heat.

Cammy the camel

I've never felt heat like it anywhere. The contrasting temperatures of the ever present air conditioning in the buildings and the oppressive outdoor temperatures was a shock to the system each time and we were visiting in the cooler season. Temperatures were now in the late thirties as opposed to late forties. It was unimaginable to me how people could cope with that heat on a daily basis.

Abu Dhabi's Grand Mosque was a sight to behold. Spending another afternoon there Karin and I donned an abaya, the traditional black cloak worn by women in the Middle East as we walked around the sparkling splendour of the huge prayer rooms and marvelled at the intricate detail of the wall coverings and chandeliers. The wealth of the city and the mosque were sharply contrasted with the sight of the many immigrant workers being bussed in and out to carry out the work no one else would do.

As so often happens, our holiday came to an end far more quickly than any of us wanted it to, and it was time to make the journey home. I was not at my best as my period had made an unwelcomed appearance that morning, and I was dreading the journey home even more than usual, knowing I would be in a lot of pain. Our flight home wasn't until 2.25am so we had all stayed up eating take away pizza and laughing at episodes of "Come Dine With Me" on their BBC Lifestyle channel.

We didn't have to be at the airport until after 1.00am as we were going through the staff check-in area. As we got into the car and the radio came on, Sophie Ellis Bexter blasted out of the speakers singing "Take me home". Arriving at the check-in desk, Peter enquired about upgrades but the staff member said the flight was full. He tried so hard for us and looked so disappointed that our trip home would be less luxurious, but we reassured him we would be fine in economy, just delighted to have had the experience on the way there. We were told to check at the gate anyway, just in case.

As we said our goodbyes and made our way through passport control, I was feeling awful: cramps and nausea and panicking about how I would get through the flight. Colin was reassuring me as best he could, but the splendour of the airport was lost on us, as all I wanted was to be home.

We waited for everyone to board then went up to the desk and showed them our upgrade tickets. The staff member said,

'There's one seat in business.'

'You take it, Susan. I'll be fine and you need the comfort,' Colin

212

reassured.

'I don't want to leave you. That's not fair,' I protested.

'Just take it please. There's no point in wasting it and I'm not going to take it and leave you in economy. Take it and get a rest.'

So I took it. We entered the huge plane and I turned left towards business while Colin turned right and made his way to his economy seat. While I felt guilty, I was in need of the comfort and privacy my booth brought. The hospitality was wasted on me, however, as the last thing I wanted was a glass of Champagne or heavy meal. I visited Colin a couple of times and he had three seats to himself so was doing fine too though missing the wonderful food that had been on tap on his outbound journey.

We arrived in Dublin safe and sound and only had a short time there before heading back on the mini plane to Glasgow. The relief I felt on landing was huge. I'd done it. I'd made it all the way to Abu Dhabi and back, had a wonderful holiday and would be seeing my wee Ronnie soon.

Morvern picked us up at the airport and in her usual kind way, provided us with bread, milk and something for dinner. What would we do without her? Colin had already texted Chris when we landed in Dublin to find out when we could pick Ronnie up. As it happened, Chris was out with the dogs and would be passing our door shortly after we arrived home so we didn't have to wait long. He came bursting into the house, but as Morvern was there too, I barely got a look in. All had gone well and Chris described him as a "wee sweetheart".

Despite it being 1pm in the afternoon, I got into my pjs, covered myself with my fleecy blanket and spent the afternoon on the couch snuggling my boy. The change in temperature had been a shock to both of us and the heating was on full pelt. We managed to stay awake until 9pm that night though there were times I didn't think I would make it. Neither of us had slept on the plane again but we had been advised to stay awake as long as we could.

Slipping into bed that night, I was so delighted to have a warm furry hot water bottle beside me and I thanked the Universe for our holiday, our safe journeys and our happy home to return to.

Chapter Twenty-six - The routines of Ronnie

There's something to be said for routines. We all have them and relish the security they bring and Ronnie is no different. Just as I have my morning rituals of coffee, breakfast, making sandwiches, feeding Ronnie, showering, dressing and hair and makeup, our little mutt enjoys his own habitual start to the day.

He's always last up. I envy his daily long lies as I drag myself from the warmth of the bed while he rolls over, burying himself deeper into the duvet. We'll be half way through breakfast before he makes an appearance. The familiar sound of him shaking the night off as his ears flap, heralds his sleepy entrance. He tentatively makes his way towards me, bleary eyed and ears back while his tail slowly wags as if it too is just waking up.

'Morning, Ronnie. How's my wee boy today?' I inquire as if he is about to respond.

I kneel down and feel the familiar warm softness of his morning coat. Something magical happens overnight as it's always at its silkiest first thing, and I love to put my face against his head and ears, drinking in its luxurious feel. Several kisses later, he's ready for his breakfast which he eats in his usual mannerly fashion, then turns tail towards his own bed in the hall. He'll happily lie there while we go about our routines, but his eyes watch our every move. As I go between kitchen, bathroom and bedroom I can feel them following me, willing me to stop and kiss him and I do, often. I need to add at least ten minutes on to my mornings to allow time for all of these early snuggles, but they're a great start to my day.

Once Colin is up and about and beginning his key counting ritual, Ronnie's out of his bed like a flash and sitting at Colin's feet. He watches eagerly as Colin counts down the list of dogs for that day on his spreadsheet, carefully transferring each of the keys from the huge Pyrex dish into his bum-bag. Ronnie knows what's coming next. The outer pocket of the bum-bag is the treats section and this has to be replenished every day. Colin stands up and heads towards the treat tin as Ronnie leaps up onto his paws like a hunting lion. Quickly regaining his composure, he thuds down into a sitting/begging pose in the middle of the kitchen floor, eyes screaming at Colin to indulge him. He knows the ropes.

'Oops, one's dropped,' Colin laughs as he plays out this daily scenario and Ronnie pounces on it, scoffs it then immediately sits again, chancing his luck. It's not difficult to get around Colin and Ronnie generally savours several treats before they head out the door to pick up the pack.

The second routine kicks in at the end of the working day. Ronnie will come bouncing through the door and make a beeline for me as I sit at my laptop at the kitchen table. He jumps up and licks my face then races towards the water bowl for a long, loud drink. While Colin settles down to a cup of tea and a quick break before taking the last of the dogs home, Ronnie will go between him and me looking to be petted and willing one of us to feed him. Our dog is extremely food motivated. Colin will often get caught up with some article or another on the internet as I watch him lose himself and all connection with what's going on around him.

'Colin, you manifested him so you now need to show him the attention he's looking for,' I'll tease.

A few months pre-Ronnie, when we were having excited conversations about the possibility of adopting a dog, Colin had sat in his usual chair in our kitchen and regularly ran his hand over the air, miming petting an imaginary dog.

'This is what I'll be doing every day and he'll lay his head here on my lap while I stroke his ears,' he enthused.

The Law of Attraction had winged its way from America big time to the UK and for a while there everyone was talking about the book "The Secret". Much of the life coaching I was trained in also practices the principle of the Law of Attraction and there is, without a doubt, something in it. I had witnessed it many times in my own life and in the lives of my clients. It's basically the art of becoming really clear about what you want, writing it down usually helps, and then visualising your life with this in it. The more vividly you can imagine it being part of your

215

life and, crucially, believe that you deserve to have it, the more likely it is you will receive it.

Another really important aspect of the Law of Attraction is gratitude. The more you can be grateful for what you currently have, the more you will attract more of the good stuff into your life. We can all get caught up in what we don't have mode – scarcity mentality - fretting about what's missing and only believing our lives will be complete when we get the next great promotion, car or whatever it is that we perceive is missing and therefore preventing our happiness. This puts us in a state of projecting negativity into the Universe so, low and behold, we attract more negative things to us to confirm our beliefs that our lives are shit. It's all very interesting stuff and I love using the principles in my work and daily life. It's become a way of living for us both now and I'm very grateful for that.

Now I was witnessing it again through Colin, who I have to say is particularly skilled at manifesting. Ronnie sits in the exact spot Colin had mimicked, is the same size and so often places his head on Colin's lap. Coincidence perhaps, but we like to think not.

I give Ronnie his dinner as Colin heads out the door again and then the evening routine begins. He lies in the hall glancing between me and the living room door as I sit, still at my laptop, winding up my day. As I finish off the last of my tasks, shut everything down and make my way towards him, he's up on his feet, tail wagging and ready to roll.

'Wait now, Ronnie,' I say as I enter the living room and prepare the couch for its invasion, lifting the cosy teddy bear blanket that will become our comforter. He stands by the side of the sofa patiently waiting for me to lie down, pour the blanket over me and get the TV remotes in position.

'Come, Ronnie, up you come wee fella.' And he's there, clamped to my side, warm, soft head on my lap. I feel such a sense of calmness lying with him as he tilts his head up towards me, ushering in another pat and offering me a glance at those stunning amber eyes. We'll lie there until it's time for dinner and the next stage in the proceedings.

I'll make my way to the kitchen while Ronnie stays put, usually flopping down into the warm space I have vacated from the sofa. Colin and I munch our way through dinner while he continues his extended chill-out next door. As soon as he hears my knife and fork being placed on the plate for the last time, he's through. How he knows when the final time is remains a mystery to us, as I often place my cutlery down during our meals to sip on a drink, but he knows. He's waiting for his second dinner. Yes, every night I save a little of my dinner and indulge my dog in some secondary dining. I can be seen carefully taking out any small pieces of onion, which is poisonous to dogs (as are chocolate and grapes) and then scraping the remainder of my plate into Ronnie's dish.

The force of the thud as he sits down in anticipation of this is dependent on his desire to eat what we have just consumed. Sausages get a very quick, loud and definite thud while tuna with brown rice and vegetables, not so much. We've taught him to sit and stay until we ask him to go to his bowl, but the success rate of this often depends on the contents. Again sausages are just too much of a favourite and the time spent sitting is often very short before he's up and savouring the break from his own food. To be honest, that's for the best as he slavers all over the floor.

One routine we have also slipped into his day is a ridiculous one that somehow just happened and we don't have the heart to stop. Whenever Ronnie comes back in from a walk and doing his business, he gets a treat. How permissive we are of him, I mean really? It would be nice if I got a treat every time I did a poo.

Speaking of treats, Ronnie displays some very odd behaviour when presented with anything bigger than a five pence piece. He will carry the huge delight in his mouth, pacing from room to room while whining loudly as if to say 'Please help me. I don't know what to do with this.' Making his way to either Colin or I, he will drop the soggy offering at our feet as we pick it up and break it into the size his lordship will tolerate. He receives so many doggy Christmas stockings and treats of all shapes and sizes during the festivities and we can be found carefully breaking or cutting them up, like the servants of a pompous royal.

As I write this, I can see just how much this little guy has wrapped us around his little paw. We have, through sheer determination, managed to encourage him to eat a daily dental stick. It was difficult the first time as

217

he roamed the flat, dental stick stuck evenly out of each side of his mouth, crying like an animal carrying its dead young, us stoically ignoring his pleas. However, we were both amazed at the speed in which he got over his trauma as within ten minutes he was plonked down on the hall floor, happily munching through it.

'For God's sake, Colin. All that indulgence for years with treats when all we had to do was ignore him a short time. We always gave in too quickly.'

'Ah well, you live and learn and it only works for dental sticks. He still won't eat any other treat bigger than a five pence piece!'

There is just something so endearing about his pleading face. He is able to slap his ears so tightly to the back of his head, that he looks bald. His expression is a cross between the piteous look Puss in Boots from Shrek was able to produce at opportune moments, and Calimero, a mournful cartoon chick my heart would break for as a child. Add to that Colin's cries of "He's a wee orphan, just like me." and there's no chance of me changing my ways even with the words of Pat, the dog trainer, ringing in my ears, 'dogs are so manipulative, you know.'

And so as the day closes we come to our final Ronnie routine, the bedtime ritual. After his second dinner, Ronnie will happily return to the soft sofa for another snuggle, but every night around 9 o'clock, he jumps off, stands in the middle of the living room and stares at me. He's telling me he wants to go onto our bed now and I will obediently get up and let him into our bedroom. He'll lie there happily until it's time for his last walk of the day, returning for his post-poo treat (which is now a dental stick) and then make his way back to the same spot. As well as being last up out of bed in the morning, he's always first in bed at night and my snuggle magnet draws me to him throughout the evening once he has left my side.

It's routines that keep us all somehow in check. Without them, we'd lose our way. I know of plenty of people who have found the loss of routine through unemployment or illness unbearable as they lose their sense of self too. I guess it's just as important to animals to set themselves routines and stick to them. I love the sense of sanctuary mine bring me and I'm sure Ronnie feels the same.

Chapter Twenty-Seven - Cats

Before Ronnie was anywhere near our radar, cats played a big part in my life. I lived in the Southside of Paisley for eleven years in a cosy wee tenement flat, my first bought property. Paisley gets a really bad press at times, but I spent many happy times there and will always have a soft spot for the town.

I had popped out one Sunday morning for some milk and as I made my way up the close stairs towards my first floor flat I spotted a gorgeous little kitten sitting on the middle step of the second flight of stone stairs. She jumped to her feet and began meandering between my legs as only cats can, meowing and rubbing along my shins.

'Hello, there. You're beautiful. Where did you come from?' I cooed as I bent down to stroke her. She was white with splashes of grey markings over her soft fur. I was revelling in the love this little cat was pouring all over me when I noticed some blood on her coat. I gently picked her up and saw that her two front paws were cut and she had scrapes on her body too.

'Goodness, what's happened to you, little one? You've been in the wars.'

I opened my front door and she skipped in behind me. There was no sign that she was in any pain from her behaviour, but I knew from her injuries this couldn't be the case. I grabbed a bowl from my kitchen cupboard and poured some of the newly purchased milk into it, placing it gently at her feet. She popped here head over it then pulled away. Searching my fridge, I found some cold meat and offered her some of this from the end of my finger. Again, she refused the morsel.

'Okay, sweetie, I think we need to take a trip to the vet. You're in great form, but there's something just not right.'

I searched for the number of the local vets and called them to explain the situation. Luckily, they had a Sunday morning surgery and told me to bring her down. I didn't have anything to put her in and decided to take the chance that she would do okay in the car, being such a lovely natured wee thing. Scooping her up in my arms we made our way back down the stairs where she sat obediently on an old towel in the front seat of my car as we made the short journey to the vets.

The vet was lovely and welcomed my poor injured find into the surgery with gentle kindness. She looked her over thoroughly and checked for an identity chip in her back.

'Well, there's no chip unfortunately, and no collar, so we can't trace where she's come from,' she said dismayed.

'How old do you think she is?' I inquired.

'She's young, about five months I'd say. It looks to me as if she's taken a tumble from quite a height, maybe out of a flat window. I think there are leg fractures but she'll need x-rays and her pallet is badly cracked not to mention all of the cuts and bruises.'

'Oh my goodness, the poor wee thing. If her pallet's cracked that explains why she didn't want to eat or drink anything. The wee soul must be in lots of pain, but she's so good natured.'

'I know. She's a lovely kitten. I would suggest you leave her with us and she goes to the SSPCA. There's hundreds of pounds worth of treatment needed here and she's not your responsibility. They will carry out all of the care she needs and there won't be an issue about her being re-homed because of her age and personality.'

'Oh I feel really guilty just leaving her.'

'You've done the right thing bringing her in. Don't feel bad. Her owners may check here and with the SSPCA and she could then be reunited with them. She'll be fine either way, so please don't worry.'

I said my goodbyes to "Lucky" as Morvern had named her afterwards. I remember asking why she'd chosen that name as to me, the ordeal this little cat had been through, was anything but lucky. Morvern explained that she had come to my door and that's where her luck had changed. I had felt awful leaving her, but was not in the position to take on a cat at that time. I just kept telling myself that she would find a good home and, with any luck, her previous owners would search for her.

A few months later, I was walking up my street towards my flat and a little black and white cat followed me to the close door. Again, I bent down to greet him and have my usual welcoming conversation. As I opened the close door, he flew past me and up the stairs. He had the most comical way of running up stairs as his two back legs splayed outwards as if he had just stepped off a horse. I followed him up and opened my front door as he entered, without invitation. As I put the bright light of the kitchen on, I got my first good look at him. He was a handsome boy, jet black with a small frame that gave him the look of a young cat and he was exceptionally vocal, talking to me the entire time I hunted for some food for him.

He polished off the tuna I'd placed on a saucer and some milk, and followed me into the living room where he curled up on the sofa for several hours before heading for my front door and requesting to leave. This became the pattern for several years. He wasn't my cat as he didn't come every day. I think he had several flats in the street he visited when he was hungry or cold and he would greet me from my car on the evenings the other doors weren't open to him. I called him "Wee Cat".

Wee Cat

Time moved on and Colin was now living with me in my cosy flat. Wee Cat was still a regular visitor. He had two favourite places to lie on his visits, one was on the cushion of a rocking chair I had in one corner for the living room and the other under a lamp on top of the piano. Colin would often arrive home delighted to see him curled up in one of these places.

Then a ginger cat decided to join in on the action. He was an old boy who again followed me up the street and into the flat and just wanted to be cuddled. His long ginger coat was so soft and he had few remaining teeth, but he had such a gentle personality you just couldn't help falling in love with him. Similar to Wee Cat, he visited as and when it suited him and for as long as he wanted. He had the most beautiful way of letting us know he wanted into the flat. Perched up on his hind legs he would softly scratch the door as if to say 'Hello, I'm here to see you, please let me in.' and we always did. Just hearing those gentle scratches at the door lit up my day. We called him "Gingy".

Wee Cat had a friend he liked to play with in the back court, a gorgeous black and white cat who was very wary of people. His two front paws were white until half way up his legs like a pair of socks. On summer evenings we loved to watch Wee Cat and his pal play together and the two of them would leap high in the air so acrobatically it was magical to witness. This new addition was only ever in the flat a couple of times, encouraged in with treats but he wasn't comfortable around humans and there was a story behind that lovely cat that we never got to hear. We called him "Socks".

By this time, buying cat food was a normal part of our weekly shop and we had an array of cat dishes lining up on my galley kitchen floor. Our neighbours also had cats; there was Smudge across from us and Milo below. Milo would often arrive at the door to join in the feline fun, but Smudge was a house cat we only ever saw staring down at us from his living room window. He was a big grey and white striped tom cat with smudged markings on his face and Milo was a huge black tom too. Our home was turning into a cattery, but we loved it.

Socks

Then one day Smudge went missing. Our neighbours asked if we'd seen him, but being a house cat we hadn't even thought to look. We didn't see him again and a few months later our neighbours moved. About six months after, we were sitting watching telly one night when we heard howling from outside. It was a strange soulful and mourning sound of distress and we immediately looked out of the window. Through the darkness we could just make out the shape of a cat cowering in-between two wheelie bins. We made our way down stairs to find a large cat curled up and looking the worse for wear.

'Susan, I think that's Smudge,' Colin said trying to get a closer look.

'Goodness, Colin, I think you're right. He looks awful.'

His coat was matted and he'd lost a lot of weight and was staring at us intently as if to say 'I want your help, but I don't trust anyone.'

'What'll we do, Colin?'

'Bring some food down and let's see if we can encourage him up.'

I ran upstairs and grabbed a cat bowl, filling it with one of the many sachets of cat food lined up on the work surface. For the next two hours, Colin gently tried to coax Smudge from his safe space between the bins up the close stairs but it was no use. While he ate the food, he wasn't for moving. But he kept coming back every night and letting us know he was there with his cries. This went on for several weeks and eventually he began to slowly trust us and edge his way up the stairs until one night he came into the flat.

Goodness knows what had happened to Smudge in the months since he went missing, but he was now displaying feral tendencies. He was hissing and growling despite our attempts to appease him and part of me was wondering if we should be encouraging this wild cat into our home. Another part of me was heartbroken to think what he must have been through and this was overtaking any fears.

He crossed the front door and ran into the living room where he hid behind the couch.

'Let's just leave food and water out for him and let him do what he needs to do, Susan. At least he's out of the cold.'

We had a litter tray in the hall for all of our little guests and we made him up a bed behind the sofa and left him to it. In the morning, the food was gone and we let him out to go and explore. Every day, he came back to be fed and sometimes he stayed the night, sometimes he would be out all night and we just let him do what he needed to do. We had no forwarding address for his previous owners, but as time went on he became more trusting again and would let us pet him and he'd curl up on the sofa with us when he did stay.

'Colin, I haven't seen Wee Cat for days. It's not like him not to pop in for a cuddle.'

'I'm sure he's fine. He'll be back when he's hungry.'

But he never did come back and I missed seeing his comical run up the stairs or watching him leap about the back court with Socks. Goodness knows what happened to him, but we never saw him again and I was feeling the loss. Then one evening I was getting out of my car after work and I heard a lovely jingle of a cat bell coming towards me. The most beautiful little kitten was by my feet meowing and purring as she said hello. Once again I was followed to the close door and she did exactly what Wee Cat had done the night I met him; ran in front of me and climbed the stairs in the same hilarious manner. I called Colin.

'A little cat has just followed me up the stairs. She's so like Wee Cat Colin, she's got exactly the same funny way of running up the stairs and her small frame is identical. Maybe it's one of his kittens!'

Maybe she was and we'll never know but it certainly helped with the loss of Wee Cat as she became a regular visitor too. We called her "Jingle".

The years were passing quickly and we had long outgrown my little flat. It was now time to move on and one of our biggest dilemmas was what would happen to the cats. We talked about them individually as we made our plans.

'Gingy goes to nearly every flat in the street and definitely has an owner as he's so well looked after. Jingle is the same. Socks is a poor soul but he's a survivor. It's really just Smudge, Colin. I can't bear the thought of leaving him here after we've worked so hard to rehabilitate him.'

'I know but we can't take him with us. He wouldn't last a day in our new flat. We're in-between two main roads and he'd be demented if we kept him indoors now. We're going to have to re-home him.'

'I know. Tell you what, I'll send an email around work and see if anyone will take him. There are lots of animal lovers.'

I got a great response from colleagues, but wanted to make sure it was the right home for Smudge. It needed to be somewhere he could get out and roam without fear of being run over and with someone who understood that this cat had had a tough time and would need a lot of love and support. The perfect candidate came forward and we made arrangements for me to bring him to her one Saturday morning.

I borrowed Morvern's cat box and with great difficulty, eventually got Smudge inside it. He was not a happy cat and was thumping around heavily making those mournful, distressing howls again. Somehow I managed to get the cat box, which was uncontrollably moving as Smudge threw himself from side to side, into my car. I placed it on the front seat beside me and as I was putting on my seat belt I saw a free paw pushing up the lid. Before I had time to push the paw back in, Smudge had squeezed his large frame out of the tiniest of spaces his paw had created and was on top of the box. We looked at each other for a split second then he was off, whirling around the car, fur everywhere and claws scratching every surface, including me. It was a disaster and we were both becoming so distressed that the only thing I could do was to open the car door and set him free.

I sat in shock as I saw him tear down the street. My dashboard was covered in scratches as were my hands and arms. I reached for my phone and with shaky, blood stained fingers, called to cancel the handover. Smudge didn't want to move and it would have been unfair of me to put him through that again.

Our downstairs neighbour knew of our dilemma and kindly offered to take over the care of Smudge. She was a vet nurse and also owned Milo. She told us not to worry and that he would be fine. We had no choice but to trust her and hope the poor wee traumatised fella would be okay.

Luckily, the person who bought the flat off us was a cat lover. We told her all about our little visitors and their routines. She said she would be delighted to take over feeding and caring for them, so that made us feel a whole lot better too.

I couldn't end this chapter without mentioning my own experience of cat ownership. I had made the decision to re-home a couple of kittens several years before I met Colin. Heading out to Erskine Community Farm with Morvern, we arrived home with two of the cutest kitties ever. The entire litter had been handed in to the farm in a plastic bag and the two I had chosen were both black and white, though very different in looks and nature. One was long haired with white paws and a white chest and the other was short haired with black and white markings all over her body. They were sisters, apparently, though I sometime wondered as they never really had a close bond. I called them "Sparkles" and "Joy".

Sparkles

I fell in love with them and together we formed a happy family unit as their loving energy filled my flat. I started a new relationship not long after bringing them home and my new partner was not a cat lover. As time went on and the relationship developed, we decided it was time for me to move in with him. He did agree that the cats could come too, but it soon became apparent that this arrangement wasn't going to work. To my great shame, I chose the relationship over my darling cats and this remains an act I feel deeply remorseful of.

Morvern came to the rescue, as she so often has in my life. She had the most amazing dog called Hamish for sixteen years. He was a Jack Russell and shared a lot of qualities and characteristic of Ronnie. Cheeky and loveable, Hamish slept under the duvet with Morvern every night and adored being kissed and cuddled. I loved that dog. A few months before I was asked to give up the cats, Hamish passed away. He was an old dog

228

who had had the best life, but it was still heart-breaking and Morvern was at a loss. When I told her of my dilemma, she immediately said that she would take them. To know they would be going to such a loving home and I would be able to see them all the time, lessened some of my guilt, but the day I gave them up was torturous.

Inevitably, the relationship I was in broke down. It was a miracle that it lasted the four years it did and there had been several break-ups and make-ups over the period. Given what had been asked of me and what I had chosen to do, betraying my beautiful cats like that, it was doomed. He was a good guy and we both tried hard to make things work. We just had very different values and had I been more secure in myself at that time, I wouldn't have done what I did. I was in my early thirties and surrounded by married friends, having babies and so wanted the relationship to work that I was prepared to sacrifice my own needs. The experience gave me so much insight and understanding for the work I now do when I support others ignoring their true selves for the sake of being in a relationship.

By this time, however, the cats were living a magnificent life with Morvern and it would have been unfair to disrupt that and Morvern felt she couldn't part with them too, so they remained with her.

Joy passed away a couple of years ago. A frailer Sparkles is still with us and as adorable as ever. While it had been one of the most difficult things I've ever had to do and a real life lesson, had I not done it, we would never have adopted Ronnie. The cats would have been living with us and Ronnie would have been rehomed with another family. That seems unimaginable to me now. And so as awful as the whole thing was and, as difficult as I find it to admit what I did, it happened for a reason. Often at the time, we do not see why things are evolving as they are, but in time life shows us what was intended. In this case our gift was to be Ronnie and Ronnie would gift to us not only Colin's business and a deep friendship, but a whole new insight into life as we knew it.

Leaving that flat after all of the years I spent there was really tough. I could have moved on far sooner than I did but something had kept me there. Perhaps it was all of those little extra mouths that needed fed and loved. Looking after the cats was a special time in our lives and one I will always remember fondly and with some sadness when we reminisce. What if the cats weren't okay? I had pictured Gingy scraping our door and wondering where we were or Jingle darting up the stairs to an unopening door. There was nothing we could do and the reality was that those cats were all survivors who would find another home to adopt out of the many others they visited.

Though I'm much more of a dog person, cats are really special too and on looking back, they were a great training ground for us in the work we now do with Ronnie Ronster's.

Chapter Twenty-eight - Different disciplines

Colin and I are very different people. Not so dissimilar in our value base, but quite opposing in our personality types. I'm more of a worrier than Colin, while he has a loathing for conflict. I'm one for getting things out in the open and facing issues head on, while Colin is getting better at this, he still finds it really tough. Unlike me, however, Colin doesn't sweat the small stuff and has a clear idea of what matters in life. I was brought up in a family that put a great deal of emphasis on putting a front on things no matter what. Colin was an orphan by the age of twelve. You'd have thought with that legacy, he would be the one with more issues, but as he said to me often, 'Susan, I've not had to live with parents setting me up against my siblings or making demands on my time. While I would never have chosen what happened to me, who knows how different things would have been …' The older I've got, the more I've realised that very few people had chocolate box upbringings and parents do the best they can.

And so we have diverse ways of dealing with life and subsequently how we discipline Ronnie. I believe Colin lets him away with murder. He thinks I care too much about what other people think. Ronnie is not a bad dog by any means, but he does have his flaws, like us all. The training classes we attended certainly helped to instil some manners in him, but he remains a determined dog with a mind of his own.

Whenever our doorbell rings, he's off and up from wherever he's lying like a rocket, barking furiously at the poor unsuspecting person behind the door. Once the door is open, despite my trying to keep him at bay behind it, he will often squeeze his way past me like Houdini bursting out of a crate. Much barking and jumping up and down then ensues as I attempt to pull him back while apologising profusely to our guest. Most people take it well, but you can also see the terror on the faces of some; those poor people who have had a bad experience with a dog in early life and are now reliving it in full Technicolor as Ronnie bounds at them.

He does exactly the same thing when out in the back court. If anyone else dares to invade his space, he's off like a bolt, racing towards them in a very unwelcoming manner. I feel mortified by this behaviour of our dog. Colin is very blasé about it. I can be found racing after Ronnie shouting, 'No, Ronnie, come here, that's very naughty, come here NOW!' and pulling him back while Colin meanders over smiling and murmuring such things as "Come on, Ronnie. What are you up to now?' with no sense of urgency whatsoever.

I've seen students on their way to the bins nearly leap in the air with fright, struggling to hold onto their recycling materials, as Ronnie propels his way towards them. Not good. While Ronnie has never bitten anyone and his behaviour is all bluster and bravado – a way of marking out his territory – it still must be terrifying to someone who doesn't know him.

'Colin, you can't just let this happen every time,' I'll say, exasperated once again.

'Oh he's fine, Susan, he doesn't mean any harm.'

'That's not the point. He's frightening people and they don't know he isn't going to bite them. He looks really scary when he's flying at them. I'd get a fright if a dog did that to me.'

'It's just his way and I always explain to people that he won't hurt them.'

'Don't you think we should be doing more to stop this behaviour in him?'

'What can we do? He's guarding and some would say that's a good thing. At least we know the house is safe when he's in it, and no one would stand a chance if they tried to attack either of us.'

'But people aren't attacking us. They're just going about their business or coming to the door. I hate it and I wish you would apologise to them when it happens. You act as if he's doing nothing wrong when he's behaving really badly.'

'I do apologise and I always speak to people and explain he's a rescue dog.'

'I don't always hear you apologise and he was rescued years ago so that excuse is running out for him and you!'

And so the argument goes on with no resolution and Ronnie continuing to scare the life out of people who don't know him and his ways. I've tried to analyse why it upsets me so much and I think it's because Colin and I are on completely opposite pages on this one. I want the ground to open up and swallow me and he couldn't give a shit. I think it comes back to our different life experiences and what we believe to be important. We definitely share the same values in that we have similar dreams and aspirations and we both possess very strong views on equality and justice. Colin just thinks that Ronnie should be free to express himself while I believe he should be better behaved. Writing this, I can see that this is also how we live our lives. I'm a bit of a goody two shoes, always wanting to do the right thing while Colin goes so much more with the ebb and flow of life, taking things in his stride.

I've worked so hard to train Ronnie in not begging while we are eating and most of the time Colin will support this. While we dine, I tell Ronnie to go under the table and he follows these instructions well, lying down at our feet until he hears me enjoying my last mouthful. If we're eating food on the sofa, he'll also take instruction to lie under the coffee table and I'm so proud that I've managed to train him in this way. I think it's only as a result of him knowing he gets a little of what we've been eating in his bowl as his "second dinner" once we're done, but it works.

There are times, however, when Colin just decides to completely go against this as he hands Ronnie something off his plate. It's pretty random in its occurrence but he always gets the same look of disdain and chastisement from me.

'Colin, what are you doing?'

'Ooops, sometimes I just forget.'

'Well, please don't do that. You know how hard I've worked to train him in this. I hate begging dogs!'

'It won't do him any harm.'

'That's not the point. He gets enough treats and extra dinners without you undoing all my hard work.'

Ronnie just leaves the room, licking his lips.

Who are we trying to kid!

Every time we have people over it all goes out of the window again. My brother-in-law, Charlie, is particularly guilty of offering Ronnie crisps and dropping sausage rolls on the floor just beside him. Most people can't resist his begging face as he sits so nice in front of them willing whatever's in their hands into his mouth. I put on a brave face and recognise it's a battle I can't win. Ronnie loves company. We've had to give up on putting food on the coffee table. I have a crystal 'Lazy Susan' dish which used to come out whenever we had a people over. The middle section of this round plate held a tub of dip perfectly while the four outer sections were filled with crisps. Similar to the "cheese" incident at one of our New Year's Eve party, Ronnie would wait until the room was clear then dive into the dip. I'd caught him a few times but wonder if there had been occasions when he had got away with it and we were all innocently dipping our crisps where Ronnie's snout had been only minutes ago. Other times there was no mistaking his cheek as he wandered around the flat with a white nose.

Sometimes he wouldn't even wait for the room to be empty. He has been witnessed slowly crawling along the rug, commando style towards the plate and once the conversation was at its most animated, his head would pop up over the coffee table and very delicately swipe a crisp, much to everyone's amusement. My 'Lazy Susan' is now gathering dust at the back of one of our cupboards.

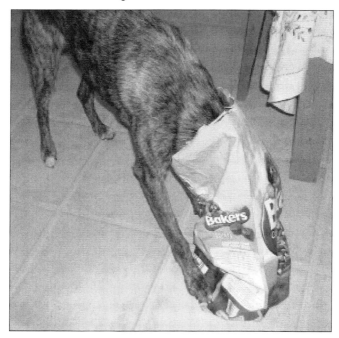

Lesson not learned

Colin and I also differ on the amount of treats we feel Ronnie should have. Part of how Colin dealt with the loss of his parents was to associate food with comfort. Food is very important. While I love eating, I was brought up differently and disciplining myself around what I eat has always been a part of who I am. I don't deny myself things, but I do keep a check on my weight. And so Colin associates giving lots of treats to

Ronnie as showing him love while I would rather give him lots of cuddles as well as the odd treat. We clash here too.

Luckily, Colin and I have a relationship that is argument free most of the time and we have found ways of communicating our differences about Ronnie without falling out. I remember when we first met we couldn't believe how easy everything was between us, neither of having experienced anything like this in previous relationships. We sat smugly on my parent's sofa the first Christmas we shared and claimed,

'We just don't fight.'

'Yes mmmm, well I'm sure you know that that's not realistic. It will change with time as you move out of your honeymoon period,' Elizabeth, my sister, said with the experience of five years of marriage behind her and ahead of us.

'Oh I don't know, this is just so different,' we both cooed.

But of course she was right and we do fight but it really isn't that often. However, on the odd occasion we do have a row, it's not pretty. Like every marriage, tensions build and external stresses can mean that the argument you originally have is nothing to do with what's really going on. It's just as well it doesn't happen that often as we can both sulk for Scotland. Stubbornness is a trait we share as well as having tempers that can leave room doors rattling as Ronnie scurries for cover. I can find myself using language that ordinarily would never come out of my mouth, but as the years have gone on, we've learned so much about each other and how and why we react in certain ways through our arguments.

We'll sit down and talk it all through once one of us has eventually 'given in' and broken the stony silence. I've learned that it cuts Colin to the core if he feels I am criticising him. He equates this to him not being good enough and that I may leave him, so the way I communicate things to him is really important. He's learned that I worry and that sometimes I just need to express this without there being any solutions. The worry can cause me to feel overwhelmed and then lash out at him for not doing the things I've asked him to do and then he feels criticised. We can get quite the vicious cycle going when we put our minds to it, but were learning all the time.

Since leaving the rat race and adopting Ronnie, our stress levels have greatly reduced as have our arguments. The couple of years leading up to my leaving my job were really tough for us as I was unhappy at work and my mum was also very ill. Now things are easier and while we may differ in our approaches to disciplining Ronnie, it's not the kind of stuff that's a deal breaker. It's everyday life stuff. How on earth would be have coped with these differences if we'd had kids?

I'm always a little suspicious of couples who say they never argue, like we proclaimed, so naively, all of those years ago. Ronnie will continue to be the child we never had and like all parents, we will continue to disagree on certain aspects of his care. It's through our differences that we keep learning and the relationhips grows.

Chapter Twenty-nine - Births, deaths and marriages

One of the many great advantages of owning a dog is that you get to meet new people. Even before Colin had set up his business, just walking with Ronnie brought him into contact with strangers all of the time. There were the people who just love dogs and want to stop and pet yours, and the other dog owners who will often stop for a chat and to swap stories about their canine friends. And of course there were the dogs themselves who just love to make new buddies, and thankfully Ronnie is a very sociable animal who has never shown any aggressive tendencies towards other dogs.

Some dogs aren't so blessed with that kind of temperament, though, and it breaks my heart to see their owners pulling on their leads, sometimes struggling to stay on their feet, as their dog barks furiously, straining to reach their nemesis. I can relate to this as Ben, the Collie we had when I was a teenager, had these tendencies. It wasn't all the time, just certain dogs, and there was no pattern to it, just random canines who were happily going about their business. It would begin on approach with a low growl which gave me the heads up to shorten his lead and if possible cross the road or move in the opposite direction. He would then rear up on his hind legs like a dressage horse and with teeth bared and bellowing barks, I would pull him along the road, shouting embarrassed apologies at the frowning owner as I passed.

Not good and the fact I never knew if or when it might happen, meant I was always on edge as soon as another dog was in sight. I've learned that dogs pick up on your anxiety and can feel the tension running down from your arm into their lead, but it's really tough not to react. I had such a lot of sympathy for Stephanie, who owned Sparkles, the dog with issues that Ronnie and Colin had gone on therapy walks with way back when we first had Ronnie. Seeing both Stephanie and Sparkles sometimes struggle to keep control brought back difficult memories of Ben. I guess, just like humans, dogs have different personalities and their life experiences will affect them too, not that Sparkles was shown anything but love.

I guess it also depends on the dog and the owner as to how much they want to enter the new world of the canine community. Some owners don't stop and talk, others do. Colin, being as sociable as Ronnie, always stops for a chat, while me, being shier and more reserved, find this a little more challenging. Regardless, those first few months of adopting Ronnie were a real eye opener for me. I had no ideas there were so many people with dogs on our door step, many of whom have now become our friends.

It was in those early days in the putting green that Ronnie met so many of the people and dogs who became instrumental in supporting Ronnie Ronster's Dog Walking Service. From Pat, the dog trainer, whose invaluable advice has kept Colin confident and in control of his pack, to Gaile and gentle Lola the staffie who became his first client, and Chris who continues to capture Ronnie's essence in photographs including the ones for this book.

We've experienced a lot over the years and have twice looked after dogs while their owners' babies have made their way into the world. Missy, the Collie came to stay when an anxious looking James dropped her off as he headed to the hospital to be with his wife, Louise.

James owned the restaurant next door to our flat, having taken it over from Dave and Steven a few years after them, and Missy was a regular as at that time they lived in Park Circus. Savanah safely arrived the next day and Missy stayed on with us until the new family got settled into their new life together. One thing we discovered, quite by accident, is that Missy sings the blues. Colin was messing about in the kitchen with his acoustic guitar one night when she started singing along, well howling really, at the top of her voice. The more he played, the more animated she became and she was loving it, though I'm not sure our neighbours were. We really should have taped it and sent it to "You've been Framed".

The following year, Eddie, the Australian Shepherd dog, came to stay while his owners awaited the birth of their daughter. Less of a regular and full of beans, Eddie bounced his way around our home for the five days he boarded. He was only a puppy and brought with him all of the enthusiasm only a pup can bring. His favourite cuddly toy was a sheep which we of course named "Sheep" and he would wander around the flat with it in his mouth making little whining noises and would not be parted from it.

All went well with the birth of little Nina-Rose and after a few days of settling back at home, Eddie joined his new little sister and I'm guessing life was never the same for any of them again.

It was nice to know we had played a small part in these momentous occasions in our clients' lives, and births are always such a time of celebration. The flip side of this is of course the other end of the life cycle. As I've already written, death is something any dog owner needs to prepare for. We had already experienced the sad loss of Peggy and now we had to get ready to say goodbye to another beloved member of the pack. Veronica, who owned Noelle and Rachelle Ann, and was now studying to be a vet in Edinburgh, called Colin.

'Colin, I'm sorry to call you with bad news.'

'What's wrong?'

'I'm back in Glasgow for a few days with the dogs. Noelle's not been too good. I'm afraid she's come to the end of the road and I wanted to let you and Susan know so you can come and say goodbye to her.'

'Oh, Veronica. I'm so sorry.'

'Only if you want to. Please don't feel you have to. It's just I know how much you love the girls.'

'Of course we'll come and see her. When suits?'

'How about tomorrow evening. I'm staying with a friend in Gibson Street. I'll text you the address.'

I was so sad to hear the news, but heartened to know we would have the chance to see Noelle again. We made our way to the flat the following evening and there she was, 'Noellelegant' as Colin called her. This gentle, graceful Whippet had been a part of our lives for the last four years, staying with us many times and sharing two Christmas and New Year's with us. She looked so well as she bounced out into the hall to say hello but the vet had told Veronica that she was in a lot of pain with her joints and she had had several seizures which were affecting her brain function.

It was a real act of kindness to let her go. She was an old girl, with many happy memories to leave behind, but she would also be leaving a huge hole in the lives of everyone who loved her.

Her sister, Rachel Ann, the miniature Shitsu, otherwise known as 'the duster', was sweeping her way around the hall too, unaware of what lay ahead. She would miss her life-long companion. We knelt down and poured lavish amounts of affection on both of the dogs. I kissed Noelle's soft warm head so many times and she was left with lipstick stains all over her white fur. When it came time to leave, I couldn't bear to look at her. Whippets have such sad faces at the best of times and here we were in the worst of times and those beautiful, soulful eyes were too much for me to bear. We tearfully made our exit, walking up the road in silence, each of us keeping our macabre thoughts to ourselves. When we got home, I held Ronnie close and told him he wouldn't be seeing his old pal Noelle again.

As well as the heartbreak of saying goodbye there have also been times of celebration. Kathryn and Skip, who now had Betty, the cheeky Cockerpoo, got engaged, and myself, Colin and Gaile were invited to their wedding reception in the Glasgow Art Club. It was a lovely evening with Betty present as guest of honour. Taking our duties seriously, even when off the clock, we walked Betty a couple of times during the festivities to ensure the new happy couple could relax, and we danced with her in our arms to the eighties music that filled the room. It was an elegant affair with some celebrities present. Gaile came back from the toilet at one point announcing that Kristy Wark had been washing her hands as she had walked in, but she had now left. I was very miffed to hear I had missed her. She had been one of my role models, having never missed an episode of the talk show "Scottish Women" when I was younger.

We also got an invitation to Veronica and Blair's wedding in Culzean Castle in Ayrshire. With Veronica being from America and Blair hailing from Scotland, the wedding was a gorgeous fusion of the two countries. It was the first outdoor wedding I had ever attended in the spectacular grounds of the castle and when Veronica arrived in a horse drawn carriage (a surprise from her mum) I gasped at the magnificence of it all. This was going to be a spectacular wedding … and it was.

The couple now had a new Whippet called Freya who, alongside Rachel Ann, was back at our home being looked after by Morvern and Chrisanna for the day. They stayed with us from the week before the wedding until their return from honeymoon. Freya was a character and a half, only being young when they got her. The new duo had both stayed with us several times so she was used to our place. She had the softest coat, as all Whippets seem to have, which was golden in colour with white flashes. We reckon that's where Ronnie got the softness of his coat from, as he is part Whippet. They also both share big bionic ears, which are a continual source of amusement.

Freya was learning fast and turning into a beautiful dog. While Veronica had told us that she now slept happily in her own bed all night, every morning we would wake up with her in-between us and Rachel Ann curled up at the bottom of the bed at my feet. I'm a very light sleeper and always wake when Ronnie moves in and out of the duvet, but Freya had mystical powers and was somehow able to climb in beside us without a stir. Colin called her "the snake" as he was convinced she slid up the side of the bed and over the top of us like an agile python. Ronnie stoically put up with his bed fellows, as he always does.

Freya and Rachel Anne

242

There have been so many experiences we've shared alongside our new friends and dogs over the years. It's humbling to be invited to be part of both happy and sad times and I'm sure there will be many more of both times ahead. Who knew adopting a dog would add a completely new dimension to our social life too. I've often thought that owning or even fostering a dog would be a fantastic thing for people who are socially isolated. It gives such a sense of purpose and opens so many possibilities in terms of new friendships. I know dogs are not for everyone, but what a difference they make in the world.

Chapter Thirty - The ripples of Ronnie

It's amazing how one decision to make a change can impact on so many other areas of your life, and on the lives of others too. Adopting Ronnie has been one of the most positive joint decisions Colin and I ever made. It's made me a better person for sure. I've learned to live in the moment far more than I used to. While this is something I teach and train people in as it's another important part of life coaching, it's taken adopting Ronnie to really show me the true meaning of it. I can be stressing about something and then catch a glimpse of Ronnie tearing up and down the hall with a ball in his mouth and realise it really doesn't matter. Whatever's going on will pass, so I push it aside and go and play with my boy.

There's no point fretting about the past and worrying about the future. All we have is the present moment we're living in and while it takes skill and dedication to master remaining there, when I see how happy Ronnie is, it keeps me trying.

I often say to Colin, 'But how did we know he was the right dog? He was the first one they showed us, yet we had no hesitation at all in taking him.'

'We just knew, Susan. There was something about him.'

'We had no idea he would change our lives so much for the better though, did we, when we walked out of the Dogs Trust with him?'

'Nope.'

'I mean, I know everyone thinks their dog is really special, like people with their children, but he really is special, isn't he?'

'Yes, he is.'

A version of this conversation goes on between Colin and I on a regular basis, and I think it's because I just can't believe how lucky we have been. You hear all kinds of horror stories about rescue dogs wrecking furniture, biting owners, or just being so mentally damaged as a result of ill-treatment that they can never trust humans again. Yet here we are with the most amazing little dog, whose light just keeps shining on everything and everyone. Gratitude is a constant in my life.

But he's not only touched our lives in the most amazing way. There have been offshoots all over the place, owing to people meeting him and hearing his story. Gaile, the owner of Lola, the gentle Staffie, watched Colin set up his business and go from strength to strength. She was so impressed with the change in him, and how happy both he and Ronnie were with their new lifestyles, that she, too, decided she wanted to try her hand at self-employment. Being a total canine lover as well, she undertook a dog-grooming course, passing with flying colours. Colin and I helped her all we could, explaining what we had learned in setting up our own businesses. She also managed to find a really helpful business advisor who supported her to apply for grants to help her pay for the cost of materials, and was just generally available for her whenever she came across a blip.

Being a designer, she was able to produce fantastic graphics and within a relatively short time 'The Dog's Paws' was up and running. She traded in her car for a huge white van that she could walk around in with ease, after all of her grooming equipment had been installed, and once her graphics and business name were added to the outside, it looked fantastic.

Herroch, another friend from the dog community, carried out all of the necessary work to transform the van into a pooch's beauty parlour. In went a bath with a shower head, a huge hair dryer, a surface to stand the dogs on while drying or clipping them, and numerous hooks with lead attachments to secure the dogs while she worked. The unique selling point of Gaile's business is that she's a mobile grooming service. She will come to your door at a convenient time, and save all of the hassle of fitting salon appointments into busy schedules. Genius! Lola travels happily around in the van with Gaile, and sleeps in the front seat while she works her magic.

Being well-known in the dog community, it was easy for Gaile to get started, and Colin has been able to pass clients on to her too. She grooms Ruby and many of the other dogs in Ronnie's pack regularly. Being short-haired, however, Ronnie has never had the pleasure of being pampered by 'The Dog's Paws', but I keep meaning to ask Gaile where she gets the coat-freshening spray she covers the dogs with just before they jump out of the van, as they all smell divine post-pamper. It's wonderful to watch someone else follow a dream.

Another offshoot of Ronnie's influence is that John, one of guys Colin meets up with every day in Bellahouston Park, decided to try his hand at dog walking too. Again, with Colin sharing all of his experience with him, and supporting him in any way he could, John gradually began building up a pack of his own to walk alongside his dog, Coisty. The extra income and change of lifestyle suits John and Coisty in the same way it does Colin and Ronnie.

The biggest surprise came from Jen, Jackson's owner. She had a good job as a teacher but was looking for a change. And so she decided to pack it all in and set up "Park Life Dog Walking Service". I must admit to having a few minutes of worry when I first heard this news. Jen lives right around the corner so the competition was close. I caught myself quickly though, remembering that there are more than enough dogs to go around. Jen would need our full support and that's exactly what we have given her. She too is now fully enjoying the great joys of self-employment and spending her days with four-legged companions.

Then there's Elizabeth and Jim, my sister and brother-in-law, who adore Ronnie, and over the course of the first year we had him, began asking questions about dog ownership. They were thinking about getting a Westie and while these are lovely dogs, we just couldn't help exhorting the many virtues of Lurchers: they don't need much exercise; don't smell; get on with other dogs and children; and are generally just lovely natured, gentle creatures. Unlike a Westie, which would have to come from a breeder at great expense, recues centres always have greyhounds, Lurchers and Lurcher-crosses like Ronnie. This brings the added benefit and all round feel-good factor of giving an abandoned dog a good home. We sold it well. One winter's afternoon, my phone rang.

'Susan, we've done it.' I could hear the excitement in Elizabeth's voice and it took me right back to the day we first saw Ronnie. 'We're just on our way home from the Cat and Dog Home, and we've chosen a dog — a Lurcher — and she's just beautiful.'

'Oh, Liz, that's wonderful news. What's her name?'

'Belle. They don't know exactly how old she is. All they can tell us is she's between eight and eleven! She's dark grey, but has lots of light grey round her muzzle and mixed into her coat because of her age. Oh, Susan, she's just lovely.'

'So when do you get her?'

'We can pick her up on Thursday. We need to buy everything in for her and she needs to gets a health check, but they've said if she's fine, then she's ours.'

'Fantastic. Just wait till you get her home. It's so exciting.'

'Listen, Susan, Jim and I really want to thank you and Colin. We would never have thought about a Lurcher if we hadn't spoken to you.'

Belle

They had five and a half years together sharing many happy memories, and Belle brought them both so much happiness, but inevitably, when rescuing an older dog, time together is shorter. She had lived far longer than anticipated as they had been told to expect about a year, in a worst case scenario. Now she was getting frailer and in pain from arthritis and we all knew what was coming. Elizabeth and Jim held her in their arms as she passed away at the vets and they began the slow process of mourning the loss of a much loved member of their family.

Like many dogs, Ronnie is acutely aware of changing moods and emotions in any environment. Dogs can be a huge comfort to people in psychological and physical pain, as well as to those who are grieving. It's one of the reasons some dogs are used for therapy in hospitals and care homes, as their calm, gentle natures appear to support the healing process. There is something so therapeutic about petting a dog and their unconditional love builds confidence and self-esteem. Charities that offer healing through dogs are now opening up across the UK and I can fully understand why. Ronnie certainly shows healing tendency towards my mum when she becomes depressed.

He's an extremely high-energy dog that bounces around from person to person when we are in company. However, it's like a switch goes on in his mind when he sees my mum sitting quietly with her own thoughts, and he just knows it's not appropriate to jump all over her. He makes his way slowly to her, then lays his head gently on her lap, looking at her with such intensity that even in her withdrawn state she can't help but connect with him. As time goes on, he makes his way tentatively from the floor to the couch so he can get closer in for a snuggle, and he'll lie there for hours, as my mum gently strokes his head. It's no cure, but it does give my mum a little relief. Who wouldn't feel a bit better with a furry friend showing such love and affection?

A final story which shows how Ronnie has had an impact on the lives of others began with a Christmas card that was sent the second Christmas after the business was set up. Colin decided to design and print personalised Christmas cards for clients and friends. Using all of the wonderful logos Gaile had developed for the website, he produced a collage of cartoon images of Ronnie, covered with holly and stars and other Christmas delights. The inside description wished everyone a happy Christmas from Ronnie, Colin and Susan, at Ronnie Ronster's Dog-Walking Service. When they arrived back from the printers, we loved them and couldn't wait to send them all out.

One little girl was particularly taken with the card. Sylvie is the daughter of my friends, Ashley and Cyrus. Ashley has been a constant source of support for me while writing this book, being a talented writer herself. Sylvie was nearly three at the time the card arrived on her doorstep. I can just imagine her opening it up, her huge brown eyes shining in wonder as only children can at Christmas time. Ashley told me that Sylvie wouldn't go anywhere without the card for months after Christmas. Ronnie went with her to bed and to nursery; he was beside her at meal times, and if Ashley left the house with Sylvie, but not the card, there was no going any further until Ronnie was back by Sylvie's side. Luckily, we had a few spare cards as the original got so tattered from all the love it had received, that it had to be replaced. It's incredible that a little card like that could bring so much joy to a beautiful little girl. Who knows what brought on the attachment to it, but it's nice to think it was down to Ronnie's specialness.

There are so many more ripples of Ronnie not mentioned here, and there will be more and more to add to the list as time goes on. That's another of the great benefits of dog ownership: you're constantly creating memories that will last a lifetime.

Chapter Thirty-one - We've only just begun

It's been so wonderful to take time to reflect on all of the great blessings Ronnie has brought us, in the seven years he's been by our sides (quite literally when it comes to bedtime). Funny how we find it so hard to imagine a time before him now, and our lives together are unrecognisable when compared to how we once lived. Again, I make the similarity, I imagine, to how a child coming into a family shapes and changes the entire direction and focus of their parents' lives.

It's not that we weren't happy before, but there was definitely more stress. Both our jobs were in pressurised environments and that, certainly in the run up to my leaving my employment, was taking its toll on home life as I struggled to sleep and enjoy the simple things I am now so appreciative of. I just didn't have the energy or motivation to try new things or feel enthusiastic about each day, being tired and overwhelmed a great deal of the time. As is often the case, it's only on looking back now that I see this, having been trapped on the treadmill of the rat race, and I'm grateful every day for having catapulted myself out of it and then supporting Colin to do the same.

Now, we have genuine quality time together as we have created a work/ life balance that has eliminated a lot of the stress. Ronnie makes us laugh every day with his hilarious antics, and caring for another living being has strengthened our relationship and brought us even closer together. I don't remember ever going for spontaneous walks around the wonderful area we live in pre-Ronnie, yet now, not taking in the beauty and nature around us seems unimaginable.

Being happier and more content with my lot has enabled me to connect more genuinely with the people I work with. Ronnie has enabled me to see that sweating the small stuff is a waste of time and energy and while this may be a work in progress, I'm definitely practicing what I preach much more authentically than before. I've always believed that love and people are what really matter in life, and Ronnie has reinforced this massively while adding the element of taking more time to just have fun and laugh … live in the moment.

Karen Carpenter's velvet voice sang 'We've only just begun', as we took our first dance on our wedding day, and the words seem very fitting all these years later. As she sang; we have shared horizons that were new to us, and watched the signs along the way. We've talked it over, just the two of us, and worked together day to day.

It's been a journey filled with many highs and some lows, but overall, I don't regret a minute of it. If anyone reading this feels the pull of self-employment, I wholeheartedly encourage you to make a plan, get some reserves behind you and take that leap of faith. It won't always be plain sailing, but being employed by someone else isn't either, and you'll always be working towards their dream, not your own. Sourcing the services of a reputable life coach or mentor of some kind also propels you towards success, and provides much needed support when self-doubts turn up in the most unexpected places. There are times I would have been lost without my wonderful coach.

As I sit with Colin and we do our weekly money count, I still have a sense of disbelief that he has been able to build up such a successful business from walking dogs. Every Friday evening, when he and Ronnie return from their last walk of the week, Colin brings his weekly earnings through to the kitchen, and then empties his pockets of any payments he received that day. He counts out loud in a funny voice and the tone gets higher and louder when he hits each hundred. Ronnie is often to be found sitting on Colin's lap watching, as if savouring the fruits of his labour. I act as treasurer, taking each pile, double-checking it, then placing it in the banking envelope, alongside the pay-in slip, once I've filled out the denominations of each pile. It's a very rewarding way to round off the week, and I'm sure we must be wearing extremely self-satisfied expressions as we go about our business.

When counting money isn't the only time Colin puts on silly voices. He's actually a Johnny Morris in the making. Every dog that stays with us has a voice of its own, and the things they come out with really match their personality and have me in stitches on a regular basis. It really doesn't translate well on the written page, but listening to the conversations between the dogs, and being spoken to by them each day, is an ongoing source of amusement and entertainment for me.

Then there's our singing to Ronnie, which we also do on a regular basis. Our favourite song is:

'We love you, Ronnie, we do. We love you, Ronnie, we do. We love you, Ronnie, we do. Oh, Ronnie, we love you.'

Colin's even developed a nice little harmony on the last line. I also like to sing *You are my Sunshine* to Ronnie just before we go to sleep. What bizarre behaviour from two otherwise reasonably responsible, well-adjusted adults.

Ronnie definitely does bring out the maternal side in me as each day goes on. Whether it be feeding and brushing him, or comforting him when he's not well, there is never a day goes by when he's isn't smothered with my love. From the moment his eyes open in the morning, I can be found kissing and cuddling him. Sometimes, when I'm sitting working and I know he's sleeping somewhere in the flat, I have an overwhelming urge to seek him out and snuggle him. It feels like a magnet is pulling me to him. I'm sure he must get fed up at times with the constant hugging and preening.

I have a saying that you should 'Stop and kiss the doggie', and I follow this advice all the time. It's amazing how taking a little time out to show some love to my four-legged friend can put things in perspective if I'm having a bad day. He's a wee tonic. I'm sure other dog owners will be able to relate to this, and I don't think it's any coincidence that the owners of a lot of the dogs Colin walks don't have children, and their dogs play an important role in filling this gap. All the love we have needs to go somewhere, and how wonderful that it can be shared with these animals that pay us back in so many astonishing ways.

I watched a programme on dog behaviour with great interest a few months ago. Research has now been done, which shows that dog owners live longer and are much less likely to have a heart attack than non-dog owners. When an owner pets their dog, the hormone oxytocin, otherwise known as the 'hormone of love', is produced in their brain, with a resulting rush of well-being. This is the same hormone a woman produces when nursing a new baby and it's really important in building the powerful bond between mother and newborn.

It turns out that not only is oxytocin produced in the owner, but tests have proved that the dog gets a rush of their own: win win. Research has also shown that oxytocin levels in humans are under threat with the amount of stress and pressure people feel under, because of the many demands life throws at us. Surely there can be no better reason to get a dog than there being a mutually beneficial feel-good factor to petting them, and it helps you live a longer and healthier life. It certainly explains my need to 'Stop and kiss the doggie' every five minutes. I'm hooked on oxytocin.

Another benefit of writing this book is that is has made me see how much I connect with the seasons, and how important they are to my day to day life. I love them all for different reasons. I love the new beginnings spring brings, as the crocuses and daffodils burst through the soil, to let us know the long dark nights are coming to an end. I love the sunny days that go on forever during the summer months, and the array of flowers that blossom at this time. I love the warm colours of the autumn, and feeling that first nip in the air as the leaves fly off the trees, telling me Christmas is just around the corner. And then the winter arrives and it's time to don coats, hats and gloves, hibernate a little and eat lots of homemade soup. Every season has something wonderful to offer and they somehow keep me in check.

The only thing that concerns me as I grow older is the speed at which they fly past. Time is moving so quickly now, and Ronnie is getting older. Neither Colin nor I even want to contemplate the day Ronnie passes away, though it's a thought we both have in our private moments. It is a really sad time we are going to have to deal with in our future, but for now, I just want to enjoy every minute with him; hence the constant snuggles.

I couldn't finish without tying up a loose end. One day, about a year into us having Ronnie, Colin was walking in Alexandra Park when he saw a beautiful greyhound in the distance. As the dog got nearer, the woman with her made her way to Colin.

253

'Is that Ronnie?' she asked.

'Yes, it is. How did you know that?'

'I work for The Dogs Trust. I remember him.'

'Oh my goodness. That's amazing … but wait a minute, is that Blue?'

We had both been drawn to Blue at our visit to the Dogs Trust when searching for a dog. On reflection, despite her being a beautiful dog, I'm so glad we didn't take her. It would have meant we would never have met Ronnie, and while I'm sure we would have had many happy times with Blue, there's just something so special about our wee mutt.

'Yes.'

'My wife nearly took Blue home when we went to the Dogs Trust. She was so upset for her. It was just that she was older and bigger than we'd wanted. Is the poor soul still there?'

'Not for much longer. She's found a lovely home with a family and is heading there next week. We're so happy for her, as she's really special. Even though she's been with us for a long time, she was treated really well, often going home to stay with different staff members, to give her a break from the kennel. You can tell your wife she's doing great, and so is Ronnie by the look of him.'

'Yes, he's a fantastic wee dog. Oh, Susan will be pleased.'

He couldn't wait to tell me about Blue and I was delighted to hear the good news. Something about the sad look in her eyes had haunted me and I had often wondered what had happened to her. It was great to hear she was going to a good home and wouldn't be stuck in that kennel anymore.

Adopting Ronnie has brought us into contact with so many lovely people and dogs, and it's amazing to think that there was a dog community right under our noses that we never knew of pre-Ronnie. Ronnie even has his own Facebook page, and Colin posts regular videos of all the dogs out on walks. Many of the owners are 'friends' of Ronnie, and are able to check in and see how their dog is getting on. I'm sure it's a comfort to see them all having such a great time.

As I write the last lines of this book, Christmas is only a few days away. I'm completely caught up in the festive splendour and our home is once again decked to the brim. Thankfully, this year the tree is holding its own. Last year we rushed out and bought a tree in haste. Never again. A couple of weeks after it had been adorned with my favourite ornaments it was practically bald. Every time I tried to water it or adjust a bauble, it shed another pile of needles and then the lights kept blowing. Taking off each set of lights to add a new one resulted in us having a very sad looking tree a week before the big day.

'Colin, we're going to have to get another tree. There's no way we can keep this one. Both our families are coming for Christmas dinner and you know how important the tree is to me.'

'Okay, we'll do it tomorrow night.'

As stage two of our tree search began, it was a hideous evening weather wise. Rain was pouring onto the windscreen while the van violently swayed in the wind as we made our way to the Cricket Club in Partick. Unfortunately, they were shut for the night. I couldn't blame them given the conditions. We headed to B&Q only to find that they had no trees whatsoever. I was distraught.

'What are we going to do, Colin? I've already stripped the old tree.'

'I don't know. We've left it too late I guess. I'll have to bring the tree back in and see if we can do anything with it.'

'Colin, we can't! It'll be soaked through and it was ruined before you even lobbed it outside. Oh God, Christmas is ruined!' and with that dramatic announcement, I burst into tears and sniffed the whole way home.

In the morning, I rose early and made my way back to the cricket ground. The guy showed me what he had left but there were no large trees to be had. He phoned his colleague at the tennis club in Hyndland to see if there were any larger trees there and luckily he had one ten foot Frazer Fir left. Thanking the guy for his help, I leapt into the van and sped up to the tennis club. There it was, standing alone amongst a few much smaller offerings and although it was a little oddly shaped, I snapped it up and managed to carry it into the van.

Once I got home, I trimmed it into the best shape I could with secateurs and left it in a bucket of water ready to be assembled later that evening. I tried to re-capture the atmosphere of my first tree decorating adventure two weeks previously by playing Christmas music, eating mince pies and sipping on a glass of wine, but it was feeling more of a chore than a pleasure second time round. However once it was done, I felt a lot better and it did look beautiful. We would have a tree for Christmas after all.

This year, we went straight to the tennis club and it's holding up well. It takes up the entire bay window of our living room and closing the curtains is a bit of an ordeal. We have one of those long wooden poles with a hook on the end, the kind school janitors use for opening and closing windows. Every night, I have to use this to drag the curtains shut, trying hard not the knock of bobbles, and the star on top is always at a jaunty angle due to being swiped by the pole, but I love it.

Christmas, wonky star and all

We also have to organise cards and gifts for all of Colin's clients at this time of year. Creating a special card with a photo of Ronnie on it has become another tradition and each client gets a card, box of chocolates and treat for their dog. It's a lovely time of year and Colin's clients are always so generous in their gifts to Ronnie and us too. Colin walks two fantastic Labs, Archie (Brown) and Bertie (Black). These two dogs have brought so much laughter and fun to the pack. They are both enormous and bound their way around the world just wanting to enjoy every minute. Last week, Colin got a text from Peter and Michael, their owners, saying that Archie would not be needing a walk that day. He was being taken to the vet having eaten his way through forty mince pies, including the foils! Thankfully, he was fine and suffered no serious after effects. The stories just keep coming.

It's also a special time because it's always the anniversary of us bringing Ronnie home from the Dog's Trust. Six years ago on 21st December was the first time he walked over our door. Little did we know then that this dog would impact so greatly on our lives and I will always be grateful that we made that decision all of those years ago.

If we'd never made that decision, I would never have written this book or experienced all of the many associations there are between dog ownership and coaching. It's rekindled my love of writing and I want to write more. There's so much to say about overcoming difficulties and leading the life of your dreams than is between the pages of this book, particularly in the area of positive mental health, and I would love to have the opportunity to share that with others.

And so to everyone who owns a dog, enjoy every precious moment you have with them. For those of you who don't, what you waiting for? As the Dogs Trust motto says: 'Give a Dog a Home'. It might just change your life, it did ours.

That's ma boy

Some other books from Ringwood Publishing

All titles are available from the Ringwood website (including first edition signed copies) and from usual outlets.
Also available in Kindle, Kobo and Nook.
www.ringwoodpublishing.com

Ringwood Publishing, 7 Kirklee Quadrant, Glasgow, G12 0TS
mail@ringwoodpublishing.com
0141 357-6872

Memoirs of a Feminist Mother
Carol Fox
"What a journey. A tough and terrific story"
- Beatrix Campbell, writer and feminist

Memoirs of a Feminist Mother
Carol Fox

As a committed feminist, Carol Fox has achieved success for very many women, but her greatest battle described in this book was very personal. Following serious fertility problems, Carol made the positive decision to become a single parent by choice, to have a child while she still could. Refused access to fertility treatment in Scotland she had no choice but to move to London. Through sheer determination and tenacity, Carol obtained treatment in England in the early 1990s and her daughter was born in 1992, following extensive fertility treatment and battles against judgemental attitudes which appear almost vindictive to us 25 years later. Her story has attracted media coverage, sparking debates on motherhood and the right to be a single parent in the UK.

ISBN: 978-1-901514-21-6   £9.99

A Man's Game

Alan Ness

On a Saturday afternoon in central Scotland, both Davie Thomson and Stuart Robertson have scored goals for their respective football clubs: Cowden United FC and Glasgow Athletic. Once team-mates in the Athletic title-winning side of 1997, their subsequent fortunes could not have been more different. Whilst Robertson had gone from strength to strength, winning titles and the love of the Scottish public, Thomson had slipped out of the team and down the leagues with alcohol and a weight problem contributing to his fall.

Whilst scanning the results, James Donnelly, reporter for the Daily Standard connected the two and remembered the tragic events which would forever link them and their team-mates from that ill-fated side.

The Gori's Daughter

Shazia Hobbs

The Gori's Daughter is the story of Aisha, a young mixed race woman, daughter of a Kashmiri father and a Glasgow mother. Her life is a struggle against rejection and hostility in Glasgow's white and Asian communities.

The book documents her fight to give her own daughter a culture and tradition that she can accept with pride. The tale is often harrowing but is ultimately a victory for decency over bigotry and discrimination.

ISBN: 978-1-901514-12-4   £9.99

The Activist
Alec Connon

Unfulfilled by student life, Thomas Durant and two friends decide to cycle the length of Britain during their summer holidays, dressed as superheroes. The experience of their short trip is enough to whet Thomas's appetite for further travel and set in motion his decision to drop out of uni and see the world for himself. Influenced by a burgeoning interest in marine conservation, what begins as a typical gap year develops into over decade's worth of involvement and participation in animal rights activism. The story follows Thomas as his journey takes him around the globe, from his first tentative steps into the life of an activist in Vancouver, to his battles with the Japanese whaling fleet in the Southern Ocean.

Jinx Dogs Burns Now Flu
Alex Gordon

Jinx Dogs Burns Now Flu is a rollicking, often hilarious, trip through the crazy world of Scottish newspapers. It's a journey that takes the reader behind the headlines of the biggest, most sensational stories of our national press. Meet the madcap characters who bring you your daily news. Prepare to be bewildered by their antics as they chase front and back page exclusives. You'll be amazed and amused by the tales that did NOT make it into print. Until now, as Jinx Dogs Burns Now Flu brings many sensational stories into print for the first time!

The Herbal Detective
Charles Gray

Strange things have started to happen in the small town of Holy Cross. Black cats, sneaking suspicions and wine-powered ecstasy lay their grip on the clueless inhabitants and local news strongly suspects witches are behind it all.

Meanwhile, poor Rosie McLeod is simply trying to deal with day to day catastrophes including lapsang souchong tea, carpet slippers and the impending doom of old age. With the innocent brewing of some herbs the frontiers between innocence and guilt, logic and magic, start to shift and events come thick and fast.

Morbid Relations
Jonathan Whitelaw

Morbid Relations is the story of Rob Argyll, an unsuccessful stand-up comedian. Following his mother's death, he returns for the first time in years to his family in their Glasgow home. Rob struggles to relate to his somewhat dysfunctional family, seeming to bounce from one mistake to another while simultaneously trying to make amends for his long absence. The narrative is a darkly comic take on modern Scottish life, family relationships, and finally trying to grow up.

ISBN: 978-1-901514-19-3   £9.99

The Malta Job
Alywn James

The Malta Job follows the story of John Smith, a young Scottish journalist with literary aspirations, who is sent to Malta to complete a sequel to the very successful MacMurder, a round-up of Scotland's more infamous homicides. Once on Malta, with the dead author's notes, he gets involved in a gripping set of circumstances involving high romance, exciting adventure and a bank heist crime.

ISBN: 978-1-901514-17-9   £9.99

A Subtle Sadness
Sandy Jamieson

A Subtle Sadness follows the life of Frank Hunter and is an exploration of Scottish Identity and the impact on it of politics, football, religion, sex and alcohol.

It covers a century of Scottish social, cultural and political highlights culminating in Glasgow's emergence in 1990 as European City of Culture.

It is not a political polemic but it puts the current social, cultural and political debates in a recent historical context.

ISBN: 978-1-901514-04-9   £9.99